BEING HUMAN BEING

BOOK ONE

"out of the village and into the jungle"

The story of a man on a quest to find himself, as he navigated through his childhood from a Third World village, into adulthood, in the big city of New York. The challenges he faced and overcame in order to follow his dreams to success, as a pilot instructor, an electrical engineer, and a professional in the corporate world. He treated every challenge as a learning experience, to be explored, and to resolve his conflict between science and doctrine. Every one of his accomplishments allowed for another opportunity for learning, as he formulated his philosophy of human existence.

His quest was to find his identity and purpose on this planet. He found himself first, then everyone else, all swimming in the sea of life. His writings concern our human existence, as he wondered about humans, and what we are all doing here in this fishbowl from which there is no escape. In this first book he offers details into the professional worlds from which he learned about us humans, especially as a pilot instructor.

His philosophy is factual, and science based, about the past, present, and the future of humanity, with emphasis on several disciplines of human existence in Book Two.

RALPH B. BACCHUS

EDITED BY: Judith Kilfoile

BEING HUMAN BEING
Book One
"out of the village and into the jungle"

ISBN: 9781090986412
April 2019

Dedicated to my sister Jan.
I miss her dearly.

CONTENTS

PREFACE

A narrative of a man on a quest to find his identity, and the truth about his existence; a narrative that was written decades ago, and now complete, as it unfolded into a scientific based philosophical account, with an autobiographical theme. This is the story of a man, born in a place, in a circumstance, and with a predisposed deep passion for all that matters in human life. I am that man. I describe how my mind was shaped from childhood, by my thoughts and feelings from all that I experienced, and how I became the person I am.

This first book is an account of my subliminal quest to understand the universe in which I was living. I wanted to understand everything from the Cosmos to the atoms, from the simple human concepts to the complicated ones, from doctrine to civil matters. It would seem fortunate that I had the opportunity to focus on this quest at every turn in my life. My attitude was that every challenge brought a new learning. I accepted the occurrences in my life, and I accepted my situations and circumstances. They all became part of me, as they also defined me, as a human being.

I wrote so as to relate and reach all humans of any belief, profession, religion, culture, country, political affiliation, age, or any other persuasion for that matter. I wrote for everyone, including those who know some science, and those who know a lot of science. I was looking to find myself, and I found everyone, and a whole lot more. I wish to share this information by sharing my experiences, and telling what I have learned in my life. I explain details from my professions, especially as a pilot instructor, where I was fortunate to be looking through the window into the human mind, and understanding human behavior. All the pilot candidates brought their own beliefs, fears, anxiety, talent, knowledge, and emotions, which became challenges for me to analyze, understand, and assist towards their goals. I gained much knowledge from them, as they were willing to trust me with their lives. In addition, I added details of interest from the stories, which would help the reader to understand the world of Aviation.

Every event in my life, small or large, had an effect on me, even though many have been at a subconscious level. Every event brought its own addition to my life, and my human existence. Every event originated from the previous events that occurred. Several events in my life firmly brought the curious question: "Why?" I always wondered about everything naturally occurring, or caused by human action. All of my adult life I yearned to understand myself; it was my personal quest. I wanted to analyze all the aspects of my being, from the life form I am, to my consciousness. I wanted to understand my feelings, beliefs, opinions, convictions, and emotions. I wanted to unify my existence, and myself, in the same way scientists want to unify the universe. I wanted to understand the forces and laws of nature, in all of its disciplines, to reach this understanding. I wanted to find the DNA of the Cosmos.

In Book Two, I explain how I found myself, and I found everyone else too, and I am happy to accept my position in this vast universe. Join me on my journey into the Cosmos, and the human mind. Read on, enjoy, laugh, cry, explore, know, and understand. Most of all understand yourself, and who we are, as humans, from my perspective.

Chapter One

I FEEL

It was a sunny and warm morning in Florida when the phone call came instructing me to turn on the TV. The children were already at school, as it was September, and I was home alone. This call was an intrusion on my time with myself, the time I got to do whatever I wanted, and at my own pace. I was being disturbed and distracted from this state of mind. What could be so important?

I watched TV during the day primarily to check the weather and such, but never for news. This had better be important. I turned on the TV and there was breaking news on every news channel. It was the most horrific thing I have ever seen in all my years of living. At first I thought it was a movie. Then I thought it was a hoax. Afterward, I thought it was anything but what I was watching. Somehow I wanted to believe I was not watching what I was watching. It was truly unbelievable. In time, I began to realize that what I was seeing was real; both of the World Trade Center towers in New York were billowing with smoke, and fire was shooting out of their sides. Struck into shock, with mouth open I watched in horror, and within a few moments tears started running down my cheeks. I covered my mouth and slowly sat down without ever taking my eyes off the TV.

In time, after I watched the smoke billowing and the fire blazing, I saw the buildings collapse. At that moment I felt as

1

though someone had removed a part of my body. I felt like I had lost something so dear to me and I will never overcome the grief of it, or be able to accept the reality of it. I felt like I had lost two friends who were most important to me, and I will never see them again. I felt like I would be mourning for the rest of my life. I felt like my head was going to explode, as a rush of adrenaline filled my being.

I was sad. I was hurt. I was terrified. I was angry. I was confused. I was also fearful. I was powerless. I was helpless. I had been traumatized. I felt pinned to the ground by a massive rock and I was struggling to escape. I shook my head from side to side, with mouth covered, and in great disbelief of what I was seeing. I did not know what to do next. All I knew was that I had to continue watching. I wanted to scream very loudly so the whole world could hear me. I wanted to run in the street and rip my shirt off, while screaming and pointing to this horrible scene, which I felt only I was watching. But, it was not only I who was having this experience; the whole world was watching. As much as I thought that something was wrong with my TV, it was my coping mechanism trying to tell me that what was on the screen was not real; that what I was watching was a fake.

Finally, I began to realize that the iconic Twin Towers at the bottom of Manhattan were on the bottom of the ground. The same two towers that I saw grow out of the ground during the nineteen-seventies as they were being built. At one point one was taller than the other. Then floor after floor they went up and became equal in height. It was such a beautiful and powerful presence they had at the bottom of the greatest city in the world. They were a lovely couple. With the Midtown high rises, including the Empire State Building, the Twin Towers in lower Manhattan, in my mind made the city balanced; as though Manhattan was attached to the sky in many places.

These buildings had become my favorite sight to look at because they offered this balance to Manhattan. I visited them many times for pleasure, and in my professional work. I would go to the restaurant at the top to eat dinner, or sit in the lounge and enjoy the view. I would fly in an airplane close to them many times when I was giving flight lessons. It was legal to fly at their height and be only 2,000 feet away. I would rock the wings of the airplane, and many of the excited visitors on the observation deck would return the wave. It was as though the towers were waving back to me. They were my friends who always greeted me every time I flew by, as I continued down the Hudson River and passing the Statue of Liberty.

Day or night, New York was a great and grand city to view from the air, especially from a low altitude. I felt the intimacy, the friendship, the warmth, the love, and most of all the welcome. The towers were my motivational tools to encourage student pilots to get their licenses, so they also could fly down the Hudson, with their family and friends, and watch this awesome city.

Now, the towers were gone, right before my own eyes. My friends who stood so tall were gone. My life would change forever. I must now accept their death. I must also now believe that on any day in the future some group who felt like it could just remove the head on the Statue of Liberty, at will. I was scared and I felt unsafe.

Eventually, days after watching the story on television and talking about it to countless people, I began to accept. The mourning turned to logical anger; the type of anger that someone thinks about; premeditated anger; like vengeance was needed. I felt like someone had to pay; I wanted revenge. But, even if they paid by being punished, the towers would not return. This is the price of anger and revenge; anger and revenge do not bring back dead people or destroyed buildings.

With all the logic of premeditated anger, it did not provide a solution. In any case, the ones who would have to pay were already dead, and on their way to the Heaven they believed in, to meet the God they believed in, who would so welcome them for their great accomplishment. At least it was what they thought. They were dead wrong. Those brutal bastards were going straight to Hell. No God would reward anyone for such a horrific act. If Mahatma Gandhi or the Pope had ordered the attack I would be more inclined to believe that

3

God was not always good. But, knowing it was a madman's plot with fools doing the dirty work it became more credible. I accepted the truth. That madman gave his God a bad name by commanding idiots to do his dirty deed, for which he was a coward to do himself.

I thought of others whom I hadn't spoken to, about how they must have felt, and what they witnessed. I thought about all those people who experienced horrific events, such as the attack on Pearl Harbor. Some people saw it on television and in the newspaper, while others saw it in person. I wondered how it was for the different groups. I thought that those who were present would be more affected. I eventually met some of those who watched the burning towers with their own eyes. Somehow, it seemed like I suffered as much as they did, and in some ways even more. Perhaps I suffered more because of what the towers meant to me; because of the close relationship I had with them, and because I never took them for granted.

I had to focus on healing, and on myself. I was still alive, but I was suffering. I was not dead, or maimed, or injured physically. I was emotionally hurt and I was traumatized. I asked myself why this situation caused me so much pain, and I had no direct answer. I did not own the towers, and I no longer lived in New York. I did not have any direct interest or connection to them any longer. Why would it trouble me so much? After much thought I realized that many people all over the world were also troubled, but perhaps not as much as I was troubled. I knew it had to do with my close relationship to the towers, my friendship with them and the lifelong memory. They were there for me night and day. I knew all the reasons why I was sad, and hurt, and disappointed, and angry; it was as though I had lost my soul.

I wanted so desperately to understand how such events could occur in our modern society. Could it be that I had simply buried my head in the sand and ignored whatever was going on in the world? Was I that naive? Did I assume too much about the arrogance and ignorance of others? Was I lost in the sea of humanity? It was not any of that; it was simply because I had a relationship with the towers that was different than those thugs who destroyed them.

I was the one on the quest to understand humans and human nature, and I had discovered what many others had already known; that there was no perfect system in any civil society that seemed to work; not political, not religious, not moral, not even common sense or human decency. Humans would always find something wrong with someone, some group, or something, and I did not understand all of that. The emotional toil of this event prompted me as usual, and gave me more reasons to wonder. With all that I had already discovered about what we were all about, I continued to wonder, and that was my only choice. I had to find the answers myself. I also had to examine myself.

As for the towers, it was my expectation of them; that they would be there at my beckoning call if I were to fly the Hudson again. It was selfish of me to expect them to always be there and to wait for me, and that anytime I wanted to visit they must be ready. I realized that I must accept the loss, and I must cherish the many lovely memories they provided for me, and all those who I took to see them. The memories were wonderful, and it was because of my memory that I would be so hurt, until it fades. If I were an alligator I would not be troubled as much. As a human being, the most important reason for my hurt would be because of my intense memory.

The imprint in my memory of the Empire State Building was its importance in marking the middle of the city, and the first iconic building I would visit after arriving in New York. In addition, during my flights out of LaGuardia Airport, on my way towards New Jersey, it was often that the clearance given would be to fly directly towards the Empire State Building. The additional comment from the controller would be: "look out for the gorilla." It was nice to break the monotony of seriousness in a serious setting. The entire city was unique and beautiful to look at. It flowed so sweetly from the George Washington Bridge, to Central Park, to the Empire State Building, to the

World Trade Center towers, and finally the Statue of Liberty. Wonderful memories of all this were wired into my brain.

However, the case for me was that I was still trying to unravel my emotions about what happened. I realized that I was especially affected and needed to look inward at myself. I needed to understand what I was feeling, and why. I also needed to understand the people who took those buildings down. I had to find a resolution, and I began to wonder, as I always did. What kind of human beings would commit such an atrocity? I needed to find out for myself. I needed to heal myself as everyone else was trying to do. It was not one person's loss, it was everyone's, and each had to deal with it individually.

I was also angry with the government. I was angry that there was no system to protect my Twin Tower friends who were so valuable, and meant so much to so many. I wondered why no one in the government had the foresight to know that knives on airplanes were a bad idea. Today, we can't even take water on an airplane. Really, can't someone know that anything that could be turned into a weapon must be banned from an airplane? Must we wait for a tragedy to take action? Somehow, I think that humans are smarter. I think that common sense must be superior to laws, and that laws must be made with common sense.

My thoughts and feelings switched back and forth between anger towards the government, and anger towards the perpetrators. The government would start the investigations to find out who they were, and at the same time pass laws to prevent this type of horror from happening again. As for the perpetrators, I wondered how they could become such horrible people. I also flew close to the buildings many times, and never once had the thought of flying into them. In their case, the actions were premeditated and deliberate, not just a casual thought, or accident. I could never do such a thing; I was a different kind of human being. I thought that maybe they were sick in their heads, or abused as children, or ordered by someone, or psychologically conditioned to commit this crime, and die for it. I really believed that conditioning was the methodology of the execution of such an act. It was most plausible to me.

They were terrorists. They were from a country that was friendly to the United States. Their leader was a defector from the same country. Perhaps he was banished, and in exile, either voluntarily or by force. He turned to an alternative method of war called terrorism; a war waged by him and his weak-minded followers. He was a Hitler. He wanted revenge against the United States, and he used religion as the basis to condition the minds of his followers; a psychological programming to convince recruits to rise up against the mighty enemy he invented, with the reward of martyrdom if they were to die. He was simply a sick man, with enough money to propagate his missions. His followers all took the bait. They would do anything he asked. He convinced them that they would get great blessings from Allah anytime they could attack the United States, or its people, or its property. The followers of this cult were blinded from the truth because they believed in the interpretation of the facts as was explained by their master. He had control of their minds. He must have told stories of prior religious wars where people died, and how Muslim warriors became martyrs. He must have told them that martyrs would get the most blessing from Allah. They believed all that. What stupid fools they were; they believed they were going to Heaven. Someone should have given them the bad news; they were going straight to Hell.

It seemed that the mastermind used conditioning to program his robots, and organized a complete plan. Many a compliment would be given to the leaders and the followers of the plan, as the entire group would be united toward the objective. Compliments would work well in this case. Compliments were the master manipulator's tool, which was camouflaged as blessings and encouragement, with the ultimate reward coming from Allah, after the act was complete.

Really, as easy as it could be for normal people to detect this as a fraud, the followers were conditioned to believe that they were on a mission from Allah himself. They were hypnotized, in a manner of speaking. Common sense would not matter to these criminals. Their religious beliefs would all be interpreted and confirmed by their leader. Their minds did not have to work. Their logic did not have to serve them. All they needed to do was to follow. It did not matter that nowhere in the Koran is it stated that the taking of innocent lives would offer a reward or a blessing. It did not matter that the act they were about to commit did not make sense. It did not matter to them that if they killed a Muslim in a deliberate attack Allah would punish them to the highest level; according to the same doctrine they believed. In fact, the deliberate killing of anyone who believed in the one God would result in the harshest penalty from the same God. It meant that if Christians and Jews were also killed in a deliberate attack, the punishment to the criminals would be Hell. In addition, to take one's own life is a sin, and a double sin during a criminal act. All of that did not matter. The logic disappeared from their brains and they did the crime anyway. It would be reasonable to believe that most, if not all the people they killed were believers in God. If each of those idiots were to get one Hell sentence for each person they killed, eternity would have to go on much longer than forever. I could only imagine if I were the God they believed in how angry I would be. I would look at them with disdain and disgust. I would grind my teeth and spit on them, as I tell them that I have not yet found the penalty harsh enough for them. I would be one angry God.

The logic of the brain of the perpetrators was no match for the mastermind. As much as they could have consulted with others in a truthful way to get a second opinion about the plot to fly into the buildings, they opted not to do that. They could have read the Koran themselves, or asked the mastermind to show them in the book where, and what was stated regarding the killing of innocent people in the name of Allah. He would not be able to, because no such nonsense was written. Manipulators could cleverly find ways to avoid showing proof or facts. That would be their mastery - the manipulation of the minds of their victims so as to convert them into criminals. They were the suckers he found to manipulate and execute his crime. They were just a bunch of stupid fools.

This incident had taken a profound impact on my life. Every incident I experienced or witnessed allowed me the opportunity to understand the many challenges in our human existence. I spent much time analyzing and dissecting the many aspects of being a human being. We are a complicated species. We are a difficult bunch of people, many of whom try to grasp the meaning of life. Who, or what are we? Why are we here, and where are we headed? Does someone or something manipulate us all? Does religion, politics, or people condition us to believe and behave a certain way? Do we have control of ourselves in every aspect of life? Can we understand why, how, and what people do in life, and what motivates them? Can we understand our world? Humans do have difficulty with the facts and the truth, as they are not always the same to us.

A philosophy of choosing facts and evidence over any other methods before reaching a conclusion, or taking any action, would seem appropriate and supportive for logical analysis. Conditioning by doctrine or philosophy that does not support facts and evidence would be contrary to understanding. As difficult as it could be, as a human being, I try to deal with facts and truths as best as possible. It became the easiest way for me to live with fair judgment of everything and everyone.

Chapter Two

ME MYSELF AND I

I must have been born a wonderer. I remember always wanting to know; "why?" I wondered by day, and by night. Especially I wondered about myself, quite often. I wanted to have an identity that did not simply include a name, number or fingerprint. I wondered who I actually would be without such identification. In my childhood I never tried to understand the purpose of life; I merely followed the leader. Fortunately for me, my experiences would reveal some of what I needed to know about my life, and myself. I would discover the world I lived in, the universe I wanted to know, and my future. As casual as my life was, or as I took it during my childhood, the meaningfulness would become clear only in my later years. Perhaps it was aged wisdom, or perhaps I was just simply slow. More importantly for me though, it was all of the history of my life that shaped my future. Beginning with the place where I was born, the parents who facilitated my existence and nurtured me until my eventual emigration to another place of abode, all of it mattered in who, and what I became, as a human being.

PRIMITIVE

I was born in a little village, which was located in the only British colony in South America. I was not born in a hospital; hospitals were for sick people. I was born in a house,

11

just like all other babies in the village. Nurse Galloway was the chief stork and mid-wife. She had a Master's in Obstetrics from the University of ECS; (Experience and Common Sense), conferred upon her by the Village Officer. The house I lived in had no running water until I was about eight years old. I went across the main road each morning to fill a bucket of water from a tap connected to the main water line, and available to anyone in the village. That was for my bath. I used the half shell of a dried calabash fruit to dip the water to pour over my head. There was no electricity until I was about twelve years old. It didn't seem to matter; it was the way things were.

When we have nothing to compare with we accept our situation, and we get accustomed to our environment, especially the environment we were born into. When the people in the entire village lived with the same conditions it was easy to accept the conditions. I was not even aware that I was accepting a condition; for me, it was the way of life; it was what my parents provided for me, and I never questioned them. I dared not question them. I accepted what was the normal. I was quite content, with food and drink, and a bed to sleep in. I walked to school every day, returning home for lunch, and then walking back to school again. That was normal for me too. I didn't mind; it was what I was born into; a way of life that I had no choice but to live.

Of course I saw movies in the cinema, which were filmed in the Developed World, with people in houses with running water and electricity. But, I knew the movies were filmed somewhere else, so it didn't matter. I did not rush home to complain to my parents about not having running water or electricity. Had I complained, the answer would have been a gentle explanation from my father that it was not possible to have those things because of infrastructure limitations. The answer from one of my sisters would have been a lot more colorful.

The milkman came daily with fresh milk from his cow. Two pints he scooped directly into our milk pot. The milk was immediately boiled to kill germs. Later that day it was boiled again; to kill more germs that may have come for a drink. After it cooled, a layer of solid cream formed on top. The lucky child who discovered this cream would scoop it out into a dish very quietly, add some brown sugar and have a mouth-watering snack that tasted simply heavenly. Eyes would be closed during consumption so as to concentrate on all the taste buds being activated by this delicacy. The child discovering that someone else was there before, and that the cream was gone, would let out a loud shriek of disappointment. Oh well, better luck tomorrow.

The doctor had an office in the nearby town. The only time someone went to see him was because of sickness. There was no such thing as preventive medicine; that simply meant to be careful. One man went to see the doctor, and when he was asked about his problem he explained the best that he could. The doctor could not make a diagnosis based on what he said so the doctor pressed him for more answers. The man replied that he was a laborer, and he knew how to work a fork and a shovel very well, but for sure he did not know what was wrong with him; it was up to the doctor to find that out. The man's mannerism was typical of people in the village who always made humor about everything, including serious matters. The doctor made house calls for the aged or sickly people who could not travel. If someone were sick in the village, a white flag would be placed near the roadside. One day per week the doctor would drive, with his bag, to the nearby villages, and he would stop at each white flag.

The village was near an inlet that led out to the ocean, and naturally there were several fishermen. They went out a few times per week, in the early morning. They would return around sunrise, and their family would start to sell the fish, while the fishermen went to sleep. The fish was loaded into a wooden cart, which was pushed by hand. The sellers would blow a conch shell that sounded like the moo of a cow, except louder. As they traveled, they would yell very loudly: "fish! fish!" If they had shrimp they would yell; "fish and shrimp!"

Housewives, including my mother, would run out to buy fresh seafood. That same evening it became dinner.

We had a fairly large yard with a variety of trees that bore fruit. In the village it was fruitless to have a tree that did not bear fruit, (literally and figuratively speaking). We had papaya, coconut, mango and guava, to name a few. The trees produced ample amounts of fruit during their bearing season, and we shared with neighbors. Some fruits had different purposes at each stage of development. Green mango was used to tenderize meat, and was often added in the pot. This type of innovation and creativity was common in all aspects of life, and was handed down from generation to generation.

There were some cars that were so old they had to be started with a crank handle in the front. It was as though I was living in a bygone era. I eventually realized that I was. The village people could not afford the luxury of new vehicles and there were none sold anywhere. There were buses that operated on a schedule to each of the villages, as far as fifty miles away. Special buses operated in the morning for high school students and workers in the town. The final bus picked up people in the town from the last ferry, which operated across the river to some other villages. Life in the area was alive and vibrant. People found ways to go wherever they needed, and for whatever reason.

Cooking was done on a wood-burning stove made of mortar. It was called a fireside, and was placed in a well-ventilated, and small rectangular protrusion of the house. The protrusion was called a "cow nose," as it appeared as such, in a crude way. Wood was used to make the fire to cook, and a watchful eye on the pot was necessary for safety. Water was always kept nearby to prevent carelessness, which was what it would be called if someone started a fire by accident. After the wood was burnt it turned into charcoal, with residual heat, which provided a wonderful benefit for keeping the pot warm.

The British sure had a good thing going. They made sure that the population they depended on to extract the resources from their colony would be able to survive in a

14

healthy way. There was gold, bauxite, sugar, rice and greenheart wood. These industries were all for the British Empire. The people in the village had lost their history through the generations. They had no idea how they got there, and they did not care; it was not important. If anyone would ask them about the British ships that brought people from the East, they would simply shrug their shoulders and say it was what children had to learn in school. The past did not affect their present; they simply joined their captors and followed their teachings. People were busy with the daily chores of life, similar to what could be found in a termite's nest, or in the African savanna. It was life bustling from the light of the day, when all creatures rose to the sun for another day of living. It was how life on this planet flourished, and most creatures were focused on one thing - trying to survive another day of living.

Weddings and funerals brought out lots of people in the village to the house that held the event. Food was cooked in large quantities for these gatherings. However, there were not enough plates, and the food had to be served on large lily pads, which grew in the canals. They were certainly the first biodegradable disposable plates. The British soldiers who occupied the area would often be invited to eat at these events, as a gesture of friendship. They loved the food, and only complained that the lettuce was bitter. They did not know that the lily pad was not to be consumed. They certainly learned for the next time.

When I was about nine years old gas stoves made their debut. We were one of the first to get one, as my father was considered a merchant, because of his business. My mother had lunch ready by eleven thirty in the morning as we all came home from school to eat. We had to be back in class by one in the afternoon. Studying at night without electricity had to be with a kerosene lamp. A full moon was also bright enough to read near the window, but my father discouraged it, as he thought it could harm the eyes. A few years before I finished elementary school a private investor installed a small generator and ran wires to the homes. He supplied electricity to the village for florescent lights only, and also for a price. The lights went out at ten each night and eleven on Saturdays.

PROTÉGÉ

I became my father's property by the time I was ten. He would shape me into his own image. He taught me everything from his doctrine to his profession. I was eager to learn, and that made me the perfect candidate. I followed him around to learn his jewelry business, and I worked in the shop after school, and on weekends. In time, it became my job, and I worked there each and every day. It became my responsibility to contribute to the benefit of the household of which I was a member. I was like a farm hand in the days of pioneers, where everyone must contribute.

I woke up each morning to the crowing of roosters. If I failed to get out of bed, the head rooster on dawn patrol was sure to get me out. My father was like a drill sergeant. Each and every morning, the same painful time - dawn. Each morning I had to open the shop and put the jewelry on display, before going to school. It was the age of obedience to my parents. I dared not refuse or question, as the fear of shame commanded me into compliance.

The schedule in the shop during the week was to make the jewelry that people ordered, and for stock replacement. Saturdays were reserved for the alloy of gold with some silver and copper, by melting in a crucible then pouring into an ingot. That process converted the pure 24-carat gold into 18-carat gold bars the size of pencils. The bars would be milled and shaped into a multitude of jewelry from earrings, to bangles, to chains with pendants, and other things that made people look nice. On Saturdays all the jewelry that was made during the week would be washed and acid treated, to shine and glitter, as gold should.

On Sundays the shop was closed. It was the law. That would be the day my father went on his rounds. He would ride his motorcycle, with me in the back, to the outlying villages to serve his clients. We would ride to the last village and turn back. Slowly making our way back, we would stop at every client's house to deliver completed orders, take new ones, and sell some of what we had in the bag. My father's reputation preceded him. He marked each and every piece of jewelry with his trademark, somewhere inconspicuous. He did that in the event clients would want to use old jewelry to be melted and made into something new. He was known for good quality and workmanship, and those virtues were ingrained in his being.

Clients often brought neighbors and friends to do business, and one of the free services was to pierce ears of babies. There was a special starter earring designed with a sharp point, which would be removed after piercing. Some babies felt very little pain and reacted as though it was a mosquito bite, while others screamed like they were going to die. I eventually learned the procedure and had to pierce many ears; something I could no longer do; simply because of the memory of the few babies who cried. I could not bear to inflict any such pain, or pain of any sort, not even to a stone.

THE BRITISH WERE COMING

When I was about ten years old riots broke out in the capital town. The British Army arrived with full supplies and gear. It was their colony. The soldiers arrived to restore order and keep the peace. The conflict concerned the disparity of wealth between the people whose ancestors came as slaves and those who came later. The ancestors of the slaves received only their freedom. It was an interesting concept; offering already free people their freedom. It would be like a merchant doubling the price of an item in his store and putting it on sale for fifty percent off - an insult, camouflaged as a bargain. When free people were taken by force, transported to other places and forced to work, it should be defined as; "atrocity." Restitution and compensation for hard labor should have been the tenets of a proper settlement by the oppressors. The history of the atrocity of slavery faded over time, but the anger from it did not stop seeping out of the psyche of the descendants of slaves, for

17

generations. They revolted by rioting in the capital town. The unrest spread to other areas. The victims of the rioting were the business owners, and the people who owned stores and shops. But, it was not their fault; the British were to blame. They created the conditions for the situation. Interestingly, in history, the past reveals the truth, and everything becomes clear.

When the British planted their flag, they made a plan for every group in the colony that was called, the land of six races. The Amerindians, who were the Indigenous People, were moved up-river to reservations. Native people do not believe in slavery, and would resist through peaceful rebelliousness until their captors gave up. The slaves were brought from Africa to work in the sugar industry. When slavery was abolished, the British needed to explore labor opportunities with people from other countries. They could not enslave these new people so they made them a deal. The new arrivals had to agree to the conditions and terms of a contract. Eventually, many of them became the landowners, and the slaves were left out. The Indo Asians, Chinese, Portuguese and other Europeans fared better with the British. They were offered wages and land, eventually owning large portions throughout. Most of the land ran along the coast and had excellent fertility. An irrigation canal system supplied the necessary water and ample freshwater fish.

History was never kind to slaves, from the time of the Pharaohs to the time of the New World, and the riots became the response to the injustice of the past. The victims were simply anyone who had a better economic position. Human emotions did not always allow for a direct or fair resolution of matters. Anger could be one human aspect, in particular, that could be escalated to violence, and be directed in a random way, especially with groups. Anger sometimes has no logic; it is a human condition, but it always has a source.

As the turmoil continued, my father quickly counted his savings and bought one-way tickets to England for two of my unmarried sisters. They would land in London and be issued papers, which would eventually lead to British passports. They were British subjects, and they were entitled as such. Many other parents did the same, and the exodus from many villages had begun. People fearing for their safety left for the Motherland. My sisters who went to England created their futures, eventually getting married and having their families. They became the trend of many people who could afford to travel and immigrate to the Motherland. They were all looking for a better life. I also wanted to go, but I was too young.

The purge from the villages continued for years into the future. The people who were able to leave were the ones who had money. It could be presumed that they were considered industrious, and they would make a good contribution to England. Perhaps it was the British plan to accept all the productive people and leave the rest behind. Who knew?

The people who stayed back had to be vigilant. A watchful eye was important for all the villagers. Fortunately for us, there was only one road into the village, and one bridge to cross for anyone arriving from the direction that was considered unsafe. Immediately at the bottom of the bridge would be a group of fishermen who kept a nightly vigil. The group had been assembling there even before the riots. There was rum, and they could talk loudly without interrupting anyone; it was their hangout. They were known to be the "bad boys" not to mess with. They were our protectors. Cars, with strangers looking for trouble, would slow down after coming down the bridge, as the occupants investigated their surroundings. The vigilantes would intercept the cars and investigate the occupants' intent, often by a simple question regarding whom they were going to visit at that time of night. It did not take long before they would be asked to turn around, if suspicion was discovered. In that time, a simple request to leave was enough to deter the would-be troublemakers, especially when a show of the force, (men with machetes), was evident. We were safe in the village, as it was known as a place not to come to for trouble. Every person, no matter how poor, how rich, or what ethnicity, enjoyed a sense of belonging, in a group that outsiders were not allowed to interfere. We were bonded as a village.

Eventually many of the European countries and England were dealing with an influx of colonial residents, who could never be denied entry and residency; they were all subjects of their respective Motherlands. England, Portugal, Spain, France and The Netherlands started to offer many of the colonies their independence. With independence, each country would have its own government, currency, flag and constitution. Each would become a separate and independent country with no legal ties to the Motherland. Most of the colonies in Caribbean islands and South America became independent countries, still preserving the language and custom of their respective Motherland.

Every week or two, letters would arrive from overseas. They would be from my sisters. We all got excited and could not wait to read them. One person would read out-loud to the rest of the family. We were all curious about them, and life in England overall. They would write about taking the bus, wearing coats in winter, jobs, and friends they had. The younger ones in my family, including me, would imagine that someday we would also be there. Then, in 1966 everything changed for everyone, and forever. The British offered independence to the colony. New currency, new rules, new rights and privileges emerged. Some celebrated, while others were sad to lose the British. But, the impact of the British could not be simply erased; it was ingrained in all those who were born under the Union Jack. It was ingrained in me. The Union Jack was lowered, and a new flag rose, like the changing of the guards. That event would alter the course of my life forever. No longer could I go to England. She was no longer my Mother.

NIGHT WATCH

One of the greatest life changing experiences I benefited from while living without electricity was looking at the night sky. When I was about seven years old my parents awakened me at three in the morning, to look at a comet. It was brighter than everything else in the night sky, except the moon. I was too young to understand any of that. It would be several years later that I would be able to comprehend such stuff.

Looking at the night sky with no light pollution was every astronomer's dream, and my dream, as a junior astronomer. On a moonless night the stars were too many to be counted. They looked like cherries on a tree that I could reach. There were so many, it seemed like a lighted canopy. The sky was glowing. I was able to see the ground from starlight. Stars, galaxies, nebulae and all that made light formed that canopy. Simply put, just beautiful for any human eye to behold. I saw the grandeur of the night sky; simply wonderful lights everywhere. I saw several shooting stars each and every night. I saw stars that looked like I could stretch my hand out and touch them. I saw the Milky Way galaxy, which looked so close, as though I could have reached up and put my hand in it. I saw the moon, not just as a disk, but also as a sphere. It was an amazing time for me. I thank my lucky stars for being born in that little village with no electricity. Everything became much clearer in the night, and clear to me as I studied about what I was seeing.

In the sky, I saw stars that twinkle. I would learn that they twinkled because of the air in our atmosphere, and also because they were so far away. I learned that every star was a sun, just like ours, only very, very far away. With my two naked eyes I saw planets, which did not twinkle because they were much closer to Earth. I saw Mars, Jupiter, Venus and Saturn. I could not see Mercury because it was always too low in the horizon. I could not see Neptune, Uranus or Pluto because they were too far away. I learned that the word "planet," meant "wanderer." The planets moved, when observed over days and weeks, against the background of stars that seemed fixed and painted in the sky. The planets moved in a similar way as the moon, as it circumnavigated the earth. It would be like holding up a flashlight in the house, and moving it around in a circle. The light of the flashlight would move whilst the ceiling lights remained stationary. The flashlight would be the moon or wandering planet, and the ceiling lights would be the background of stars. Each night I gazed at the sky and

21

wondered. I was the wonderer amongst the wanderers; I wondered by day and I wondered by night. Whenever I wandered into the night sky I would wonder even more. I simply could not stop wondering about what, and why all that stuff was there.

I saw fuzzy groups of stars called galaxies. I learned about a Frenchman named Charles Messier who, a long time ago, wanted to study the night sky without those fuzzy objects. He labeled each fuzzy object with a number. Today, astronomers can thank him for labeling the galaxies and nebulae; which in his honor are preceded with an "M," such that M31 is the Andromeda galaxy. It is the closest spiral galaxy to our Milky Way galaxy. The Milky Way got its name from the Greeks who thought it looked like milk. I saw it in the blackness of night, as a beautiful ribbon of light, stretched across the sky, with a multitude of colors. It had a glow, which looked like artwork, done with milk and mixed with colors, and soft background lighting, with individual stars peering through. Truly beautiful, especially on a moonless night, in a place without light pollution. It could rate as one of the ten things people should see in their lifetimes.

Electricity came to the village when I was about twelve years old. It was turned off at ten each night, except Saturday nights, at eleven. People just went to sleep after a hard day's work and dealing with the heat of the day. As for me, I couldn't wait to gaze at the sky. I could not wait for nighttime with my newfound hobby. Each night I saw constellations like Orion and Cassiopeia, and I looked for more with a star map. The names of the constellations came from ancient peoples, mainly the Greeks. Many of the individual stars have Arabic names. Orion is one of the brightest constellations in the night sky, even if viewed in a city. It consists of three bright stars in a row with about equal luminosity, and almost equidistant from each other. They form the belt of Orion, the hunter. Above and below are the other stars that make up the constellation, which has the shape of a hunter with his arrow and bow. The brightest night star, named Sirius, could be found after finding the three stars of

Orion's belt; they seem to point to it. It is clearly brighter than any other star.

I saw the big dipper in a constellation officially named Ursa Major; the big bear, and I saw the little dipper, officially named Ursa Minor; the little bear. They both form the shape of bears and dippers in the sky. Two of the stars in the big dipper point to the North Star, Polaris. This star stays on top of the North Pole continuously as the earth turns around it. It marks north, and has been used by navigators since the beginning of time. In the Southern hemisphere where Polaris is not visible navigators use the Southern Cross constellation for navigation.

The most bizarre observation I made whilst star gazing, and studying Astronomy, was how far away the stars were from Earth; light years away. As an example, the three stars that made up the belt in Orion were not the same distance away from Earth. In particular, the one in the middle was hundreds of light years away from the others. Quite a mind-blowing concept. But, it was science, it was fact, and I already accepted the scientific principle. This beginning would mushroom into my exploration of every facet of science. I wanted to understand the world of the cosmos, and eventually, I also wanted to understand myself in this human race.

I learned further that the sun was 93 million miles away from Earth, and it took just over eight minutes for the light to reach Earth. That meant when I saw the sunrise, I was looking at the sun in the position it was over eight minutes ago. I did the math. The speed of light is 186,282 miles per second in the vacuum of space. I divided 93 million by 186,282 and got over 499 seconds, which is over eight minutes. The moon is about 240,000 miles away from Earth and the moonrise takes under two seconds to reach Earth. The more I learned, the more insatiable my appetite for scientific information became. I wanted to gobble it all up.

I remembered what my third grade teacher said about space. He defined it simply as; "The farther you go the farther you see." That was hardly scientific, and an eye opener for me a few years later. What I wanted to learn was not going to be from school, it would be from the countless hours in the town library. In my later years it came from scientific books, research papers, journals, history books and such publications.

The concept of distance and time was fascinating. Scientists have pondered over these concepts for hundreds of years. Einstein's ideas are now the accepted values. As I learned, I started using terms, such as light year, cosmos, sunspots, luminosity, declination, axis, and a host of others. My vocabulary expanded, and most of my friends did not understand my findings, simply because they were not interested, or that it was outside the school's curriculum. I was the wonderer amongst them, but I still fit in with the boys on the backbench, trying to be cool throughout high school. The backbench was literally a bench in the back of the classroom. It was the place for the cool dudes, who preferred to be quiet throughout class, and who did not wish for the teacher to ask them any questions. That would embarrass them and they would not be "cool" anymore. During break time, I could never speak about my secret of stargazing. Had I mentioned it, I would have been considered weird, and be told by my friends that I should be doing my homework at that hour in the night.

Night after night I gazed at the sky and learned that most of what I was looking at was not in the same place any longer. The light coming from these objects started the journey millions of years in the past. Just as it took eight minutes for the light from the sunrise to reach me, so did it take millions of years for the light from them to reach my eyes; I was looking in the past, the distant past. I also learned that the distant past was not so long ago on the cosmic calendar. In fact, the beginning of the universe started billions of years ago and these objects were only millions of years in my past. These concepts, as hard as they were to imagine, just drove my quest to want more and more. I wanted to let my imagination be challenged constantly, and most of all, I wanted to know. It all made me wonder, more and more about the being that I was, who I am, and what we were all about. Sometimes at night, all alone, looking at the night sky, as I thought about this huge universe before me, a feeling in my body would emerge, where the hairs on my skin would rise up. I felt my presence in the grandeur of the universe, and I was in total awe.

I was amazed at what I saw in the night sky with my naked eye each night. It was a very huge universe right in front of me. By daylight the sun would make the entire universe disappear. The entire village would wake up with the voices of people going about their daily routine, totally oblivious to the grandeur of the world. They cared only about what they had to do. They did not care about anything I was discovering. I cared about the universe, and wanted to know who made it, and why. How did all the stuff; planets, galaxies, stars, and all of what I saw come to be? Why couldn't I see the God who made all this stuff? But, the people in the village could care less. Perhaps they would also tell me to do my homework, instead of getting drunk on stars each night. But, I could not help myself. I was addicted.

Past civilizations looked at the night sky, named constellations, and made Gods from the heavens. They had a God for water and one for fire, and one for every other thing they needed to give thanks for, or to complain about. That was their system. In the village, it was the one God feature playing. According to the villagers, all the Greeks and ancient peoples were wrong; it would be voodoo or astrology, not religion, to name Gods from stars. In voodoo and astrology the future could be foretold based on rituals, or the position and configuration of celestial objects. In religion it was forbidden to foretell the future. Only the one invisible God knew the future. Mankind must only worship the one God and live a proper life and be invited to Heaven as the reward for being good. I was caught up in a massive confusion regarding religion, astronomy and astrology. Nobody in the village wanted to hear about the night sky; to them it was fictitious, contemptuous, and a ridiculous waste of time. In all the religious books I read, there was no mention of anything scientific, or about stars and galaxies, except the star, which the three wise men followed while looking for Jesus. That hardly qualified as scientific; at a stretch it could be called celestial navigation.

Somehow the God who commanded humans to follow religion did not want any human to understand anything scientific. Yet, he gave us the brainpower to understand how to build cities, roads, and machines, in order to live comfortably, and all of that was done scientifically. This whole thing did not make sense to me. If I mentioned astronomy in the village it was interpreted as astrology; I could not win. Sometimes I felt like the fool. But, I realized that I had learned more than the past generations, and the past civilizations. I was privileged to have inherited all the science that had been discovered, and I knew at that time that I was not a fool.

Many people, especially my father, had tried to mold me. There were teachers, preachers, neighbors and friends. They all had opinions about doctrine, life, and choices in professions. They wanted to tell me what to do. But, I was rebellious and resistant. Perhaps it was my wonderings about the vast universe, which I saw at night that empowered me to resist other points of view. Perhaps it was my defiance to authority; an authority originating from doctrine and civility, which was handed down from generation to generation, and forced upon me. I could not help questioning whether they were lost, or I was lost. They questioned nothing. I questioned everything. I rejected my father's teaching out of sheer adolescent and juvenile rebelliousness, propelled by the science I was learning. But, I would have to appease him, and others, without revealing my night secret. I accepted, but I would not relinquish my resilience with regards to science. I continued to further my education in school, as anyone should, while reading books in the library and always keeping an eye at the sky.

Eventually, between my research at the library, and my classes in school, I discovered that I could also acquire the knowledge of all the great scientists who came before me. It was all written in detail. I learned about Galileo Galilei, Nicolaus Copernicus, Charles Messier, Isaac Newton, Michael Faraday, Johannes Kepler, Louis Pasteur, Robert Boyle, Edwin

Hubble, Archimedes, Pythagoras, Leonardo da Vinci and countless more. I was in awe. I confirmed that I was not crazy. Moreover, I confirmed that the scientists were not wrong. Their names and theories were published in books, and they made sense. I was with them on the quest for the truth, much of which had already been proven.

Interestingly, every great scientist was published quite widely, except one named Charles Darwin. He was not allowed in the library. He was not allowed in school either. He was not allowed at home, and he was not allowed to enter the minds of the people in the village. Charles Darwin was not allowed to interfere with the daily blind grind of the people in the village. They had to be allowed to simply stay constructive and ignorant, without ever considering evolution. They had to be left in darkness during the brightness of daylight. But, I was keeping my secret of the brightness of the sky in the blackness of night.

BACK TO THE GRIND

I knew someday I would have to leave the village and find a venue that would accept my interests, as I kept my secret sacred. Really, no one wanted to have a boring conversation about stars and galaxies. That would be a conversation for nerds, or scientists in a lab. What I saw when the sun came up each morning was not the same place I saw during the night. I dared not tell anyone that there were stars millions of miles away from us. They would tell me that I was wasting my time and that I was crazy, or something to that effect. I felt as though the whole village was drugged to believe in only one way of life; life without questions. For hundreds of years these people lived this way, and I was certain it was the same before that.

Humans have been the same for thousands of years; living life without questioning the existence of the universe they lived in. They just didn't seem to care. There were never any discussions or questions relating to their own existence in the village. If I would even try to talk about the universe that I saw in the night they would dismiss me, and tell me to focus on the God who made everything. They could not explain anything scientific to me, and only insisted that I read the Holy books instead, as those would provide guidance on how to live. It seemed like mass hypnosis. There was so much more to see and wonder about, and investigate, and they wanted to read Holy books on how to live. What fools I thought. I thought they were all so lost. The whole universe beckons their call, but there was no convincing them to change. I had to leave them shrouded in the darkness of daylight. I was going back to the light of the darkness of night.

To these village people, the universe was made up of the schools, the houses, the churches, the buses, the cars and the carts led by donkeys. Yes donkeys, really. The leaders were the parents, the teachers, the priests, the policemen, and the civil servants. They were the masters of the universe, the masters of my universe. The village people focused on traditional life. They had a ceremony or ritual for every birth, every wedding, every death, every holiday, every cough, every sneeze, everything, and I mean, everything. That was their system. It was what they accepted, and their belief could not be changed. These were the same people who would look at the night sky briefly and just comment on its beauty, never going beyond that, and never wanting to know how far away objects were, or how they got there. To them the one and only God did all that, perhaps for their enjoyment. There were objects larger than our sun and they could not comprehend it, nor cared to. They just thought God made all that stuff, and only he knew why he made it. The whole thing was simply bizarre to me. In their minds, God would make all that stuff for the enjoyment of humans, like he had nothing better to do. I could only laugh, as I cried for help. I had to accept that it was their condition. I had to ignore their beliefs in order to prevail. I was alone in my quest. I had to wait for my time, while I did my time.

I rode a bicycle everywhere, including to high school, and I became proficient at riding. Many schoolboys wanted to drag me. "Drag" was the term meaning: "to race." I beat every one of them, as I rode happily to a cheering bunch of teenage schoolmates waiting by the schoolyard fence. I did not realize I could ride that well, but it sure felt good to win, and that gave me a bit of arrogance. Soon however, the races would be forgotten and something new would have the stage in my life.

At night during a full moon it was easy to navigate the familiar area, and riding a bicycle at night was safe by moonlight. The moon was really bright and eyes got adjusted quickly. The only problem riding at night was encountering an assembly of dogs in someone's yard. These dogs would chase after anyone and anything, even cars. Dogs owned by people were allowed to roam free. There was no leash law. There were no leashes to begin with. Riding at night meant knowing who had dogs, and identifying the position of the dog assembly long in advance. Many times the dogs would be by the roadside and easily identifiable. The technique to avoid the harrowing experience of a pack of fierce barking animals in pursuit was challenging at best. The first step was to ride as fast as possible, and then lift both feet up to the highest point as the bicycle used the momentum to pass the danger. After passage, the dogs would continue running along with the bicycle down the road, and barking at their loudest, while scaring the living daylights out of the rider, who would be wishing it was daytime. After some distance they would turn back, and a well-deserved sigh of relief from the rider would follow.

I continued my grind in the village hoping to leave someday. Where I lived was close to the equator so there were only two seasons, the rainy season and the holiday season. The sun rose around six o'clock in the morning and went down around six o'clock in the afternoon. By eight o'clock in the morning it was already hot, but manageable. By three o'clock in the afternoon water would turn to steam on the road surface. By ten o'clock in the night if you were out and about, you were either a night worker, a thief, or you were looking for trouble. Every day seemed to be the same. Life was just a routine that everyone was obligated to follow.

Some people thought it best to leave the village and move to the big towns. A couple of my older sisters got married and moved to the big towns, which had running water and electricity. During school holidays I would go to visit them many miles away. There, I would learn to swim near the mouth of a river, across the street from the house. It was a fishing village with a tidal rise of almost ten feet of water, which slowly crept up to the shore to a concrete wall barrier. The technique for learning to swim without lessons was to wade out to an anchored fishing boat, with a friend, and jump into the boat. After about an hour of rocking around in the boat, the tide would raise the boat high enough that only swimming could have saved me. It would be time to jump into the water and swim to shore. My friend who already knew how to swim would jump off the boat first, leaving me to ponder about taking that leap of faith. I had no choice. Had I chickened out, my friend would be sure to tell everyone around, and I would be laughed-at. I jumped into the water and knew I was swimming because my feet could not touch the ground. It was easy to swim; as a human I was already predisposed to being able to swim, using my long limbs to propel me, and my lungs for buoyancy. I survived, and I gained much confidence.

ADOLESCENT REBELLION

One of he most rebellious actions as a teenager that I masterminded was to convince my brother to join me on a bike ride to visit our sister, about fifty miles away from home. We would be going for a few days and it would be a secret, like leaving home. He agreed. We had to tell someone for the sake of safety. We told our mother, and left it in her hands to face my father when he questioned our whereabouts. We had to leave the house before my father woke up. We decided on four in the morning. It was better to ride in the morning anyway and avoid the afternoon tropical heat. We had to operate with the least amount of noise so as not to wake my father. If he woke up from noise at four in the morning he would immediately consider it to be robbers in the house. The last thing we needed was the impact of a stick across our backs for being suspected robbers. To be extremely quiet was no easy task in the pitch-black darkness of a house with no electricity. We got dressed, got the bikes and made it out.

We began riding leisurely to conserve energy, and after only a few miles, my brother's clothes that were wrapped in newspaper and tied to the handle bar, began to disassemble. That slowed the trip down considerably. I had to disregard the paper and simply strap the clothes into a bundle and secure it. Hours of painful riding with a partner, and some frustration, and we finally arrived. I was disappointed that it took so long. Days of laziness followed, and were welcoming to us. We had nothing to do but have fun and relax. My sister was married and had a few children. She took good care of us while we played with her children.

A few days into the trip and bad news arrived. That would be a message that we should return home. Our father needed us to do work in the shop. We agreed on a particular travel day, but my brother agreed not to ride back. Instead, he would go with public transport. I was happy. I wanted to ride, and so I did, after packing and giving him my clothes to take home. The road was not in good condition; some of it asphalt, some stone, some sand, and lots of holes. It was a rough ride, but in four and a half hours I made it home, and in time to attend a small birthday celebration for one of my other sisters.

Fifty miles of riding was unheard of in the village, especially when there were buses that would take me, and my bicycle, for a small charge. If people found out that I rode fifty miles, they would consider it strange, and me, crazy. The village people could not fathom expending extra energy for anything except purposeful work. I kept it quiet. It was something I wanted to do for myself. I wanted that record in my memory, and that made me happy.

WAITING GAME

It was not yet my turn to leave the little village. It was also not my time; I was too young. I would have to wait. In any case my father never wanted me to leave. He needed me. The first reason was that he had lost an only son before I was born. Now he wanted to keep me close and guard me from anything that could take me away from him. I had other brothers, younger than me. But, I was the first son to be born after my brother had died. I became the replacement. The second reason my father would not let me go was that he wanted to groom me as his protégé. He wanted a replacement for himself. It seemed like an instinctive feature of fathers to show the world the product of their masculinity, and perhaps their pride.

Grooming me also meant that I had to work after school in the family business; the business that had sustained all of my siblings and I, in our house, in the little village, for all of our lives. It was a jewelry business where I learned how to use all types of tools.

I learned how to alloy gold and shape it into fine jewelry. I could take a piece of alloyed gold and mill it into thick wire, then stretch it into fine wire; fine enough to make a lady's chain. I would then have to curl it into the size of the links. It looked like a long tightly woven spring. I would break out each two turns on the spring and heat them to remove their hardness. With two long fine needles I would position each piece of the spring and twist to into an "S" shape to form one chain link. Each newly formed link had to be perfect, meaning that both sides had to be equal. Any mistakes would result in the melting of all the pieces back into one piece of gold and starting over. The work had to be done with accuracy and skill; there was no forgiveness for sloppiness. After each newly formed link was complete it would be opened on one end and connected to the end of another, then closed. The linking was done with a pair of pliers with fine points. Eyesight had to be excellent or magnifiers would have to be used. After all links were connected, the chain was inspected and finally placed in a mild acid bath. In about fifteen minutes it became a yellow, shining handmade eighteen-carat gold chain.

OLD MCDONALD

A farmer friend of my father gave him a few-months-old lamb, as a gift. His fleece was white as snow. He had to be fed with a bottle, like a baby, and it was exciting for everyone who fed him, or watched him drinking. We watched him grow really beautifully. He was a bundle of joy. Eventually, the lamb would jump and run quickly, then stop suddenly. It was a good show for all. The lamb grew quickly until it became apparent that the time for some company would be appropriate. Soon it would be a grown teenager, then an adult. Some other sheep were then brought in. They all flocked together, and slept together in a shed in the backyard. They were supposed to be kept as livestock, but for us boys they were our personal pets. We even had names for several of them. But, they did not respond to their names; to them it was just noise we were making. Their brains were not wired for articulated sounds from humans.

It was amazing to study these animals. Each morning we would hear the bleating as they became restless to get their day started. Sometimes they would begin fighting inside the shed. The males would tend to show-off to each other and chase one another, whilst bumping into the females and the young ones. Sometimes it became chaotic, with the heads of rams ramming the walls. We were afraid they would break out of the shed. Noise in the backyard was the warning sound that the shed needed to be opened immediately. One of my brothers had the chore of opening the shed. We would watch the sheep come out with a sense of urgency to escape the battle inside. First to exit were the mothers and little ones, followed by the single females, while the fighters would continue their duel inside the shed. Someone had to go in and get one male out whilst holding the other inside, so that after a few minutes, they could forget that they were fighting.

Animals do not hold grudges. They don't feel anger. It would be reasonable to accept that anger would be a prerequisite to grudge. This was such a behavior to study and compare to humans. I was living in a laboratory. As soon as the sheep forgot that they were fighting they went about their business, friends as usual. They would all make a complete walk around the house eating anything that may be of interest and taste. They were tame animals that never responded to the names we gave them; they only responded to food. They loved to eat the inside of a squeezed orange. We would turn the half-cut orange inside out and hold it firmly. One by one they would come to the door and eat right from our hands, pulling on it with their teeth and then chewing. We made sure each of them had a taste. We would experiment with all different types of food to see what they liked. After their tour around the house they would all walk to the pasture.

One of my brothers was told at school that a good way to build muscle was to take vitamin B. We were teenagers and our bodies were paramount in our interests. The only source of supplemental vitamin B came in a spread, like butter, which could be put on bread. It was used primarily for flavoring food when cooking. It smelled like hell, and tasted like death. I could not eat it, and my brother would not eat it either. I decided to give it to the sheep to investigate their behavior towards food recognition. I found out that sheep were not stupid. Each one of them took a good whiff and walked away. I could not even force it on them; it was like giving medicine to a toddler. A good piece of bread loaded with vitamin B, and the sheep kept walking. Time to take notes on this study. Why did they not like the bread with the spread, and how did they know that their physician did not recommend it? Most humans would try anything, even as a dare. Were we the stupid species? That was my question. The sheep went to the pasture to eat grass, which they instinctively knew would nurture their bodies, ignoring any new cuisine offers, especially those being used for scientific research.

34

I would never realize how important my childhood circumstances would be until I became older, as I pursued my goals in science. I was lucky to observe animal behavior to a maximum, no different than if I were in the wild, except that there were no predators. There was a daily dose of rooster pursuing hen, ram pursuing ewe, and the laying of eggs, and the hatching of chickens, and the births of baby sheep and baby cows. I could see the hen pecking the eggs to get the baby chickens out. They were very yellow, very cute, and so soft to hold to my face. It was a wonderful feeling. The mother hen would always attack if anyone were to reach for one of her precious babies. Sometimes it would be a two-person operation to try to get a baby chicken to hold: one to pick up the baby, and the other to keep the protective mother at bay. It was nature at its best, and a lesson on evolution for me. In a few weeks this hen would not care about her offspring. She would be moving on, and making more chickens. What a strange creature the chicken was. As for the sheep and the cow, they stayed longer protecting their young and feeding them milk.

I would watch the babies grow when I went to the pasture. I would see baby sheep and baby cow meet face to face and stare at each other as though one wanted to know about the other. In a short time, after a brief observation, each would run back to their respective moms. Since these babies only drank milk and did not have to graze, they had all the time to explore, find friends, and get into trouble; a challenge for mothers trying to eat while watching over their young. What a laboratory I was living in, a wealth of information to ponder. I did not realize it at the moment; it had to simmer for a few decades. It did simmer and now it's very ready, and it is time to make all the connections between galaxies, animals, and humans too.

The sheep came home at dusk every day. They worked their way from the pasture right to the shed in our backyard. I wondered about their memory and navigation skills. I was amazed that they did not just stay in the pasture all day and all night. It could have been so simple to just wake up where the food was and started eating. They came home every day, one behind the other, to sleep in the shed. Perhaps they felt safe, perhaps they felt peaceful, or perhaps it was what they knew. I could never know, as the sheep would never tell. I realized that their behavior was one of the reasons they were called livestock. But, how did this happen? Who trained them? Was it in their DNA? I always wanted to know the "why" in everything.

There was a pasture on both sides of the main road. Houses lined this main road one after the other. Each house had at least two or more directly behind it. Behind the last house was a man-made ridge upon which people and animals could walk. Behind that was a small drainage canal, and finally the pasture. The Dutch settlers built the ridge and canal for irrigation and drainage, years prior to British occupation.

The elementary school I attended was located at the diagonal end of the pasture, accessible by a small road, about a quarter of a mile away, which connected to the main road. It was a longer walk from school to take the road, and sometimes students would cut through the pasture. It was more interesting, and took less time, except when I was with friends; it definitely took longer because we would play around.

Walking through the pasture had its own challenges. Large holes in the ground called, "cow-holes," made when cows stood on the soft ground, had to be avoided in order to prevent an ankle sprain. Small drainage ditches that ran crisscross in the pasture were sometimes concealed by overgrown grass. These had to be avoided so as not to come home with mud to the ankle. Finally, care had to be taken to avoid the plate sized plops on the ground left by cows. That mistake would require a walk into the canal for a temporary wash. The worst portion of the journey home was yet to come. Walking in-between the houses we would have to pass the pig farmer. That would be the time we held our breath, clenched our jaws and walked as fast as possible. The stench was "deafening" from holding our breath until our ears hurt.

PLAYTIME

I worked for my father after school and on weekends. I had very little playtime. But, I made good use of whatever time I had to play. I played ball in the yard. I climbed trees and picked fruits. I jumped over canals as a dare to the other boys, and I did a host of other boyish things. Boys had to be boys. Finally, I organized a team of boys to do experiments. Two brothers and couple of neighbors joined. I wanted to do scientific exploration and experimentation. One great benefit of this idea would help everyone realize accomplishments, learn about teamwork and gain self-confidence. At the same time we would be learning something new. I was the ringleader, and we would do things never before seen or done, in our village, or many other villages in the area.

The thought of making the largest kite ever seen by anyone in the village was our project. It would be over six feet tall. The boys all agreed and the project was underway. The construction of our kite took many days. Excitement grew, and the boys showed up for work at every chance they got. They followed instructions carefully. We worked secretly in the shed in the back yard where the sheep slept. The sheep had to be sent to my uncle because they multiplied into a flock too large for the shed. We had to clean it out and lay cardboard on the floor. I was certain that my parents suspected an ulterior motive when we started cleaning the shed, as that would certainly be something we would never do voluntarily. We were designing our laboratory. We kept everything secret so our parents would not command us to finish chores, or homework. Every member had separate tasks to acquire parts for the frame, glue and paper, along with high strength cord.

The inspiration for the construction of such a kite originated from one of the movies with Sinbad, the sailor who attached himself onto a large kite from his boat, and was lowered and delivered on shore. I wanted to build that kite, one large enough to carry a person. As the kite began to take shape I dared not reveal the thought, which came to my mind; that perhaps we could attach my little brother to this kite, like Sinbad. He was light enough. As much as this would be funny and exciting for the team, I had to recompose myself, and do my best to take that teenage daredevil mission out of my head. I am sure the "boys will be boys" saying came from such things as I was thinking. I could only imagine the repercussions of such an act, especially from my strict and rigid father. I would have been in so much trouble. We would all have been in so much trouble.

The secret of the kite came out when we unveiled it. Meaning, taking it out of the shed in the backyard and preparing it for flight. Several boys had to carry the kite to the pasture to launch it. When the kite rose majestically into the sky, it made a sound never before heard. We had a special feature built-in to purposely make that loud sound. People came from the entire area to look at this kite as they heard the sound. They were all in amazement as to its size. It towered above us and took two boys to hold the cord attached to it. The kite flew several times until we got tired of the whole thing. It was time for something new, some other new project, and some other new adventure.

THE ACID MIX

I again assembled the team together to do an experiment with a practical result. It involved dangerous acids, and careful planning had to be implemented. We had access to acid from my father's supply, which was used in the jewelry making business. But, we needed a large quantity, and he would certainly have noticed if we took the quantity we needed. If he discovered that we took the acid we would not prevail with the experiment. More importantly, we would have one angry father asking questions. We could not have that. No! No! No! Time for a new strategy. We would go into town to buy the acid ourselves. But, acid was a highly regulated substance, and sold only by licensed individuals. Time for the secret agent move. One positive point was that the man at the shop where the acid was sold knew me, as I was the one who came to buy the acid for my father so many times in the past. Ok! Game on. As we rode our bicycles into town carrying the container for the acid, a new challenge arose. What would we say if the man questioned the large quantity we were buying? We needed at least two pints. One pint was more than enough for most people. Our quantity could raise the red flag of suspicion or curiosity. Well, since we worked with our father, and we did most of the work anyway, we would simply say that we had a lot of jewelry work to do. Simple. Done! We continued to the store and placed the order whilst making small talk to distract the man from asking any questions.

The acid purchase was completed with success. Whew! We prevailed. And now, after spending what was equivalent to our entire monthly allowances, we must now transport the acid to the laboratory, the shed in the backyard. Not only was the acid corrosive, and would burn skin on contact, it was also in a glass container, and we were on bicycles. Carefulness to us was as paramount as sending a man to the moon. Constant checking of the container and the acid made for a safe passage. Upon arrival at home we must pass the guards; Ma and Pa. Finding an appropriate camouflage for two pints of a deadly liquid to avoid our parents from discovering was no easy task. We figured it out; get the neighbor to keep it in his yard till nighttime, and hope that he did not ask what was in the package. We had to be like spies during wartime, trying to accomplish our mission without getting caught. Our parents would not only have questioned what we were doing; it was also that they would think we should be spending this time doing chores and homework. Bummer. For this experiment, top secrecy was paramount. We were dealing with a dangerous container of acid and if we were caught it would certainly mean jail time.

Once night came it was time for our clandestine operation to continue. We had to retrieve the deadly substance carefully, in the darkness of night, and transport it to its designated hiding place in the backyard shed. Each person had a task, one to retrieve the package, another to open the door to the shed slowly so there was no squeaking, and one to keep a lookout for the guards. It was already suspicious for anyone of us to be outside at night. If several of us were outside, the suspicion of conspiracy would be certain. Whisper was the manner of communications. Coughing was the warning sound. Loud coughing meant termination of the operation. The time and route were already planned out to the backyard shed. The door person for the shed would watch the progress since he was at the best vantage point. Finally, when the package arrived, the transporter would place it at its designated site and confirm that it was secure. The lid had to be closed, and it had to be placed level in order to prevent spills. Hearts were racing and breathing was rapid. Finally, after the slow and staggered return of each agent, a sigh of relief. Smiles were painted on our faces as confirmation to the team that the operation was complete and successful. We all learned some valuable lessons on clandestine operations, and the power of teamwork. We could probably have applied for spy jobs. But, such thoughts did not enter our minds. We were going to be in science.

The next challenge for the experiment was to obtain enough of a metal to be used for the reaction with the acid. The metal was zinc, and could not be purchased. It was not available in its pure form, only as an alloy. We needed pure zinc and we knew exactly where to find it - in flashlight batteries. We had to start collecting dead batteries around the neighborhood. No one would give us a good battery; it would be like throwing money away. Each battery had to be stripped from the outside. That was simple. It was mainly paper, and soaking in water made it easy. After the paper was removed, the battery had to be cut open like a fruit. Zinc was soft so it was easy to do by hand, with a knife. Once opened, the stuff inside the battery had to be completely removed. That stuff was a black carbon paste which was slightly acidic and smelled really, really bad. The zinc was just a shell wrapped around the battery. The black stuff had to be dug out and discarded into our special toxic waste storage facility - the bushes. We used an old spoon, a very old spoon, to dig out the paste. This task had to be completed when my mother was not in the area. We feared that she would have thought that we were using a good spoon from her kitchen. This would have posed serious additional challenges to our mission.

When the black carbon was removed, the zinc had to be washed thoroughly. It would take the form of a sheet of thick metal about the size of three business cards placed side by side. The next challenge was to extract the pure zinc by melting it and allowing it to drop into the shape of peanuts. But, this had to be done in the absence of our father, which was when he was taking his nap. Even though the zinc had a low melting point, we needed to use his gas torch in the shop. Several issues arose. Firstly, my father would banish us if he found out that we had any type of metal other than gold in his shop. He feared contamination as much as a surgeon feared infection. Secondly, if even a small amount of the black carbon from the batteries were present, which always happened, it would burn and make enough smoke for a fire department call. In a village that did not have a fire department, that meant neighbors would start yelling out of their windows about the smoke and possible fire. Aside from that, the smoke smelled like something that could wake the dead. My mother would be the first to inquire what we were burning, as the smoke would spread throughout the house first. Fire was the one thing everyone in the village feared, and was careful about. The houses were all made of wood. Chastisement beyond redemption would be the penalty if we were caught. In a hurry, we melted the zinc and made all the pieces for our experiment. Afterward, we did a thorough clean up, including removal of any and all traces of questionable tools and materials. The precious pieces of zinc were placed immediately into our vault, which was the shoebox under the bed.

The day for the experiment had to be chosen carefully. Many factors had to be considered. Firstly, we had to choose a day when all team members were available, and would not be interrupted. That meant all of our chores had to be completed. Secondly, and most important was the weather. It had to be sunny skies with no rain in the forecast, and light winds preferable. We consulted the best weather report available. We looked at the sky and read the report; it was written all over the sky. Thirdly, we had to be sure that our parents would not be out and about in the yard. For my father that was easy to find out, he took a daily nap right after noontime, and he never missed. One secret agent could easily verify that our suspect went to bed upstairs, and then make haste for the lab. As for my mother, we were not too concerned. We would sometimes tell her that we were doing schoolwork experiments and she would shrug it off. If she insisted on further investigation, one of us would blurt out a chemical formula, or a complex scientific theory and she would leave in total confusion, knowing well that she was no match for one of her teenage sons in high school. Poor Ma; we knew how to play her, as she was such a pushover. But, she accepted the way things were, and she accepted her situation.

The day had come. Blue skies, light wind and no guards about; parents were at bay. Our equipment included three empty gin bottles, balloons, and a couple large buckets of water. Of course, top of the list of items would be the acid and the zinc pieces. The large buckets of water were used to cool the bottles during the experiment, as they would break otherwise. Each man had his task. Acid was already in place in the laboratory. I had the zinc and the balloons. Next man had the gin bottles, completely cleaned. Finally, the water boy, with the buckets of water, and we were ready.

The procedure had to be exact, and the orchestration precise. First, I would evacuate the air from three balloons by sucking and shrinking them, and holding a strong squeeze at the bases. Second step was to pour about a half of a cup of acid in each of the three gin bottles. Third step was the most precise event. One man would hold one of the gin bottles firmly in the bucket of water. Another man would put several pieces of zinc into this first bottle. The third man, me, would open the end of one balloon, without allowing air to enter, and place it around the bottle opening. The last man would hold the balloon in place. These steps continued for all three of the gin bottles. When we combined the acid with the zinc, a violent boiling reaction started, which allowed the zinc to combine with the acid, thereby releasing the hydrogen, molecularly bonded in the acid. Hydrogen, being a gas, occupied more space than solids or liquids. The expansion and expulsion of the hydrogen was forceful enough to inflate the balloons directly from the gin bottles. There was no helium for balloons at that time in the little village. We had to make hydrogen from scratch for such fun, with the chemical formula of $Zn+H_2SO_4= ZnSO_4+H_2$^

It became time for suspense, anxiety, and waiting in anticipation. We would watch the balloons expand, one by one. The gin bottles got hotter and hotter as the reaction between the zinc and the acid created an enormous amount of heat. A spare bucket of water was necessary to ensure the integrity of the process. We had learned from a prior failure of a gin bottle when the acid mix was ejected into the bucket of water. Clean up on aisle two was not pleasant. Finally, after each balloon was at the right size, I would tie the base into a knot to prevent any gas from escaping. We would do about three to six balloons in the same experiment. After the balloons were secure we would join three together, then two, and one solo. It was time for the display of our success. It was time to make a big announcement in the neighborhood for everyone to watch. It was showtime.

Our entire family, neighbors, and any strangers about were summoned to the main road for a display, the unveiling of a successful experiment. A display that they would enjoy, ponder about and ask questions, and perhaps never forget. It was a simple experiment with young boys from the hood. For us it was not a big deal, but for them it was a mystery, or magic. They would see something they had never seen before. When we released the balloons they would see all of them rise into the sky, and continue upward, rising into the atmosphere. The balloons would not drop back down to the ground like any other balloon filled with air. The balloons were not filled with air; they were filled with a gas lighter than air; they were filled with hydrogen. The balloons rose above the surface and continued rising until they were too high to be seen. They eventually went out of sight.

The questions then began from the onlookers. They asked about the kind of gas that was inside the balloons, the method of inflation, the ingredients used to accomplish the task, and on and on. We could explain all we could, but they could not understand. They did not know that when the acid was combined with zinc metal, the result would be a molecular and chemical reaction. This process would separate the components of the acid, during which hydrogen would be extracted and released from the acid. They did not know because they did not go far enough in school to understand the concept, or to learn the chemical formula. Even my father who worked with acids and metals could not grasp it. He just knew how to use the acid in the jewelry making business. My father somehow knew though, that we had done something contrary to the practice of making fine jewelry, but he asked nothing about it. He accepted that his young sons were doing something constructive, and not making mischief. I believe he did not want to know the details; he simply wanted to feel that sense of pride for our great accomplishment, and for something he himself had never seen.

The thought of people not knowing something, but accepting whatever explanation was given, seemed like a fertile environment for conjecture. No matter how much we tried to explain the experiment, there was a blockage of information flow, simply from the lack of knowledge. We could have told them anything. Perhaps it was how early humans explained natural phenomena, by just assuming the best guess of an explanation, which after some time became the accepted belief. That would be of course, until sometime in the future, when a more plausible explanation was presented and the facts became clear, most likely from scientific experimentation.

HOT STUFF

The scientific challenges came one after the other, I was a juvenile with a curious mind, and I was easily bored. Card games and cricket became second and third choices. I had to find challenges, and things that were never before done in the village. The next opportunity came from a souvenir sent to my family from a foreign person. It was a photo plaque with an alcohol thermometer attached. Just what we needed in the village near the equator; something to measure hot and hotter. Eventually this thermometer broke and the alcohol with red dye leaked out. For a young scientist this was called, "opportunity." I got the team of boys together and proposed an idea. We could make another thermometer from the broken one, but we would have to calibrate it. All good. That would not be a problem. We would use mercury as the liquid inside the tube of the thermometer, instead of alcohol. Mercury was a liquid metal at room temperature and had a linear coefficient of expansion. We already knew that mercury was used widely for thermometers from experience at the doctor's office. Additionally, we had access to mercury.

I orchestrated the plan. First, we had to be sure that the gas torch used in the shop was hot enough to melt the glass of the thermometer. That was easy; we simply fired up the torch and pointed it at the top of a soft drink bottle. The heat from the torch at the most focused point turned that glass into a ball in no time at all; piece of cake for our project. Now, we could show the soft drink bottle to people in the village and ask them to explain the deformity at the top. We loved doing such stuff, especially telling them that the bottle was left in the sun for several weeks and the glass melted. The villagers would seriously consider our explanation, while at the same time knowing in their guts, that they must disbelieve it, as their logic could not accept that the bottle would melt from the sun's heat. At least for us, it kept them thinking, until the next day when they would ask how the bottle became deformed. We loved every minute of it.

I organized the team to slightly heat the thermometer to evacuate whatever air would be in the tube and bulb, which formed a vacuum in the process. We had to use tongs to hold the hot thermometer. We then placed the open end of the thermometer into the liquid mercury so that it could "swallow" the mercury by letting the vacuum that was formed inside draw the liquid in. We made sure that it was filled with mercury, and no air bubbles were present. We placed it in hot water to check how much the mercury would rise. Too little or too much mercury would render the thermometer useless. We gauged the amount, and made sure that there was just enough to exceed the boiling point of water. This meant that our thermometer would be able to measure temperature above the boiling point of water. It was not a necessity, but a benefit. Now the challenge came. We would have to seal the top of the thermometer glass tube without trapping any air inside. That meant we would have to heat the mercury until it expanded to the top of the tube, while at the same time melting the glass on top to seal it. That was accomplished with a simple candle at the bottom of the thermometer, while I used the torch at its highest temperature on top of the tube to melt it and cause it to close, just as the mercury rose to that point. The assurance that air was not present in the tube was to allow a small amount of mercury to overflow from the top while it was being sealed. It was exactly what we did.

The bigger problem was the clean up. Mercury is a liquid at room temperature and if one drop of it falls on a surface it would split up into a thousand beads, like what happens with water. The loss of the mercury was not our concern. It was the contamination of it with the gold inside the shop. Mercury in gold alloy will pose a significant problem for a jeweler to the point that the gold mixed with mercury would have to be discarded and written-off. It would be unusable. Mercury has a devastating effect on humans also; it could wreck havoc with our nervous system, if ingested.

It became time to calibrate the thermometer. We would need to mark two points on it, the boiling and the freezing points of water. Not really too difficult. We placed the bulb of the thermometer in some ice and waited until the mercury contracted and stopped moving. A quick pen mark followed by a mild passage of a thin hacksaw blade over the glass tube marked the spot. We allowed the thermometer to warm up to room temperature then repeated the process a few times in order to verify that the mark was correct. That was the scientific principle, and we followed it.

In order to mark the boiling point we would have to use the stove in the kitchen, my mother's domain. We boiled a small pan of water and immersed the bulb of the thermometer into the water and verified that the mercury stopped rising inside the tube. A quick pen mark did the trick. We allowed the thermometer to cool and repeated the process and verified that the mark was correct. Again a quick passage of the hacksaw blade completed the mission. It was important that the thermometer bulb was in the water and not above where there was steam. Steam would be the water vapor cooled by the surrounding air, and was not the same temperature as the boiling point of water. Another consideration we had to make was that the calibration had to be done at sea level, and we were already there.

Water boils at a lower temperature at higher altitudes and that is why food takes longer to cook there. A correctly calibrated thermometer would show that the boiling point of water was 100 degrees Celsius at sea level and lower on a mountaintop. It would also show that the freezing point of water would be higher than zero Celsius on the mountain, but only slightly higher.

At some point, as usual, my mother would enter the kitchen and inquire what we were doing. Her concern was that we were not going to burn the house down. We had no answer for her except one word; "experiments." One of us would even venture to indulge the old woman and start to explain how we were calibrating a thermometer. She would simply sigh and walk away. The poor woman exited school to be married at sixteen. She could not possibly fathom our venture. The concept in matters of science was far beyond her reach. In this light, we often made fun of her, and she would easily laugh it off, acknowledging her limitation, all the while being proud that her sons were in school, and being educated. We would get a chuckle when, knowing well that she did not know the terms used to describe what we were doing, she would try to repeat it.

If we were to say "calibration" she would repeat it as "caltration," "coloration" or something similar, but never accurately. We would laugh as we repeated what she said in a teasing manner. It was fun, and she was not the least insulted. She understood her limited education; it was her circumstance and she accepted it, while being proud of her sons.

We later colored in the hacksaw marks on the thermometer with a dye. We had successfully marked the two extremes of the thermometer, the zero-degree mark and the 100-degree mark. We divided the distance between the marks in half, and marked it as the fifty degree Celsius point. We continued dividing until we had enough marks for the thermometer to be usable. The first few days we watched the thermometer work, magically displaying the temperature in the house. It moved up and down from approximately 30 to 25 degrees. In other words it barely moved. It was like watching grass grow. What could we expect? We lived in the tropics where the nighttime temperature was hot and the daytime temperature was simply hotter. A gift of a thermometer to a person who lived in the tropics would be equivalent to a gift of a snowball to someone living in an igloo. At least the thermometer became useful for our boyish curiosity.

We lost interest in the thermometer after a few days and left it on the wall to continue its fluctuations. I wondered about it afterward that, even though no one was watching, or cared, it still continued to work. It had no purpose of its own in the world; it just did what it did, as it was designed. It was no different than the sunrise, or water dripping slowly from melting ice. All the processes in the world were automatic, like each situation knew what to do. This was nature following the rules of the universe, while no one was watching. This was how I wondered about the universe. All the systems were derived since the beginning of time, forming slowly, and always surely following the rules of their formation, the rules of science; the rules of the universe. Before the beginning of time we may never know; it is the curtain pulled across the stage of our existence, and behind it is forbidden to see. If we did someday

48

find a way to take a peek, what would it matter? Would we then have purpose and objective in life? Or, would we just find more areas to explore in our never-ending quest to find ourselves?

TIME TO THINK

The explorations I started were not only with scientific experiments. I was curious about everything. I wanted to know about animals, trees, stars, galaxies, matter, energy, weather and a host of other stuff. Especially, I wanted to know all the reasons why, and how these things existed. Human behavior was one of the most prominent of my searches. I had such a difficult time understanding people and their motives. I could not fathom, for example, the rejection by many young and old people, for my exploration of the night sky. Some of them even associating my studies with astrology. This would be voodoo in the one God society I lived. I just gave up trying to convince anyone who was not interested. I could only imagine the suffering that Galileo went through, a few hundred years ago, being accused of heresy, because he confirmed that the earth orbited around the sun. The Catholic Church held the belief that the earth was the center of the world. Wow! I am no Galileo, but still in the twentieth century I could not get villagers to see the facts of our world. They did not care. They did not need the sun for anything else except for its light and heat, but not so much for intense heat. They were able to live their entire lives in this ignorance and still feel that they were complete, some even thinking they were the top dogs of society; simply because they were the most knowledgeable in divine and spiritual matters. No one dared mess with the top dogs. My father was one.

THE CHICKEN WITHOUT THE EGG

One of a parent's worst nightmares must be having bored teenage boys. Mischief would seem to be in front and behind them continually. Chores were not the antidote for this condition, only a mere distraction. In-between our chores, I mustered the gang and assembled for another one of our thrills. We were clandestine operators, and snuck in operations as soon as eyes were not upon us. We decided to take one of my mother's healthy male chickens to check its ability to fly. As was normal in the village, many people had livestock, and my mother raised chickens and ducks in our yard. We had a variety to choose from, but the selection had to be careful. We had to be sure that the chicken would be safe and unhurt for this experiment. We could never indulge in behavior that hurt animals, and for that matter people, or even trees and plants.

We assembled the group of boys and picked three volunteers who would quickly go up on the second story of our house to launch the chicken out of the window. Quickly, meaning before any of the adults could see, and also to avoid any clean up from a nervous chicken. My parents would have our heads if a chicken were brought into the house. The offense would be much more serious if the chicken relieved itself in the house. I knew that none of the boys would want to clean it up either. Precaution included careful orchestration. Three boys went to the second floor; one holding the chicken, the other holding a piece of cardboard under the chicken, just in case, and the third came as a lookout. I was sure to place myself in a position as though I was not involved in the prank, inasmuch as I was the ringmaster of our circus. Execution of the plan had to be precise, and that was part of the teamwork.

Finally, the moment came that the chicken would be placed on the windowsill and the boys would stand behind to release and observe. The other boys would be at ground level. It did not take long for the chicken to decide whether to jump in or out of the house; three boys behind it were convincing enough. The chicken took the leap of faith, believing that surviving the descent was the lesser of the two evils. The chicken flapped its wings vigorously and clucked continuously all the way down. It landed gently and un-hurt nearby some other chickens. Those chickens simply ran out of the way while looking at the flying chicken as though it was a crazy animal. Soon after, the flying chicken went about its business as though nothing had happened - the benefit of a short memory. During the exercise, the laughter was deafening, from the moment the chicken left the launch pad. Stomachs began to hurt from the ludicrousness of such juvenile mischief. When my mother showed up to investigate, we became serious for a moment, until someone confessed that we threw a chicken out the second floor window. She was serious at first, and soon after started to giggle with the humor, while accepting that boys will be boys. She would dismiss the whole thing, while walking away, and reminding us how we could better spend our time. I doubt that my Ma ever fathomed the trials and tribulations she would have to endure by having boys.

If Pa had found out that we threw a chicken out the upstairs window he would have probably chuckled at first, then referred the matter to Ma; chickens were not in his department. Pa did not care about chickens or kitchens, and for sure he did not care about flying chickens, except to have a laugh. His jurisdictional boundaries were precisely marked.

Shortly after the chicken landed and all was calm, a thorough analysis had to be done. These would be mental calculations, no paperwork or formula. One of the boys would start the discussion as to why the chicken did not fly. One other boy would make the simple and accurate conclusion that the chicken was too heavy for the lifting surface of its wings. The discussion would go on to aerodynamics, and on with the analysis of birds that fly, to flightless birds; like kiwis and penguins. Evolution entered briefly, but again we were not ready for prime time with that subject; it would turn into another heresy accusation from someone, if they had heard about our discussion. In the village, there was some kind of blockage to ideas or investigations about facts. All conclusions had to accommodate the norms, common acceptance and visual validity. Any conclusion on the contrary would be deemed contradictory, and be rejected. Everything I could be interested in was a conundrum; such were the circumstances.

51

OLE MAN SHANKS

There was an old man living in a shack immediately next to our house. He had only one eye. No one ever asked him how he lost his eye, but he kept the other watchful eye on us whenever we made noise or mischief in the yard. We called him, "Mr. Shanks." He would come quietly out to investigate if he heard any type of noise. His hearing certainly compensated for his one eye. We would simply see him standing near the fence with hands on his waist, and a very serious look on his face. Often, he would inquire as to what we were doing. Somehow, he saw everything with that one good eye, and he already knew that we were up to mischief.

He represented our parents, and that commanded his role as elder in the village, with authority and privilege, conferred upon him, after being duly qualified as such. If we defied or disobeyed him there would be a complaint lodged with our parents, and that meant double trouble. Mostly, he was concerned about our safety, and would tell us such things as to get out of trees we had climbed. One trick we naturally devised when he showed up was to "freeze" our positions and hope he did not see us, until he finally gave up and walked away. If he happened to see us, and were to ask what we were doing, we would simply not reply. After asking for a second time and not receiving a reply the old man would say; "Who am I talking to, a ghost?" Finally, one of the boys would reply that we were not doing anything, which was true. He could not deny it, as we would not be moving in our frozen positions. As soon as he disappeared we would resume our mischief.

He became frustrated when we ignored his commands and would revert to calling one of our parents, primarily my mother. But, by the time she would show up, we were at ease and had already abandoned our mischief. He would look foolish. One particular day he ordered one of the boys to come down from a tree and the boy refused. He called out for my mother, and the boy replied, "She is not home." He then called out for my father, and the boy happily responded, "He is not home either." With laughter all around, the poor old man simply sucked his teeth and retreated to his shack. The juvenile philosophy of young boys in the village interested in making mischief was; "when the cat is away the mice will play." We lived that philosophy and became vigilant in always looking out for the "cat."

Mr. Shanks was a baker of bread and sweet cakes, which he sold for a living. He had a clay oven in the back of his shack and when he was baking it smelled nice everywhere. My mother and sisters would occasionally ask him to put a dish in his oven for baking. He never refused. That was, until one of my sisters gave him a glassware dish to put into his oven. The poor old man had not been aware that glassware had made its debut into the oven. He thought the glass would break, and he questioned my sister as though she was playing a joke with him. She insisted that it would be fine in the oven, but he still did not believe. He immediately summoned my mother and questioned her. She also confirmed that the glassware was fine in the oven. Ole man Shanks shook his head in disbelief as though the world had gone crazy, and proceeded to put the dish into the oven. I could only imagine that it was placed at a safe distance from his bread and cakes. After the baking was complete, he eventually accepted, and got used to the new technology of glassware for the oven.

The old man's shack was on a piece of land that was owned by my father. It was not unusual for people to build houses on land belonging to others who were willing to offer a long-term lease. His rent was fifty cents per month. That was a very, very long time ago in a place that was still in a time zone far in the past, when a candy bar would cost ten cents.

My father had several properties for rent in the village, and I collected the rent from tenants when they came to the shop to pay. I wrote a receipt for them and marked the payment in a big book my father kept for records. As I flipped through the pages curiously I could see which tenants were up to date with their rent, and which ones were behind. I noticed the only

53

one who was years in arrears was no other than Mr. Shanks. My father never asked him for rent, simply because he did not have the heart to do it. I also felt sorry for this old man, and often I would use my allowance money that I saved to pay some of his rent. I would put the cash in the drawer, write him a receipt and deliver it to him. He was gracious for my gesture and thanked me very kindly. I also noticed that he never seemed encouraged to discuss the subject of the arrears on his rent. He seemed dismissive when I mentioned that I would pay some more, with my future allowance money. He was slightly embarrassed, but I also believe that he believed that my father had recognized his presence as more valuable than the rent money. I believe that he was right. My Pa recognized this old man as a contributor to the neighborhood, and the greater good to the entire community, and left him in peace. My father also never discouraged me from paying his rent with my allowance money, as he preferred that I be compassionate towards an old man and exercise charity towards him. I was being taught, without words.

Mr. Shanks' baking schedule in the clay oven was weather dependent. He would have to wait for inclement weather to cease before lighting the wood to heat the oven; wet wood and fire did not mix well for Mr. Shanks. Some days it would get dark while he was still baking. He relied on a powerful gas lamp that worked with pressurized kerosene. It had a pump at the base, which was used to add pressure to vaporize the kerosene in the tank. This vapor then flowed through brass tubes into a jet at the top. The jet was lit, and the hot gas exhausted through a thin fabric filament to show the light. This type of lamp was a remarkable invention. The lamp could be hung on a wire hook attached to the low ceiling, or carried around. The lamp was also wind proof. The intense heat from the old man's lamp would cause it to fail when parts became warped or jets became blocked. He would ask me, or one of the boys to fix it. That would be a delightful request for boys who loved the challenge of experimentation. We would disassemble the entire apparatus and soak it in a mild acid bath in the shop to clean it. There were plenty of tools in the shop for any project or type of fixing, and my father did not object to us helping this old man. In fact, he thought it was noble of us, and he felt some sense of pride, as evidenced by his acceptance. In due time we would have the lamp lit, with parts we would sometimes have to pay for ourselves. We did not mind; the opportunity he gave us was worthy of the cause. We would deliver the lamp with new instructions as to its operation, based on whatever rigging we had done. The old man would be delighted, and he rewarded us with pieces of fresh cake. The freshly baked cake was made with coconut and brown sugar, and was delicious and mouth-watering.

A TIMELESS PIECE

The strange and crazy village still preserved its constructiveness. Everyone in their respective position and profession was productive in their jobs and goals. Fathers went to work, students went to school, and housewives stayed at home to cook and clean. It was ultra traditional, and stuck in the past. Everyone had a role in the village, and hustled for a dollar. There were few complaints about anything, and one in particular could be about the price of something from a merchant, while haggling for the right price. Aside from the seriousness for survival, there was lots of laughter from people who were simply funny. One man made sure he read every page of the newspaper so he could get his money's worth. Another would not open his new umbrella for fear of getting it wet. Yet, another wore boots when he traveled to the town and was told that he had to walk on "Water Street."

In the evening some people went home, got dressed and went to the cinema. It was an occasion to be social and to show off new fashion. One such fashion item was wristwatches, when they became affordable for the common man. They sold like hotcakes. One middle-aged man wore one, even though he could not tell time. Yes, there were adults who were capable of building an entire house, but were unable to read a clock. The only time workers cared about was quitting time. Time was estimated by the angle of the sun, as the village had a fairly regular sunrise and sunset, being near the equator. We also had an almost equal day and equal night throughout the year. The overhead sun marked the middle of the day. Other times were estimated according to the angle from the horizon, or from the high noon mark. It was the days of celestial time-keeping.

In this crazy village it was not uncommon for people to make fun of each other or tease someone, in a gentle manner. It was not uncommon to accuse a friend of robbing the bank if he had a lot of cash on him; both knowing it was a joke. If a villager said that he liked my shirt it meant that he would like to have one just like it; preferable the one I was wearing, and for free. I have taken the shirt off my back for such an occasion. If a man said that his comb had some broken teeth, someone would tell him to take it to the dentist. If someone said, "your head no-good" it meant that you were crazy, about what you were saying. It was all taken as fun.

As for the man who wore his watch for fashion, but could not tell time, he was teased daily. Everyone knew he could not read his watch, and many would first compliment him on the beauty of his watch, then immediately ask him what time it was. The poor fellow had only two answers; "It's late man, it's late," or "It's early man."

I could not tell time either, as any other child, until I was able to understand the concept. My sisters would ask me to tell them the time if I could see the clock in the house. I merely told them the number that the short hand was pointing to and the number that the long hand was on.

THE HUMAN ELEVATOR

My father was a very industrious man and he did not depend on one source of income. His jewelry business provided most of his income, but he had slowly purchased and added land, and small rental property to his portfolio. Aside from collecting monthly rent, the property had value like a bank account. He could have sold a piece of land if he had found himself in a difficult financial position. On the land he owned, which became under joint ownership because of his marriage to my mother, there were several coconut trees. Coconuts had a variety of uses in the village. Young coconuts had ample drinking water, full of minerals and jelly that was delicious and sweet. The older, dry coconuts were used for cooking and baking. The hard shells of coconut were also used for arts and crafts. Villagers found many other ways to use coconuts, including extracting the oil from the nuts. Coconut oil had many benefits and was used primarily as a body lotion. It was good to rub the clean body with coconut oil to bring out the lovely tropical tan, with an almost reflective sheen.

In the village, the coconut trees were tall, and only individuals with special skills could climb them for the coconuts. It was sort of a profession. The one individual who was an expert climber kept a watchful eye on all the trees in the village. Individual trees always had young and old coconuts together. He would approach the prospective owner when it was time to reap the nuts. He received payment in cash, plus coconuts. He sold the coconuts for a profit. This was a man who could take a coconut in one hand, a machete in the other, and in one minute have you drinking the water; as may be seen on a Caribbean island.

The man who could climb the trees was short and slim with a low body weight. His name was Bang-a-Lang. In the village it was customary to address people by their names, but never to ask how they got their names. Many people had false names, which originated from aspects such as their anatomy, manner of speech, manner of walk, profession, and such. The man who raised sheep was named, "Woolly." The man with one short leg was called; "Hop along." Any young boy was called, "Smally." The milkman was named simply, "Milkman." The son of the milkman was named, "Milkman's son." The man with a hoarse voice had the name; "Husky." The man who repaired furniture was called, "Chairman." The man who fixed sewing machines had the name, "Singer-man." My Pa was called, "Goldsmith," because that was his profession. Most of these people simply accepted their names; it was the norms of the society. Somehow false names worked well, as several people did not even know their real names. When births were registered, a birth certificate, which also had the false name of "born paper," was issued, and most likely placed in a forgotten location. Only for official matters like marriages, or court cases were real names important. That would be the time when the digging for the "born paper" would be undertaken.

Bang-a-Lang would consult with my mother to receive permission to climb several trees while negotiating his payment. One of the boys, most likely me, would have to accompany him as a lookout; so coconuts did not fall on people's heads. He had a cart to transport the coconuts. I would watch him as he climbed, and climbed diligently, as naturally as an animal that lived in a tree. The tree swayed in the wind, and the wind was strong. The higher he went the more he swayed. He held on as though he had suction cups in his palms. Within a couple of minutes he would mount a tall tree and reach the top. He would stand on top of the tree and start to push coconuts towards the ground in all directions. When he returned down, we would collect and load them up in his cart. Some of the coconuts were pushed in a direction far from the tree, which he would expect me not to notice. After he delivered the coconuts to my mother he would return to get those; that was his bonus. Everyone was in on his game, and that was the way it was for the coconut picker. Who else would climb the tree for coconuts? Bang-a-Lang had a talent few people possessed, or dared to even try.

On one of our trips I noticed that he reached the top of the tree, but did not stand on top of the tree. Instead, I saw a man hugging a tree and descending like the fastest elevator I could imagine. When he reached the bottom, I questioned him about the issue, and reminded him that there were several coconuts on that tree. He told me that there was a snake in that tree and he did not get along with snakes.

THE DIAMOND DEAL

I was working in my father's shop one afternoon when a man, who was in a similar business, came to visit him. The man was a miner, and he wanted to sell diamonds. My father did not make diamond jewelry; he was strictly a goldsmith. The man had some diamonds to show, which my father looked at as a courtesy, and out of curiosity. They were raw, and of different sizes; they looked like pieces of dirty glass. As the man finished with my father he expressed gratitude for the discussion. He packed up his valuables and was about to depart when he looked at me and asked if I would like one of the small pieces of diamond, as a gift. He thought that I could make a piece of jewelry for myself. I accepted. I was overjoyed and excited. I thanked him enormously. He gave me a gift I could never find, or purchase, and he was delighted at my response to his gift. What he did not know was that the piece of diamond was worth much more to me than he thought. It was never going to be made into jewelry. He gave me the one thing I needed to prove about what I had learned regarding geology and the formation of rocks.

Geologists have poked holes in the earth and dug into it multitudes of places. We have learned so much about this earth from science. Sedimentary rocks were formed in layers, igneous by heat, such as volcanoes, and metamorphic was formed by heat and pressure deep inside the earth. It was in the metamorphic rock that the carbon mineral was pressed under extreme pressure to form the hardest natural substance known to man - diamond. After millions of years the diamond came close to the surface during earth movements. The same carbon mineral could be as soft as a number two pencil, or as hard as diamond. Diamonds on the streets of New York carried a great value; in the little village their value was negligible. It was gold the people wanted. Gold held its value, and it was a form of investment.

I had received a gift of the substance that would prove what I had learned. If that piece of diamond were real, then it would be real hard, and that meant harder than steel. Without my father looking I placed it on an anvil, and I used one of the old hammers to hit it gently. It did not shatter like glass. I continued hitting it carefully so that it would not slip away, and it still did not shatter. I was in awe to have confirmed what I already knew. I was amazed at my new discovery, which I could not wait to share with others. My excitement waned when I looked at the anvil and the hammer; they both had dents from the impact with the diamond. I was in big trouble with my father, as he would not tolerate dents in tools used for fine jewelry making. I sanded the hammer down, and did the best to smooth the anvil also.

The best part came when I would dare the carpenters in the village to break the stone with their hammers. They thought it was just a piece of glass. Each time they would strike it, harder and harder, and simply be amazed at such a hard stone. After several attempts I would tell them it was diamond, and they became more amazed. I would tell them to look at their hammers and they would see the dents. The carpenter's hammer did not have to conform to the precision of the jeweler's hammer. They accepted it calmly. As for the value of the lesson, the diamond was worth its weight in gold, so to speak. The man had done me a great favor.

NUTS ABOUT NUTS

In the little village, peanut butter was called, "nut-butter." Simply said, it was because we were not used to other nuts, except coconuts. Cashews, almonds and hazelnuts only came at Christmastime. We would be lucky if each of us got ten of those nuts as a snack during the season; they were rare and very expensive. When we said the word, "nut" we meant peanuts. Oh, the things I take for granted at this point in my life. At this moment I can walk to the pantry and have all the almonds, peanuts and cashews my stomach could hold. Yet, I am not enticed; they are not scarce items; they are not expensive items. They are not precious to me anymore. Nuts and nut-butter were all we had as a treat, a special and tasteful snack for a child.

Peanuts came in a raw form and had to be placed in an oven to be parched. Leave them just a bit too long in the oven and they would come out like burnt charcoal; black as carbon. They would disintegrate when touched. Burning the nuts would be a disaster with great consequences. Each and every little boy and girl would have a serious complaint to the person responsible for such a horrible mistake. Unless it was our mother. Then lips would be sealed, stomachs would growl, sadness would prevail and saliva would flow freely. We would be mourning the loss of a dear snack, without the expression of disappointment and emotions. Our only consolation would be to wait till the next time. But, the next time was so very, very far away. Our memory would have to fade, until eventually we would be excited again, when the time for nuts came.

As I reflect, I realize that it was a good lesson on the stages of development in humans, and the circumstances that generate our thoughts, feeling and anxiety as children, where the present was the most important time. As an adult, these things became less important. Today, I must be concerned with political, financial, health and other issues. What I would not do to be that child again. But, if I were to be a child again I could not be writing now. Another paradox of life.

Life in the village was not necessarily difficult or horrible. The circumstances were certainly more challenging for some than those in the Modern World. But, most people were content with their conditions and circumstances, and accepted life as such. They seemed happy, most of them, to me at least. There were some people who had a more difficult upbringing than those in my family. I admired their perseverance and drive to succeed; it was their human endeavor.

Every person has his or her own set of circumstances to deal with. All of the events I experienced became the events that shaped my condition, and my circumstances; from seeing a shooting star and wondering what it was, to observing the behavior of the man with a watch who could not tell time. All the experiences had affected me and made me wonder, and wonder more. I would be defined by these life experiences, along with my curiosity. It was my curiosity that commanded my quest to find the DNA of the universe.

AMERICAN INVASION

The plan for my future had to take a different approach than a one-way trip to England. The exodus from the village had stopped because England was no longer the Motherland. In the village, it was as though the sun had set on the British Empire. But, as one giant turned its back, a new force awoke, as the colony was still quite important for its resources. More importantly, it was vulnerable to new propaganda, especially from those with false promises, and bad intentions. The risk of a new communist alliance had to be mitigated by the one force on the planet that would not accept or tolerate it - the United States. The USA could not possess the colony, so they opened their doors to immigrants after the British gate was closed. It would be their way to establish an important mutual relationship and dependence, which would inhibit the colony's friendship with other aggressive rivals. It was their way to protect themselves, as well as the exiled British colony. A new sun had risen in the village, the American sun, and it shone brightly, and offered hope.

I almost had to learn to despise the British, as I felt they did not care about me anymore; they left, and they left me back. Additionally, I would have to follow the rule of local politicians who needed some lessons on governance. I decided that I had to look for a new country for my future. I was already one of the people who just wanted to leave the village, like others, and try to find prosperity and success elsewhere. I set my sights on America, and accepted that I could also change my perspective on culture, instead of holding on to the British values, which in summary, to me, was simply being polite while holding resentment. It was not my cup of tea. I preferred diplomacy where I could tell someone how I felt without insulting him or her, even though it may be unpleasant.

A few of the new teachers at my high school were good examples of why I should love America; they were from America and they were easy going, down-to-earth and mostly cool. Some of my history classmates suspected that they were CIA agents keeping an eye on the new and vulnerable country. Of course in the nineteen-sixties the United States fought tooth and nail to stop the spread of communism. Cuba had already folded to Castro, and America feared a communist anchor in South America. That matter was for the Government people as far as I was concerned. My business was about my future and me.

I thought America was a friendly force showing its face, starting with the lovely teachers. Perhaps the teachers were keeping an eye on the youth, as we would be the easiest group that could be conditioned by an enemy with a different agenda. Smart people, the Americans, and practical too. The Americans contracted to build the entire road system, which was in horrible shape when the British left. It was so horrible that on open stretches of roadway drivers would drive on the wrong side of the road thinking that it was the better side. The oncoming car would do the same thing, and as they approached, the drivers would switch to the correct side, pass each other, and move right back to the wrong side of the road. It is amazing what the human mind can concoct to alleviate a problem. I call it a mind game, as the road was the same on both sides.

Undeniably, the Americans made a big presence in the former colony and the people began to like them, and like America too. It also gave the Americans the right to invade, in the event of communist aggression, in order to protect US citizens who were working there; a formidable option indeed. That tactic assured the Americans that no communist would set foot in the ex-colony. They were in, and they were respected and loved. The people were not going to turn their backs on their friends whom they loved. That was how we grew up in the village; we looked after each other.

I was learning to like America while, at the same time, trying to lose my allegiance to the British Empire. It was how my mind was being shaped, by my circumstances and my goals. Perhaps it was normal for my mind to work that way, and not necessarily as the story of the sour grapes. I would not shun the British simply because I could not go to England; I genuinely liked America. Especially, I liked that whatever could be possible with human endeavor would be possible in America first.

I had every reason to love America already; they were going to the moon. I followed every launch, every astronaut, and every space vehicle. There was no television, so I listened intently on the radio for launch countdowns and any other related programs. I had to imagine I was watching a spacecraft rise from Cape Kennedy as I was listening to the roar of rocket engines and people, on the radio. The next day the newspapers would have photos of the event, and stories of which I read every word. I knew the names of all the astronauts, and I was sent a full color photo of the first Apollo crew that landed on the moon. I was beginning to feel that America was encouraging me and liking me already. I was ready to make my giant leap for the kind of man I wanted to be.

THE GAME PLAN

I contacted a pilot school in America, which then sent me many encouraging letters, and flyers with pictures of nice looking airplanes. I went through all of them as though I was studying for an exam. As a youth, I could only dream of learning to fly. I never thought of the cost of such an endeavor; that to me was a parent's responsibility. I had fallen in love with America. It was the place where anything was possible, even if it were a dream; America was the place where dreams came true.

As I waited for the opportunity to go to America for any scientific career, I continued my investigation of the world by doing many activities, which always involved the other boys, especially my brothers. I wanted them to help with projects and experiments, and also to learn. Some of our activities did not easily conform to my parents' rule of discretion, or common sense. By involving the other boys I was not always blamed for something my parents would discover. The blame was shared, even though parents always wanted to know whose idea started the activity; they wanted the ringleader.

I am certain that my encouragement of the boys helped form the circumstances that would help one of my younger brothers, in later years, to follow his scientific educational mission. He would eventually receive a scholarship to attend a university in Switzerland, where he successfully pursued a PhD in science. It was the same university that Albert Einstein attended, after failing the entrance exam. Who said that someone could not be a genius after failing an exam? Genius comes from; "imagination is more important than knowledge," as said by Einstein. My family was proud to have one member attend that university, and it was a significant accomplishment, years after our boyhood thrills.

I learned more about America every day in the following years after the British relinquished control of the colony. Of course there were more and more stories in the newspapers about America. People developed more interest in America than England, and it seemed that America was developing stronger interest in us. It seemed a natural process, since there was no English control any longer. America encouraged the educated youth and talented adults to join the American culture by immigrating. The exodus from the village switched destinations as many began leaving for America, since the door to England was closed.

I truly did enjoy the description of the difference between British and American cultures by the local people who also started to like America. They would say that if you wanted to get something done ask an American. If you wanted to talk about getting something done, ask a Brit. Americans made everything easy; nothing was supposed to be difficult, and it all made sense. The British would say that the prerequisite for a candidate to learn to become a pilot was advanced knowledge in Math and Science. In America, the only requirement was to be able to read, speak and understand English language. Wow! I was sold. I picked America, the place where dreams come true.

Chapter Three

THE GREAT ESCAPE

New York City in February, when I landed there, was a bitterly cold month for anyone born anywhere. I was a native of the tropical latitudes where people shivered at sixty degrees Fahrenheit. That month in New York I shivered like a person with a disease. Every second I spent outside I shivered. I shivered indoors also when my tropical body could not feel heat. I suffered greatly, but I was fortunate to have youth and perseverance. I was determined to prevail. It was a dear lesson on how people with diseases would feel during an episode of their condition. It would be a new learning experience for me, which would help me to appreciate and understand people with medical conditions.

My attitude when I first arrived in New York was that of Jabal Tariq, the man who named "The Rock" after himself. He landed with his army on the southern tip of the Iberian Peninsula over five hundred years ago with the determination to invade. He succeeded, and to this day the rock still bears his name - Gibraltar. He brought with him Moorish architecture, culture and cuisine; like tapas. I was Tariq in New York on that cold month of February. There was no going back for me either. The only things I brought however, were my clothes. I did not have an army, and I did not possess the desire to invade. I just wanted to survive, and I was determined to stay the course. Manhattan was going to be my Rock, and I was going to leave my name on it somewhere. Or, perhaps the Rock was going to leave its name on me.

Going back would not have been an easy choice anyway. I would not be welcomed back. I would not be educated if I returned. I would be embarrassed and ashamed for failing, and my family would consider me a loser. The worst part would be that I would have to go back working for my father in the jewelry business; not the most exciting profession for a person who wanted to be an engineer, or a doctor, or a pilot, or an astronaut. I had big dreams, and the cold winter in New York was not going to stop me. In addition, I was trying to escape from the village life, which had no potential for me. The seriousness of my father, and his convictions to his beliefs was also another factor. I did not want to be conditioned by doctrine, or culture, or tradition. Those things were enough to convince me that I needed to make it in New York. Had I returned to the village there would have been conflicts ahead for me.

In my mind I kept convincing myself that I had broken out of prison and I was free to choose my own course in life in the big and cold town. I would do all the suffering needed not to go back. I did not want to return like a dog with its tail between its legs. In New York I would have to learn how to be self-sufficient, no different than a newly emancipated prisoner. However, I still felt the psychological umbilical cord connected to me, as I felt my father's presence everywhere I went. I thought he was watching me the whole time, following close behind at every corner. I felt as though he was like a prison warden looking for me to make the first mistake so I could be placed right back into the slammer. But, my Pa was not a prison warden. He wanted me to succeed. It was all my imaginary response to the thought of failing my family, and myself. I had to compose my thoughts and feelings, and ditch my fears, so I could focus.

As difficult as it was because of the cold weather, I became encouraged when I saw so many people living and working in the same cold climate. They were walking in the same cold weather, as I was walking to school. I was convinced that I was not going to die. I was convinced that I had to get tough, because New York was a tough place to land up, and I had to buck up for the New York challenge. Once in the groove, the challenge would become more manageable. It would be my great accomplishment, living in New York and knowing the city, with all the tricks of traveling and surviving in it.

I settled in at the abode of a relative who had agreed to keep me, for a small rent, until I could get out on my own. I had to find work. I started packing shelves in a supermarket. I lasted about a week; I simply could not do mundane tasks. After that, I worked in a factory that produced plastic objects. I had to operate machines, which became hot enough to melt the plastic. I almost melted my hand. Naturally, I received minor burns when not adhering to the safety measures. That was my incentive to move on, and I was gone within days. I was willing to try anything, but I was more the type to do some kind of office work. I had to survive; it was my human nature, so I kept looking for better jobs. The cost of a New York City subway ride was about thirty-five cents. That was a lot of money when there was no money. I occasionally borrowed five dollars from Charlie, the one good friend I knew, and I always paid him back. When we first met we had that natural affinity to become pals, and so we did.

I went to college at eight o'clock in the morning till four in the afternoon, from Monday to Friday. I was lucky that my high school education under the British system became an asset to my educational future, even though I was not very serious in high school. It would seem that all the information must have entered my brain subliminally, but I didn't care how it got there. College was serious business, and not a place to neglect. It was necessary for a profession. More importantly, I had to pay for it, and that became my motivation for paying attention, especially in class.

BIG APPLE BLUES

After school I had to work part time to keep up with my expenses. I was able to find a tolerable job. I served food in a cafeteria on 42nd Street. I said tolerable, not glamorous. I wore a white outfit and a white hat. It was a uniform and a health safety requirement as well. Each night after closing, the walk to the subway train station, in the bitter cold, would be one more challenge before my day was over. It was an experience that could not be erased from my memory, especially that bone chilling wind blowing on my face and entering each and every crack and opening in my coat. The wind came in through my sleeves and flowed up my arm, then down my back. I shivered then, and I could feel the shiver all over again, just thinking about it. It was simply painful. My fingers froze, or so I thought, and my lips got chapped. There were things I needed to learn about surviving in cold weather, and I had to learn fast.

I could never fathom the desire of anyone wishing to live in such an environment, let alone the millions who did. I wondered how they prevailed each day. I thought about the people who lived here hundreds of years ago and did not have the convenience I had. They must have suffered more. They prevailed. There must be something special about the place. I also thought about those who came thousands of years ago, as the first settlers. They would have suffered much more than anyone. That human endeavor and drive must be accepted as a remarkable example of adaptation and perseverance. We are here on this planet because of all those who came before us. All my suffering gave me an insight of our human condition, and the improvement to the comforts of today. It was suffering that helped me understand people's feelings about difficulty, as it was the comfort I experienced that made me understand the difficulty of those who came before me.

Somehow after I left the little village and came to a big city I did not see much difference in people's behavior. I was shocked. Everyone did the same thing - that daily grind. Yes, there was running water and electricity, and it was convenient. But, people jumped on a rush-hour train rushing to work, then after eight hours, rushing back home to eat, sleep, and wake up to do it all over again the next day. I heard that the term for that was; "rat-race." I had to join the rat pack for school and work.

At night, the flood of city lights blacked out the night sky. The universe I used to see became almost invisible. My whole being was shifted. I had to follow a new direction; first to survive, and secondly to get an education and a career path. Life involved serious considerations, and a big change for a youth who spent his evenings staring at the night-sky, without a care in the world.

YANKEE STADIUM

I changed jobs from serving the food to collecting the money for the food. That was considered a career move for a struggling college student on his own. The new location of my cashier position was a cafeteria located under Yankee Stadium in the Bronx. I qualified because of experience with handling cash from my father's shop. In this job it was necessary to remember the price of each and every item in the cafeteria. It was opened twenty-four hours a day, every day of the year. I had the weekend night shift. I started on Friday night with the dinner crowd, and then continued with the midnight crowd, finally finishing with the breakfast crowd. The food in the cafeteria was made fresh daily, and it was good. As a special privilege, I got to eat anything I wanted, at no charge. I brought schoolbooks to study during slow periods.

The faces of the patrons became familiar as time went on. They were mostly night shift workers and essential services workers such as policemen and firemen. There were few women in those jobs in the nineteen-seventies, and I never saw a single one in the cafeteria; the world was still asleep about women's potential in those days.

After a few weeks on the job the owner wanted to see me in his office. I thought I was in trouble, and I hated to be in trouble; it would be like being with my father all over again. But, he wanted to see me for a good reason. He wanted to compliment me on my work. He said I was efficient, accurate, punctual and fast, and he was happy. He also said something that he did not have to share with me, but he had strong feelings that I was honest, which I was. He told me that each time he hired a new cashier for the register he had to employ the services of a detective agency to verify that the individual was not going to take-off one day with all the cash in the drawer, never to return. It was quite possible that a detective followed me home to verify where I lived, as part of the inquiry. In addition, he told me that he received the report from the agency, and that one detective visited the cafeteria and observed me, to be sure that I didn't pocket any money, or gave food away. I did neither, of course. The owner was happy to tell me all that, and it made my day. He was a nice man, and I was a happy cashier.

THE SKY FROM WITHIN

In my first year at college I had applied for, and was accepted to a science internship at the Hayden Planetarium in New York. It was going to be my grand entrance into the world of the Cosmos. The reality of being in a totally scientific environment, and the opportunity to meet the masters of the universe would be my glory. I was excited, not just because I had passed the acceptance process, which required being in a science major and having good recommendations by several professors, but also for the opportunity that would unfold unto me. I would be learning and interning inside the Hayden Planetarium, a most prestigious institution for studying the science of the sky.

I eagerly awaited the end of the school year, finishing all my final exams, while trying to review astronomy, cosmology and related fields. Then something happened. I looked at my bank account balance. It was too low for me to be able to sustain myself through the summer. The internship was free for me, and free for them too; meaning there was no pay. I could never ask for help from family; that would be considered failure. I had to inform the Planetarium that I would not be attending, and that I had to get back to work. I was so very disappointed, because I had looked forward to such a great opportunity, which was so rare, and did not come easy.

BIG SHOT TEENAGER

By the time summer rolled around it was time to look for work. I was happy to have gained enormous experience in business and accounting from my father's little establishment. By the time I was twelve I ran the show, opening the shop, making jewelry, selling it, managing the money and doing the books. The confidence from that, and the experience from the cafeteria job encouraged me to apply for a cashier position at an insurance company. I was interviewed and accepted. I thought it was a dollars and cents operation with loose coins. But, that was not the case; I would not be dealing with small change. This was a titled position involving big bucks; a quarter of a million dollars on some days went into the bank downstairs. It was a kind of a strange cashier position, but what did I care; the money was good; real good. I was one of four guys responsible to process insurance payments from companies around the country. The other three men were old enough to be my father. I was a teenager in love. I was in love with a new job.

I had no idea this was a big job. I had my own desk in a separate section with the other cashiers. I was stared at a lot by the other college students who were older than me and working for me, and wondering how the heck I got the big chair. I felt out of place, but I got the work done really well. My colleagues loved me and thanked me daily, and bragged about me to others in the company. The boss was proud of me too, but more for himself; he got a top-notch cashier for a third of the going salary. That would be his mistake, since I accepted the job as it was offered to me. I never stated that I was in college, and it never came up during the interview. Perhaps I would have liked the job to the extent that I would quit school and make a career of it. I did not know that as yet. But, it could have been real good; with promotions, salary increases, and pension. I felt that I was given the opportunity to try it during the probation period, while still retaining the power of the decision about the future.

I learned really quickly and was on top of the job in no time at all. My colleagues were really happy, as I was also fast and accurate in a business that needed both. I often had to reconcile other cashier's work when there were errors. I must have had a knack for numbers, and my work reflected it. I was often thanked for the work I did; a concept that I did not really understand; thanking me for work I was being paid for. What I learned as a child was that "thanks" were for when you did a favor. In any case, I accepted the gratitude and learned some new and valuable concepts in American culture.

In due time, as my probationary period was closing in, I had to make the decision about the future; whether I would stay with the company or quit. The starting salary, even though high for my standards, was too low for a career opportunity with this company. I considered every option seriously and I made my decision to continue with school. I turned in my notice of resignation. Sparks flew everywhere. My colleagues were extremely disappointed, and in total disbelief. They asked me why I was leaving and I told them the salary was too low. They were shocked when I told them the amount of my actual salary. They made an emergency meeting with the headman to try and resolve it, and they also slammed him verbally with their firm discontentment. He made me a new offer, with much more pay, but still not enough to skip my education, and still not enough for a career future there. I confirmed my resignation, with great disappointment.

A new man was hired quickly, and I trained him. He also could have been my father. I was happy that I didn't leave them high and dry. I was also relieved that before I left, they had already filled my spot with a fully functional and "mature" cashier, who filled the big chair much better than I did. I knew he was not faster than me though, because I trained him, and that's how I knew, and I liked that I knew. I was a young and arrogant little stinker. But, it was not my fault; they were the ones who made me feel so important, with their compliments. It is what compliments can do; offer a false sense of entitlement. I lost the feeling quickly though, and humility returned to my character, right after reality checked in on me once again. After my two weeks notice, I parted on good terms with my group, the other colleagues, and college kids; who probably suspected that I was one of them too. Oh well, this kid was out of there.

TWO-MAN AREA

During the summer evenings and weekends, I had found a sales job. I just did not know how to be idle; that would be for guys doing time in prison. I needed to use all of my time productively. I began selling burglar alarms from door to door in Harlem. It was the early nineteen-seventies. The math does not take long to calculate the risk involved with this job. I traveled with about four other men to a predetermined location. We went off in pairs. One pair took the south side of the street and the other pair the north side. The headman went by himself. Each pair entered a building and knocked on every door. I would take odd numbered floors and the other guy took even numbered ones, or vice versa.

It was difficult to get the residents to answer the door, much less to open it. I had to talk my way into the door. The people would look through the peephole to verify the caller. I wore a tie, and it helped. I had to let them think they were obligated to talk to me. My typical phrase would be; "We are wiring up the entire building with alarms and I have a unit to show you." They were eager to find out about this safety device, which they thought would be free. That was my ticket through the door, and into the apartment. I carried a briefcase, and I looked professional. Inside the briefcase was a large alarm bell that worked with a battery. It was used to demonstrate the alarm system. It was no system; it was just a loud bell, which I turned on to startle the clients into submission. If they liked the bell it would be encouraging, and they would sign the contract. The compensation for one sale would be the equivalent of one day's pay for me in a normal hourly job. Not too shabby for talking the talk, to the people who listened intently.

I wondered about the people who lived in these apartments and could have afforded the few dollars per month for the alarm system. I wondered if they couldn't afford to just move out to a safe location. Perhaps they could not afford the rent elsewhere, or perhaps they had family in the area. Perhaps they would not be accepted elsewhere. I was always wondering. Burglar alarm sales were conducted in depressed areas whilst encyclopedia sales were conducted in affluent areas. That was how it was. I did both. It seemed so cut and dried. Affluent people would buy educational products for their children while others, not so fortunate, would buy burglar alarms. The monthly cost for each was about the same. What was it about us humans that we acquire traits that eventually dictate our condition? Or, was it that our condition determined our traits? Perhaps it was not a trait; instead, a circumstance, delivered to us through the events of our past. If you were in a burglar alarm circumstance then you would buy a burglar alarm. Maybe it was simple after all.

BALL DROP

My job situation had to change to accommodate my school schedule. The one place for a college student who needed to work at night was a restaurant. I found employment as a cashier and greeter in a large restaurant chain. I was delighted with this job for the one big benefit; free food. I went to different restaurant locations as required by the company. One assignment placed me in Grand Central Station cashiering for donuts and coffee. It was warm down there in winter, and the train was right inside the station. I called that, "comfy and sweet." Another assignment placed me in Times Square on New Year's Eve. I was the host and greeter. Hours before midnight people squeezed into 7th Avenue like sardines. The manager told me to make sure that the restrooms were for patrons only.

Many of the tables were full, and people ordered mostly hot chocolate, coffee and pie. They were all waiting for the stroke of midnight. Several others came in only for the restroom. I simply told them to order a cup of coffee.

The line to the restaurant got longer, as people just ordered coffee so they could use the restroom. One girl walked in, looked at the menu, and requested to return after the restroom. No problem for me; I was not a bouncer, and certainly not a person to refuse an urgent biological condition. When she returned from the restroom, she approached me closely, gave me a kiss and said; "Happy New Year." Then, she went right out the door. I smiled. It made my day, and my night, and it made me happy. That was my New Year's kiss, and the only kiss I got for the New Year, and for the whole year too. I was a teenager in love, even if only for a moment, and if only with one kiss.

Soon after, I heard the roar of the crowd, as the ball started down. I must have caught the last ten seconds of it. I was just happy not to have to be in the freezing weather for hours just to experience the ten seconds of glory. I was inside a warm place with free food and coffee. That was not too shabby for a Times Square evening on the greatest moment of the year.

OFF BROADWAY

I had become acquainted and friendly with one regional manager of the restaurant chain I worked for. He was happy with my work, and offered me a better position in an upscale steakhouse, owned by one of his family members. I started there and found myself in the upper tier of society, as wealthy people came in to dine on top steaks. I met the staff of cocktail waitresses, waiters, chefs and bus boys. I would meet a maitre' d for the first time. I saw movie stars and musicians who were top of the charts at that time. During Broadway show intermissions the bar in the restaurant became packed, with those who wanted a quick one, or two. Many famous people, with household names, came in for drinks and dinner. In New

York it was not unusual to be at the same venue with celebrities. New Yorkers were very casual about such encounters. It was nice to have been close up with a member of one of England's most popular rock and roll bands. John came in with his wife. I was happy to have laid eyes on him, as he died some years later, right in New York. I was crazy about their music when I was a teenager, and I had joined the movement of youth whose parents could not accept the new sound; rock and roll. What the heck, I fell asleep to the music my parents listened to, literally.

Cash was king in those days, and credit cards were rare. Being an upscale restaurant with upscale patrons, several credit cards were presented for payment. There was no swipe or chip technology. In fact, there was no technology. A manual imprint of the credit card was taken with a signature request, and that was it. There was a hot-card file, which was a list of all the credit cards that were stolen, stopped or cancelled. I had to look up each number from a book that came weekly. I found a few bad cards in due time, which could not be returned to the patron, by law. They had to be cut in two and mailed back to the credit card company. It was a good fortune for me each time I caught one. I received a bonus of twenty-five bucks from the credit card company after I mailed it in. That was more than a day's pay for me in the restaurant.

At this same work location I befriended a woman twice my age. I called her, "mother," but only silently. Everyone should be lucky to have one or two, or three mothers. The more the mothering, the better the child. "Heaven lies at the feet of mothers," was the saying I heard while growing up, from my own mother also. She was thousands of miles away, and it was nice to have someone locally to relate to, and share success and pain - someone who was trustworthy and caring. This new mother always encouraged me, guided me and gave me hope. Whether I was going to further my education, build a house, or fly to the moon, that sweet encouragement from someone who believed in me made all the difference. She always told me that I would be fine, and I would find my way. I don't know how she knew, as I didn't know my future. But, she knew, as mothers always know. I miss her.

ON A DOWNTOWN TRAIN

I was always thinking of ways to improve my condition, and saving every cent was important. I decided to move near to my college where I could walk, instead of taking a train. The subway train was the one thing about New York I hated with a passion, especially during rush hour. The trains were mostly late, crowded, smelly and exhausting. Arriving at work after a trip on the train could make anyone feel like it was quitting time, not starting time. In addition, care had to be taken to avoid being pushed into the wrong train by the uncontrollable crowds on the platform.

I rented a room from two guys living in an apartment on Eight Avenue in Midtown. I ate garbanzo beans and white bread for many dinners. It was my college years. After a few months at this place, the building was condemned by the city. Everyone was given notice to depart. The guy whose name was on the lease still collected rent from me, even though there was a rumor from the third fellow that after the notice to vacate arrived, there was no rent to pay. I had nowhere to go, and the last thing I needed was to be asked to leave. I paid whatever the negotiated amount was. New York was so full of challenges. Before the vacation date arrived I had to find another place to live. It was just one other challenge, like the saying goes; "If I can make it there, I'll make it anywhere." It should also say; "If I can drive in New York I can drive anywhere." I became determined to make it, and drive it, and conquer it, and never ride the subway trains again.

RIDING NEW YORK

I looked at places to live, but stumbled on difficulty, one after another. I did not want to move out to the other boroughs, I wanted to stay in Manhattan. Greenwich Village was too expensive and so was the East Side. Alphabet city was a bit scary with some bad dudes in the area. I finally had to settle for an attic room in Queens. Back on the subway trains I went. This time, with the hoards of suburbanites trucking into the city, some with newspapers folded for reading, while avoiding eye contact with others.

I thought of buying a motorcycle. That would save some time and travel costs. I did just that, and I began to ride to school and to work. Riding anything in New York took a bit of guts. The traffic was intense to begin with, and to add insult to injury, the taxi drivers were the worst. Constant vigilance was especially necessary in that sea of yellow cabs. Aside from them crossing three lanes of traffic for a fare, anticipation that a passenger could open the door as I passed made it necessary to stay well clear. Then, I had to be aware of the spitting out the window from some drivers. I made sure to rev my engine as I approached an open window of every vehicle, so as to assert my territory. Riding saved me money, and eased the transportation challenge in the big city; it was all good experience.

The riding was fine until fall weather, when the wind-chill temperature became unbearable, and I felt frozen when I rode. My hands and feet became so stiff that I needed to thaw out like a frozen turkey each time. The motorcycle went into storage, and I promptly bought a bicycle. I was determined to save transportation costs, at any cost, and not ride the trains again. The wind chill would be less on a bicycle, especially because my body would also be generating heat from exercise as I rode. The most important consideration was the distance to school and work. I was good at bicycle riding from my earlier years, and I accepted the challenge. I would have to cross the Queens 59th Street Bridge every day. In rush hour it was easy because the traffic was slow and I could squeeze in-between easily.

There were few bicycles in those days, so much that bike riders waved to each other as an acknowledgement of the "crazy people's club." The riding went fine, with the biggest challenge being getting over the bridge on my way home each time I finished work, after rush hour. The traffic was not heavy. But, the cars went fast, and that was the problem. Timing was everything. I would wait to cross when the traffic light was red on Second Avenue, where most of the traffic for the bridge originated, then take-off as fast as possible. It was a tough ride uphill to the center of the bridge. By the time I reached there the traffic would have started to flow and I would be coasting downhill quite fast. I made myself visible with leg and hand movements, especially at night. On occasions, people would yell out of their car window to say something to the effect that I was crazy. Crazy I didn't mind, as long as I didn't get hit. Actually, I welcomed the screams out of the windows; it meant that the drivers saw me, and that's what I cared about.

LONDON CALLING

In a couple of years I became used to living in the big city and things became smoother. I decided to take a trip. It would be the first trip I took on an airliner after arriving in New York. I would travel to London to visit my sisters and their families. My parents were also visiting, and I would get to see them as well. I was not afraid that my father would ask me to return to the village, as I felt emancipated to the point of no return; in body, but not yet fully in mind.

I remember buying the ticket in New York at the Pan Am office, which was on the ground floor of the Pan Am building. Pan Am was the world's largest airline at that time. The price for a round trip student fare was two hundred bucks. That was quite a bit of money for me, but still a lot less than full price. I would get to fly in the largest airplane in the sky at the time, the iconic 747-jumbo jet. I was in awe. I was excited. Maybe one day I would get to fly one; as a pilot, so I thought. It was all right to dream while young.

No one in London knew I was coming, except my sister Jan. I wanted it to be a surprise for the whole family. I arrived early on Sunday morning. After a taxi ride to the address, which cost me the equivalent of two days' pay, I was knocking on the door. My father opened the door, looked at me, and asked how he could help. He did not recognize me, simply because he did not expect me to be there. I entered only after the others realized who I was.

It was a happy time for the family to be together. I was supposed to stay for one week, but they convinced me to stay for two. A quick visit to a travel agent and my ticket was changed, with no additional cost. After that was done, I sent a telegram to the place I worked to notify them of my late return. Those were the days when time traveled slowly, and easy street was everyone's street.

The family treated me well, and I learned a lot more about them. I realized how my sisters emigrated out of the little village, including all the undertakings that had to happen to accomplish that. My father took that leap of faith to send his daughters to the Motherland, where they would be safe and productive. He was a proud father. When I arrived in London he was again reassured that he had made the right decision about me. I was certain that he would have been disappointed and surprised if I had the inclination to return to the village.

I enjoyed the time in London, and went sightseeing to many places of interest. I also enjoyed the time being with several members of my family, as it was difficult, if not impossible, to be together with everyone at the same time. After my two weeks in a new land, my previous Motherland, I flew back to New York, on my twentieth birthday, as my teenager status vaporized on the flight. I was able to celebrate it two times, because of the time difference.

Upon arrival, reality checked in quickly, especially when nobody in all of New York cared that I just flew back from London on a jumbo jet. I wanted some bragging rights. The glory for this young man's trip faded as quickly as a coin down a slot machine. New Yorkers could be the nicest and most helpful people in the world, but they are not easily impressed. It was time to grind again after a couple of weeks without money. New York could chew me up and spit me out in pieces, but I would have to get up and go again.

MOVING UP TO THE EAST SIDE

I caught a break when I got a job as a bank teller on the Upper East Side of Manhattan. It was a huge bank with twenty-three teller stations. Cash was king, and that was what checks were for, to be cashed. The experience I had acquired with cashiering in restaurants, and in my father's business, doing the books and handling the cash was an advantage. I did well, always accurate with transactions, and balancing at day's end. I was a fast cash handler, and it was a benefit in this cash society.

The line of people, before the bank opened, went around the block. When the doors were opened, the customers ran to the tellers like birds running to breadcrumbs. Individual lines of people would begin to form for each of the twenty-three tellers. Eventually, I noticed that my line was quite often the longest. I figured out the reason, after I kept seeing familiar faces. Manual signature verification was required for every withdrawal, or check presented for cash. That was done by accessing one of approximately thirty drawers; filled with signature cards. It was a tedious task, and tellers simply always preferred deposits. That meant they didn't have to get off their butts to go compare a signature.

The familiar faces I saw were people I knew from serving them several times. I knew their full names, and I recognized their signatures by memory. Any cash transaction with these people meant that I did not have to run to the drawers to verify their signatures. Several were surprised when I addressed them by their names, before they could give me their transaction. People on other lines looked at those on my long line as though they were fools. That was, until my line kept shrinking like spaghetti being sucked into a toddlers mouth. Seriously, I completed transactions in seconds, and I would ask the next customer to give me the transaction as the current one was counting the cash. I had a good system, and soon, other customers from other lines would join my line, and expecting speedy service. I felt compassion for the people who had to wait at the bank; it was an inconvenience. I was proud that the supervisors always let me close last because they knew I would balance quickly and accurately. I was happy to have done a good job, as it was all about my pride.

GOT TO FLY

Shortly after I started to work at the bank I discovered a pilot school, and I wanted to attend. I registered and started learning to fly, (with my own money of course). The school was located at LaGuardia Airport. It was the only one allowed on the airport, and a Navy veteran operated it. It was exciting to operate among big airline jets. Taxiing a small plane between jets was a bit intimidating, but it offered a sense of power and command. Quite often the ground controller would notify the airline pilots ahead that there was a small plane behind them, and not to use excessive thrust during taxi. The airline pilots could not see behind their airplanes; rear view mirrors are not standard equipment. Taking off behind an airliner normally required waiting a few minutes for its wake turbulence to dissipate. In the presence of a crosswind, the wake would flow with the wind, and the waiting was shorter. Our time on the runway was usually quick, and we always turned immediately into the wind to avoid any turbulence left from the departing airliner.

On my first flight lesson I watched the ground move away from beneath my feet, when we took-off. I looked down to get the view; something every first flight candidate does. I held the controls and felt the airplane as we climbed out of the area. I was expecting a thrill. There was no thrill. It bordered on being boring, and I was not impressed. I wondered about what I was doing. I wondered more about why I was doing it. Perhaps I wanted to learn as much as I could learn. Perhaps it was my ego. Perhaps it was my curiosity. All I knew was that I had to fulfill my lifelong dream. I had to at least try it.

The flight school did not last long at this big airport, because of the restrictive nature with airline jets, and had to move to a nearby smaller one. I rode my motorcycle to the school during warm weather, and when it got cold I would ask the instructor to pick me up. I continued flying until I would run out of money, and then had to start again. I kept on flying without figuring out why I was doing it. Finally, I stopped flying because of low funds. I also had to focus on other challenges in my life. I had to save money. I continued my stint at the bank, and I continued to go to school.

JALOPY

I was fortunate that someone gave me an old car as a sort of payment for some electrical work I had done at his house. The car was in working condition, but it made noises like an old rocking chair. Every passenger asked about the annoying noise, which came from underneath the car, inasmuch as they should have appreciated being transported by the same car, and not a subway car. I so desperately wanted to find the part under the car that was making that annoying sound, and beat it mercilessly with a hammer. I would have banged the heck out of it, until it was deformed to the point of being forever silent, just to appease my frustration. Perhaps, I should simply have appreciated the privilege of having a car in New York, as I took friends, and had fun going places. It was convenient for me, as I lived in Manhattan and worked in the suburbs, at my new job. It was a perfect arrangement, especially that traffic out of the city was good, and parking was not too much trouble.

I crashed this car while driving in a snowstorm. Foolish youth I was. Soon after though, I purchased another car for a few hundred bucks. I was so used to the convenience of car transportation that it became difficult to live without. I promised myself that I would take care of this car, and I made sure to visit the auto store often. I even ran a charging wire to the trunk of the car, and connected a used battery, which I purchased for about seven dollars from the executive salvage company; better known as the junkyard. Batteries were often stolen because the hoods of cars did not have locks, especially in a 1963 model. Some people used chains and locks for security of their car hoods. Sure enough, one day as I merrily walked to my car and tried to start it, and nothing happened. The battery was gone. I simply fetched, and connected the spare battery from the trunk and drove off. It was New York style surviving.

Another easily stolen item was car wheels. I was certain no one would steal one of my car wheels; they were not attractive. But, sure enough I went to my car one morning and found one of the rear wheels missing. The one reason for stealing my car wheel was that the thief had a flat tire, but did not have a spare tire. My car was sitting on the brake drum, and the wheel nuts were left there. I guess "thanks" would be in order, for the thief leaving the nuts. This moment was not time for anger or panic, as neither would get me anywhere in New York. I also could not worry about the seven dollars I paid for the wheel at the junkyard. I had to focus on resolution. I simply opened the trunk, jacked up the car, and installed one of the two spare wheels I kept. I drove off, and was on my way within ten minutes. Surviving in New York meant always having back-up.

THE TWENTY-FIVE DOLLAR SPECIAL

A mechanic friend I knew had an old car to sell, and he offered it to me for a few hundred dollars. I already had a car, so there was no incentive for spending extra money, plus having the hassle of selling mine. However, when my car died a few weeks later, incentive came quickly. I was determined not to go back to the subway trains ever again, so I inquired about this car from the mechanic. Apparently, the car had a chronic electrical problem that nobody could figure out, even the great mechanic. Occasionally, the car's engine would quit when the car was stopped, and would not immediately start again. The problem was intermittent. The condition of any intermittent electrical problem had caused many people to take a sledgehammer to their cars and start banging. I was always amused at people who beat inanimate devices when frustration cancels logic. I must admit that I have been guilty of the same behavior, but I used a smaller hammer.

The car for sale was at the shop, and had a new battery installed. The owner must have given the car to the mechanic, as payment for all the work done to fix the problem that was not fixed. I went to inspect it and found a few minor issues. The mechanic recognized the issues, but was so desperate to get rid of this car that he simply reduced the price. He told me to take the car for a measly twenty-five dollars. Correct-o. Right-o. Exactamundo: only twenty-five bucks. That's right - two five - twenty-five. Going once!! Gone!! He had just supplied ample encouragement and inspiration. "Sold," was the word of that day, and off I went with a perfectly running car. The mileage was low, and the engine purred like a pussycat. She was nice, the car. A few days of driving and no problem occurred.

I had to do some minor work, one of which was brought to my attention by the back seat passengers. They told me they could see the road under their feet. The floorboard was rusted-out and pieces were falling on the road, leaving holes in the floorboard. I joked with the passengers that eventually if their feet reached the road they could push the car along, like in the cartoon. I immediately went to work on the problem by cutting two pieces of wood to fit the areas, and covering them with carpet. I was then able to reassure my passengers that the car was safe, and fitted with real floorboards; made of genuine wood. It was laughable.

I had much fun driving everywhere, until the moment of truth about the car arose. I was stopped at a traffic light, and the engine quit. I had to ask for help to push it off to the side. That was not an uncommon sight in New York. After waiting a few minutes the car started, and off I went. That was the problem the mechanic had mentioned. My mind became that of a detective. I had to analyze the problem thoroughly. I was the electrical engineer, and I had to apply my engineering skills to investigate. I traced the wires from the battery, and followed them to their connection points. Voila! There it was, the main accessory wire from the battery, which ran to a connection point under the headlight housing was loose. I had found the needle in the haystack. This wire supplied power to the entire electrical system of the car, including the ignition coil. Within fifteen minutes I had tightened the nut, and verified the connection. This car never ever again exhibited the behavior of cutting-off when stopped.

Many friends and family built memories with this icon in my life. It was not the most attractive car, and that definitely made it; "New York." The car was always reliable and fast. It always worked, and never left me stranded on the road. I took extremely good care of it, and I did my own oil changes and tune-ups. There were no computer controls in those days, only the driver. The ignition timing of the cylinders had to be set manually with a strobe light, and I always advanced the firing when setting the timing. It would be like turbo charging, in a crude way. The acceleration could be felt significantly when driving with this engine setting. In New York City, the first out of the gate, meaning when the traffic light turned green, had all the options for the next few blocks.

I drove one friend to his civil wedding ceremony in a snowstorm. The champagne was kept cold in the trunk, and the celebration was in the car; with the newly wedded couple and their witnesses; one of which was I. Many friends, after many years, would reminisce and ask about this twenty-five dollar car, as it was known. Ten years and 100,000 miles on New York City roads, my faithful companion served me well. The mechanic who sold me the car would shake his head in disbelief whenever I would visit to get work done. I was sure he felt some sense of disappointment that he could not fix the car, since he was the mechanic. I explained to him that the problem needed an engineer and a detective, neither of which he was. He would simply smile. He was a nice guy.

My dear twenty-five dollar companion was starting to lose her master's favor. She was getting old and tired. I became restless, and was interested in newer relationships. I was the master who finally had to let her go, my beauty, and my good old reliable. I gave the car to a friend with all the instructions on how to handle her. In a few months he called me humming a song of disappointment, riddled with complaints. He couldn't handle her. He took her to her final resting place. She was surely missed.

RETROGRADE MOTION

The New York City skyline was beautiful, but the sky of the city was not like the sky of the village. I tried to view whatever was visible as I walked at night. I was probably the only person looking up. New Yorkers do not generally look up; they reserve such activity for tourists. I was able to see the bright stars of Orion, and some planets. I saw Jupiter and Saturn from the street, between streetlights. I observed them over a period of weeks, and noticed that they both seemed to be moving backwards against the stars. I wondered about this anomaly. I did my research and learned that I was observing retrograde motion; the apparent motion of outer planets, as the earth passes them in its smaller orbit. Parallax was the explanation, because the stars were extremely far from the earth and the planets. It would be similar to driving in the desert where there are mountains in the background, far away on one side. If there were a tall tower ahead, just a short distance from the roadway, it would seem to move rearward as the car passed it, and eventually it would be in the rear of the car. The car would be Earth, the tower would be an outer planet like Jupiter or Saturn, and the mountains in the distance would be the background of stars. When I explained this phenomenon, and showed the planets to friends, their reactions were similar to the people in the village; they seemed disinterested. I gave up trying to tell people about the universe, as they were the same everywhere, in the village, or the jungle of New York.

COUSTEAU

The night sky disappointment in the sea of lights of New York City prompted me to look for other avenues to

89

explore. I registered to become a certified Scuba diver. I wanted to know what was under the water, as I wondered about everything. I took lessons at one of the few large indoor swimming pools in Manhattan. It was on the East Side, in Midtown. There were classroom instructions as well as pool maneuvers, mostly about safety and survival.

One firm concept I took away was the buddy system. I was already in on that one, to never go into water without a buddy. That became my philosophy for swimming, hiking and especially for walking in some parts of New York; the parts of the city called: "two-man areas," where no one walked alone.

My open water dives that were required for certification were conducted in New Jersey; in an abandoned quarry, which became filled with water. The water temperature was about sixty degrees Fahrenheit, (fifteen degrees Celsius). A quarter inch neoprene wet suit did not save me from the shock of such cold water. The wet suit was supposed to retard the cold water on the outside, while a thin layer of water on the inside became warm by body heat. Rest assured that warming up from body heat was not a rapid process, unless I had a two hundred degree fever. The first few moments after jumping in were sheer torture. As nature would have it, and every diver quickly discovers, there is a much faster way to heat up the inside of a wet suit. The natural reaction of the body to cold temperature would be the constriction of the blood vessels in the extremities, to conserve heat. This condition would result in an excess amount of fluid in the vascular system, as the extremities shrunk. The blood volume would be excessive in this condition, and the excess fluid would be transferred to the bladder. A full bladder could be considered a diver's delight. I would assure anyone that relief followed quickly, and it felt good. The immediate heat inside the wet suit, and the release of bladder pressure were both welcoming. It was a double benefit, deserving a rewarding and long sigh of relief - ahhhh!

The quarry was void of any form of life. There was a couple of old cars at the bottom. I am not sure how they got there, but there were no dead people inside. I stayed down for an hour, with my buddy, who was a girl, then exited the quarry to a nice warm fire in the building. It felt really nice.

FLIGHT TOURS

With the scuba diver's certificate secured and nowhere to go diving, simply because the water in the area was too cold, I proceeded to complete my pilot certificate. I found a new school that was not too expensive, and well suited for my budget. I got it done and I became a fully certified pilot. But, I had nobody to share it with. My friends in New York were not interested in seeing New York from the sky. They had already seen it from the Empire State building - a right of passage for newcomers to the city. In addition, there was so much more to do with groups of friends, instead of the one or two. Some people were also afraid to fly in a small plane. I was finally able to take some passengers, mostly friends and family, for sightseeing rides. The Hudson River corridor offered the best views of New York City, and each passenger came with camera in hand. I did not enjoy doing surface tours for my visitors, so I would offer a sky tour and send them off to do their own sightseeing on the ground.

Most times the passengers would pay their fair share for the airplane rental without hesitation, and it was a good way for me to save money. I could not legally let them pay the whole cost, as that would have meant that I was operating for hire. It would be one of the fastest ways for me to be removed from the list of active pilots; my license would have been suspended.

ANCHORS AWAY

My next curious venture was to investigate the marine environment from the surface of the water. I was fascinated by boats, and thought they were such a dynamic method of transport. They could go slow, fast, or simply stop, with plenty of room to maneuver, or park. I discovered and registered for a free course offered by the Coast Guard Auxiliary. The men who operated this organization were retired mariners, with lots of experience. These guys were the real deal - old sailors. I learned a lot about boats, navigation into and out of channels, and dangers of the sea. Upon completion, I was presented with a lovely signed graduation certificate, fit for framing. But, I did not have a wall to hang it on, and I did not have a boat either. How would I experience seamanship without a ship?

I started research on boats for sale within my budget of a few hundred dollars. Indeed, I found an old wooden boat, and engine for the right price. I was lucky. A man on the South Shore of Long Island in New York had this old boat, which he drove around occasionally, in the bay, for leisure, with his children. The children had grown up and they no longer cared about boats. The man must have been happy that he could get rid of this old floater. After we completed the transaction, he kept thanking me and advising me on how to operate on the water, as though he really appreciated me for buying his boat. It dawned on me much later when I read the saying: "The two best days in a boat owner's life are the day he bought it, and the day he sold it." The man was happy because I had made his day; the day he sold his old boat.

I had already done thorough research, as I checked dock space availability and affordability at marinas in Brooklyn. I especially enjoyed visiting the marinas and watching boats in the water, and boats being removed from the water with a special crane. The marina I selected was convenient, and the owner explained everything, including the cost for wet dock, dry dock, and launching of the boat. While the boat was on dry dock; during winter and spring, I was free to clean, paint, repair, or even sleep, at my leisure. I never did the last mentioned, perhaps only for a short nap, after being tired from working on the boat.

The boat I purchased was ready for water, so in it went, and the fun started. That was, until I could not get anyone to join me. There was nothing worse than being on a boat alone, especially if it was still docked. I was off from work on weekends, and I finally took some groups out. I almost had to beg them. I learned a lot about boats, tides, and waves. The bay was wide open and protected, and the water was mostly calm. I ventured only once into the ocean to reach a point of interest for a passenger friend. It was not pleasant, as the water was rough, and I did not like taking such risks. After that trip I ventured only into the bay. It was routine, and a bit boring, but much safer. Many of the friends and family who came never cared to return for a boat ride; their curiosity was satisfied, and interest faded. I became the lone sailor once again - alone by the sea.

I felt the same as when I became a certified pilot - no one to share it with. The expenses associated with boat ownership brought the thought of selling the sinking ship, unless I could explore some sort of excitement for my passengers. I thought of an idea; I had received a gift of a portable aviation radio from an aviation related membership. I brought the radio on the boat and started taking trips several miles east - towards the end of the bay. That was the location of JFK airport, which had runways jutting right into the bay. The planes could be very easily observed. I listened on the radio when airplanes were cleared on those runways and looked out for them. Since the boat was close enough to the airport I could hear the tower controller clearly on the radio, as he issued clearances for takeoffs and landings.

A big surprise came one day as I heard a clearance for an airplane called, "Speed bird." There was no airline name or flight number associated with this airplane, as was normal with the others. I waited in wonder until it appeared. It lifted off the runway and flew right over the bay. It made the loudest noise from an airplane I had ever heard. It shook the windshield of the boat so much that I had to keep holding it to prevent rattling. The airplane passed a short distance from my boat and I recognized it; the Concord had just taken-off. I watched as though my eyes were glued into position. I saw fire coming out of the engines. It was like watching four jet fighters taking off all together, as represented by the four engines. Ears had to be plugged, as the noise was deafening. It was downright scary. I actually thought I was in danger, and that I should not have been that close. But, there were no warning signs, and there were also other boats not very far from mine.

It slowly became quiet again, as the Concord flew out over the ocean and the noise relented, still being clearly noticeable. The trip turned out fine, and I watched many other airplanes take-off, one after the other. Then, I heard another roar. It was another Concord - this one going to Paris. I had found the hook to entice friends to join me for trips on the boat. Over and over through the summer I drove the boat to see two Concords taking off within one hour of each other. The Concord takeoffs were the surprise I waited for on each trip, as I did not tell the passengers on my boat until the moment arrived. They were all surprised. I was fairly certain that people on my boat had the closest view of a Concord on takeoff, except for airport workers, and passengers on an airliner taxiing nearby. In fact, on my portable radio, we heard the tower controller tell pilots on taxi that the Concord was nearby their airplane so they could share the view with their passengers.

I took many trips on that old boat. Every spring I had to scrape the bottom and paint it with marine paint. I found a paint supplier who was a nice fellow, selling by the gallon, at the old Brooklyn Navy Yard. Such intense research required lots of perseverance, especially while operating on a tight budget. One faithful friend always came to help me prepare the boat for the summer. Somehow, we had much time do all that, and it was rewarding for both of us. It helped our friendship grow stronger. Charlie was a good friend, and a friend to keep.

Those were fun filled days with friends. I thought it would become my life; I could fly, I could go on my boat, or I could ride my motorcycle, all on a budget. I must have been dreaming. I could not be living this life of leisure, as a man in his twenties, especially, when each and every dollar in my wallet had to be considered seriously, several times, before spending. And what about my career? Would I simply settle for a bank job for the rest of my life? I had to snap out of it. I had more ambition, and a college education; I had to do better.

CAREER MOVE

I had graduated in Engineering, but my experience in business overtook my career options. My experience in banking became paramount in my future, and I was offered a position with a fast track to a bank manager. Who said being a teller during college years would not be rewarding? I thought it would be the height of my career; being a bank manager. I had already known all the aspects of banking from previous experience, so my track should have been fast indeed. Not so fast! This management program apparently had no management personnel to manage it. I was stuck doing mundane banking tasks with no career advancement. Until, something happened that changed my circumstances. The bank had decided to upgrade all the computer terminals, at every branch, to a more modern version, with a different manufacturer. Voila! I was the man, and the man indeed. I had learned from prior banking experience, and my engineering education, about computer communications in the banking industry. I had also solved several communication problems in the past, and my record was exemplary in this area.

I was assigned to this major project. My engineering knowledge simply made me the expert. I trained the entire staff, troubleshot problems, and coordinated with upper management. I also wrote the manual for the staff to use. I coordinated the conversion of every branch of the bank, in four boroughs of New York. The bank did not have branches in the fifth borough - the Bronx. Let's leave that explanation mum; we're talking about the Bronx in the nineteen-seventies.

By the time the project was complete, and all the branches were up and running smoothly, I received an offer of employment from the manufacturer of the computer system. It was a natural occurrence; they wanted my expertise. This company had several other banks interested in their system. I took the job and received a handsome pay raise. Nice! More importantly the office was at Rockefeller Center, overlooking the skating rink and the Christmas tree. It was a nice place to work, but for me, just a place to work. I had to battle hoards of tourists, daily, as I left for lunch, or left for the day. It was their vacation, and they were all excited to see the cathedral, the skating rink, and all the flags flying around. All I wanted to do was simply to get out of the area to have lunch. I may have seen the lighting of the tree ceremony from the office only once in all the years I worked there. There were so many things to do in New York, and many conflicts with schedules. The tree ceremony went to the back burner. I wished I could have offered the view from the office to the people on the street waiting in the cold for the lights on the tree to be turned on. I felt for them, as I was also a tourist in many places at one time or another. I did see the tree after the lights were on. Quite lovely.

I worked on the leading edge products of this company, which were ATMs. I designed and documented the functional specifications for the banks, one of them being the second largest bank in New York. I was on top of the world; the marriage of my engineering and banking skills placed me on top of the charts. There were so many tasks I could get done for this company, and I became the "go to" guy. I traveled everywhere in the country they wanted, as I supported the sales force. I designed, documented and conducted testing of the client bank's specifications for all transactions, and supported the technicians who did the installations. Many small and large contracts were signed, and I was the man to complete the jobs. I was their man, and I was a lucky and happy man.

I stayed for a few years, but the salary leveled off. It was the dawn of the Information Age, and it was not unusual for specialists to switch jobs every few years. It was time for me to switch. It was time for more money in my wallet. I placed my resume out to big companies, and was hired within a few months. I was greeted with a handsome pay increase, and a career path, with the largest company in the world. I had finally broken free from the games of career pursuit. I was free to follow my newfound future. It was a sense of liberation from bondage that I would not have to hustle to look for a better job, or change professions. I was in good company, with a good company.

COSMOS

What I thought I could never escape from, and when I thought I could never escape, came to me in one of the most profound moments of my life; when I heard Carl Sagan say that we are all made of the same stuff; the stuff of life. I could still envision him on the TV screen as he spoke those few sentences that guided me on my way. He said further that the trees were my cousins, and that I was related to sharks and monkeys, as well all other humans; all at the same time; because I possessed the stuff of life - DNA. I was blown away. I was amazed that I could finally consider an alternative philosophy of life - one with understanding of the world, instead of blind faith. I could begin to resolve my conflicts between doctrine and science. I was liberated from doctrinal bondage, and I was free, free at last. I had found what I was looking for. I thought about what I had learned, and soon after, I switched the philosophy of my life to science. I was thankful that my father had exposed me to doctrine, but I was seeking an alternative system. I wanted to understand the world, and everything in it, and doctrine did not do that for me.

I felt like I had broken free from jail, and I had made my great escape. I was cured, but not healed. I would have to exhale all that I inhaled during my youth. But, I could not simply erase what was pounded into my head for almost three decades. It would take a long time to reprogram my brain. I would have to search and verify. I would have to always be vigilant that something I accepted could be wrong for me. I would have to be prepared to continue my quest, realizing that it could take decades. I would have to make the commitment that every opportunity I received, personal or professional, should be used to explore human behavior, and the world around me. I would have to find the commonality in humans, animals, trees and the entire universe. I would have to find the DNA of the universe, as Carl Sagan described it for life on this planet. It was at this time that my writings began. I made notes about all the science I could find, and I kept them, securely, like a lover keeps a diary, knowing someday they would be read. I was in love, and I was on my quest. More importantly, I had finally broken free from the bondage of doctrine in the philosophy of my life.

Within a decade of landing in New York I had acquired a college degree, obtained a pilot's license, and became a certified scuba diver. I owned a car, a motorcycle and a boat, all on a budget. I landed my dream job, with the best company in the world. I was on my quest to succeed, and it was America that made that happen. I was living the dream, the American dream. I was also learning about the many facets of humans, in all of the environments I ventured. I was curious to know. But, I didn't know why I wanted to know. I just knew that I wanted to know.

Simultaneously, as my professional and personal lives made their final turns, I felt as though I had just received my license for living, with a new and different perspective. There would be much learning ahead, as I acquired experience in life, in a similar way as every newly licensed driver or pilot. I had arrived at the future that was charted by the occurrences, circumstances, conditions and situations in my life. No longer would I be chained to the chair of guilt. No longer would I have to listen to humans who do not support the facts of our existence. New York shaped the future of my professional life, while my father and Carl Sagan shaped the future of my philosophy. I had become whole, as I changed course, and I was happy about that. It was time to live free. I had finally made the Great Escape.

Chapter Four

PROFESSIONALLY SPEAKING

I was fortunate to have found the profession that I enjoyed, and with a company I trusted. I worked for the largest company that ever existed, at that time. I was at the forefront of the Digital Age, at the beginning of the digitization of voice for telephony, transmission of data, and development of networks. I was an engineer, then a designer. I progressed to marketing manager and project manager. It was the dawn of the Information Age and I was there. It was exciting to be part of the evolution of what became this global infrastructure. It was a strange twist of the future I had envisioned, for myself. As a youth, I always wanted to be in a strictly technical, non-business environment. It turned out that my business skills proved to be my strength, and I was fortunate to be placed in a position where I could utilize both skills. I was also fortunate that I was employed in a leading edge technology discipline, and the wave of the future. It was rewarding to have been in the "right place at the right time." Perhaps it could be called luck. But, luck to me would be a series of incalculable, but fortunate occurrences or events. Either way, I accepted it all graciously.

THE DOG AND THE BONE

Just as I started my job with the largest company, in which my professional business career was quite certain, I received a letter from the Federal Aviation Administration (FAA) that I had been selected to be an Air Traffic Controller, and would be assigned to the best location on the planet to be an Air Traffic Controller; the Terminal Radar Control center in New York. The TRACON placement with Air Traffic Control was not something to be easily turned down; it was like hitting the jackpot. New York airspace, being the densest in the world, would offer challenges, and I would never be bored like some controllers in remote areas where the towers closed at eleven at night.

I had a good grade on the controller's written test some years back. I had also passed the physical, psychological and background tests. They considered me physically fit, with a better than perfect vision of 20/17, psychologically stable, and safe. When the air traffic controllers went on strike in the early nineteen- eighties, the President of the United States fired all of them, unless they showed up for work. The President was unhappy that employees of a government organization had the privilege to go on strike, especially considering that it would result in massive disruption of essential services for flights, and a huge economic loss for the country, and the world. Most of the controllers did not return to work, and they lost their jobs. They were locked out of federal jobs for their defiance. The opportunity arose for me when the largest hiring of air traffic controllers occurred.

I was high on the list because of my grade. That made me proud of myself to have been selected. In addition, I considered myself fortunate that they selected me for TRACON. But, I was conflicted. When the agent called me to inform me that it was time to register for training in Oklahoma City, I told him that I would have to think about it. I am sure he wondered about what there was to think about, as he was offering me one of the best positions in the system. I said that I would call back in a couple of weeks. It became time for me to seriously consider my options. I had just started a professional position with much room for advancement. The job as a controller would have been schooling in Oklahoma City, then training in New York. In addition, there was a rotating shift because of the twenty-four hour coverage for an essential service. I was not encouraged, and I was not sure as to which profession I wanted. The answer came to me when I realized that I was already on a great career path with one big company, and I would be able to start an additional career as Aviation ground teacher at a school I was attending. I had already made arrangements for the teaching position, and started the process for certification.

The FAA agent called me back after a couple of weeks and confirmed that all the paperwork and reports on me were complete and verified, and all he needed was an affirmative or a negative response from me. He would have to move on to the next person on the list if I refused the job. I was still hesitant, and perhaps greedy, as in the story of the dog and the bone. I wanted it all. How could I make a decision between two of the best job offers someone could ever have? It was difficult, but it was also time for me to hold on to one bone, and let the other go. I was compelled to make a decision. Finally the agent simply asked; "Is it yeah or nay?" I replied in the negative and my Air Traffic Controller's career was over before it even started.

GOLDEN HANDCUFFS

My time in the corporate world was exciting and interesting. I was working in a business environment that required a technical qualification. I was a young professional who joined this large company as it prepared to retire most of the employees. They were mostly veterans from the Second World War. I would be one of the replacements. I had the great privilege of listening to stories of these veterans who were mostly from the Air Force, where they acquired the technical knowledge that qualified them for employment. It was almost as though I was enlisted in the military; the managers would be the senior officers, and the technicians would be the enlisted men. I would guess that the Engineering department of the company,

101

and the entire technical work force consisted of these male veterans. Most of them were in the military during wartime. I heard stories of some who were stationed in England, and servicing P-51 Fighter planes, and others who were gunners on Bombers. Common for all of them were the incredible noises they had to endure, both inside and outside of the airplanes. These guys were the real deal; a generation of the past who would always be remembered as part of the strongest fighting force the world had ever seen.

Upon their return to the USA they would be faced with challenges from a war torn country on its way to recovery. There would be difficult years ahead for them, even though they had endured great difficulty already. They would be faced with challenges such as shortage of food supplies, and placing hot bricks under their beds when nighttime heating was turned off for wartime conservation. They endured, and became part of the recovery, and were the light of a nation emerging from a catastrophe.

In time, their candlepower began to fade, and others had to step in. I was one of the fortunate ones to light a new candle. Their stories were mostly humorous, and perhaps it was the best way to deal with the misery of war. The only story I could have told them about myself was that my military service draft number was not selected. I did not have to go to Vietnam because that war was over, and so was the draft. Almost every week there was a retirement luncheon for one of these Vets. Within a few years they were all gone. The last one for me was my best friend, who was a cavalryman, stationed in France. We stayed friends after he retired, and until he died. I miss him, and all of them too, and I cherish the memories and my time with them.

NIGHT SCHOOL

In due time I accepted the opportunity to advance my secondary profession, in Aviation. I started advanced pilot training, and at the same time took all the tests for professional pilot and ground instructor. The results were very favorable, and I immediately accepted the ground instructor position. I started to teach in the classroom, and I loved it immediately and immensely. I felt like I did not have to go fly anymore. I did not really enjoy flying to begin with. This teaching thing could be my cure; the cure for that drive I had from within. I taught evening classes several times during the week, and it fit perfectly into my schedule with my corporate career day job. The combination of day job and night teaching was my fancy.

I loved teaching so much that I focused on flying very little, and my professional pilot training slipped by the wayside. A student in one of my classes made a suggestion. He was a successful businessman with a major company and I took his suggestions seriously. He inquired as to when I would be teaching in the airplane. I replied that it was not on my front burner. He offered to pay for the training so that I could start teaching him. I was touched by his confidence in me and I replied that it was not financing holding me back; it was time. It was something he could not give me. In any case, I asked him to be patient.

MY VIRGINITY

I accelerated my professional pilot training after being prompted by several students in my classrooms. Finally, I became a flight instructor. The certification process required the training and demonstration of a high level of mastery of the airplane, which was necessary in order to be able to recover from any unusual situation that could be induced by a student or pilot in training. Additionally, it necessitated the knowledge on all of the academic aspects required for any level of pilot licensing, and of course the ability to teach all of it.

My faithful student was my first victim. He did not know what he was getting himself into. New flight instructors were tough, simply because we also had to learn in the process, and did not want to make any mistakes. This student progressed very nicely through all of the maneuvers and completed the requirements for his pilot's license. We became good friends during the time he was training with me.

He had reached the completed point of his training, and it became time for his flight test. I would have to review all the required maneuvers before I could authorize his flight test with the examiner, who would be the one to issue the license. I asked him to prepare for his flight test, and for him to assume that I was the examiner during the flight. I called this a practice flight test. I mentioned to him that my test would be more difficult than the actual test, since I would be having him do every required maneuver. The examiner would request only a sampling of them.

During the practice test with me he failed one of the simplest and basic maneuvers. I expressed my firm and sincere disappointment with a hint of disgust. He responded with the statement, "I thought you were my friend." I waited until we landed to address his concern. I told him that I was his friend on the ground, but in the air I was his instructor, and further, I treasured both privileges. I did sign the authorization for his flight test, after which he made an appointment with the examiner.

Upon his return to the airport after his flight test, the examiner would have told him whether he had passed or failed, as it was customary. The examiner approached me as she was walking away from his airplane. I was preparing for a lesson with another student. With a face of disappointment, she told me that he needed more training. She left and went into the hangar without further discussion. I was shocked, naturally, and disappointed; perhaps more shocked than disappointed. I was thorough with this candidate, and I thought he would make a good pilot. Within minutes, my friend walked over to me with a perfect smile on his face. My first thought was about how odd it was for someone to be smiling, after just failing a flight test. He told me he had passed. I wanted to punch him, but it was only a feeling, not requiring any action. He had told the examiner to play a joke on me, and that she should tell me that he failed. She did not want to lie, so she did the best to play his little game. He had gotten me back for the discomfort of my explanation of the friendship and instructor relationship earlier. I did not take it seriously, and we stayed friends anyway; it was a big boy's joke.

My friend had become a pilot; the first pilot trained by me, and he was free to fly. He wanted to fly everywhere, and he often asked me to accompany him for fun, and for safety. I lost the privilege of being his flight instructor, unless, and until, he wanted to advance his training for flight in clouds, meaning instrument training.

FOR THE BIRDS

Humans were not born to fly. We do not have the instincts and capability of birds. Humans learn to fly, at their own pace. My job was to facilitate the student's progress without prejudice. Age, race, education, wealth, profession, gender, religion, dress code or any other characteristics were not for me to judge. It was up to me to understand that human mind, with all its aspirations, fears, and feelings, and mold it in the direction of flight. I would have to understand the states of mind, and conditioned fears, like those handed down by a protective parent, such as the fear of flight that my father handed down to me. I knew it well, as I felt the tap on my shoulders by a man thousands of miles away, reminding me not to fly, whenever I entered an airplane. But, I had to overcome it, as I would not let it get in my way of teaching someone. Many people are susceptible to perceived fear instilled by parents whose wishes were that they did not fly. This fear plagued me many, many times and I wonder if it was this same fear that contributed to the tragic death of America's Prince, the famous president's only son. Fear mongering and guilt were powerful influences that were important for me to extract subtly from my students, in order to be an effective teacher.

The airplane was my office. The student was my subject. The session was psychoanalysis. I had just found my dream job; I was a flight instructor. My job was to coach every candidate, all with the same human brain, and teach them to manipulate the controls of an airplane in order to become the pilot in command. After this accomplishment, each of them would have to learn all the aspects of flying from one airport to another. Most of the learning would be academic. My job was to transfer the academics, from the classroom to the airplane, and explain the operation of the airplane, and flights in the airplane. In retrospect, I realized that I was subconsciously satisfying my mission to understand human nature. The first clue was that I did not really enjoy flying an airplane, since my very first flight. I enjoyed the challenge of teaching, first in the classroom, and again in the airplane. It was the teaching that planted me next to the student. The second clue was that I took great interest in the progress of all students, as though it was my sole responsibility to help them succeed. It was as though their failure was my failure. It was not just because I cared, it was because the students were giving me an opportunity to look inside their minds, without question.

I flew with those who simply wanted to be a private pilot, and those who had airline pilot aspirations. I did not judge. It was my code of ethics. One airline pilot candidate terminated his career in less than ten minutes of his first flight. He was fine and wonderful until the takeoff. Then on climb-out, not even five hundred feet in altitude, the panic stricken student insisted on getting back on the ground immediately. I wished I could have turned the airplane into a helicopter. I had the painstaking task of landing the airplane as quickly as possible while trying to keep this frantic person calm. I was certain this guy picked a different career after his trial, and tribulation, of his airline pilot aspiration.

I flew with doctors and lawyers, civil servants and vice presidents, policemen and firemen, office workers and social workers. I flew with businessmen and clergymen. I flew with women, men, adults and youths, and people from all over the world. Some were Swiss and some were Swedes. There were some Germans, Indians, Brazilians, Moroccans, and Italians. I flew with Jews, Muslims, Christians, Buddhists, and Atheists too. I flew in a tin can with Americans, Venezuelans, Belgians, Mexicans, Puerto Ricans and Africans. I flew with Japanese, Surinamese, Portuguese, Guyanese and Chinese, but never Milanese. I flew with Saudis, Pakistanis and Bangladeshis. There were also Colombians, Panamanians, Bahamians and Palestinians. French, English and Irish all came to fly. Let me also mention Thai people and Israeli people. I flew with people from every continent, except Antarctica. I discovered from a documentary show that residents of Antarctica do not fly. The students all came to fly with me in the tin can with wings called an airplane, and they loved it. They all gave me the great opportunity to learn so much about human beings. I learned about their fear, anxiety, excitement, and the gamut of emotions that came with being immersed into a medium that was not natural for humans. I was lucky. It is true to say that the one who learns most from teaching is the teacher.

EXPERIENCE COUNTED

I saw the seasons change from the airplane, from hazy green through the trees in summer to beautiful orange and red in autumn. I flew in winter and saw snow on the ground, frozen lakes, and the black of the streets and roadways against the white of the snow. I was fortunate to have the experience to land on snow, and I would let students try it; the landings were soft. It was much easier to spot a freshly cleaned runway in the distance; it would look like a black strip surrounded by white. I saw the sun go down behind the horizon like a coin in a slot machine, as the winter sunset turned very quickly into night. I flew in the spring and saw a clear sky and lush green trees on the ground. I flew at night, and I flew at dawn. I just wanted to fly, all the time teaching.

Many people just wanted to try out flying an airplane, and soon stopped after a flight or two. Others went on to fly solo, then stopped. Approximately half would continue, and then some of them would simply fade away. Finally, out of ten, perhaps two or three would finish the licensing course and get certified. After the license, one or two would stop flying altogether. It was the accomplishment they wanted - that piece of paper that said, "Pilot" next to their names.

My experience in shaping the mind by training people in an airplane was valuable in my analysis of human behavior. Firstly, the environment of an airplane brought out many new emotions and feelings from a person. I had to assess and manage every issue of each student. Secondly, it was important that I learned as much as possible about each student in order to facilitate a successful training program. I made sure that my interests were focused on training the students. This meant keeping a schedule of tasks to be accomplished in a progressive manner, and building on each lesson by adding on previous accomplishments. Considering the amount of time a student traveled to the airport for a one-hour lesson, it was prudent for me to be sure that they learned as much as possible each time, and that they recognized their progress. I encouraged them as best as possible, and they came back over and over again to quench their thirst for flying.

The airport was the watering hole. I had become more important than sleep sometimes, especially to my male students who gravitated like magnets to the airport. I became the "other woman" in these men's lives. I became the one they were having the love affair with - the love of flying affair. I was the envy of their wives and girlfriends, as these guys placed them on the back burner to go flying. I often recommended that the guys offer the wives and girlfriends a quick flight lesson with me to cure the tension. It worked well, most times. I was dealing with a host of human issues, and I loved it. Thank goodness the female students came with no issues, and good listening capability, offering a more relaxed atmosphere.

MACHO MAN

I had immersed myself into a male dominated activity during my training days in aviation. As I reflected on the day I was to make my first solo flight, the instructor simply asked me for my logbook, signed it, and got out of the airplane. As he departed he told me to do one landing by myself. There were no preparations, no pep talk, and no questions, just go do it. I appreciated his confidence in me, as I also thought I was qualified for the task. I would learn later in my career that this type of macho behavior, which lacked any psychological considerations, was improper. Many accidents had occurred simply because of male machismo. The advent of terms, such as "team work" and "cockpit resource management" (CRM) would make their debut to help men, and some women, manage the psychological aspects in aviation.

My first exposure to this human characteristic, in a professional way, was addressed during the testing for my professional licenses. Prior to the issuance of any pilot instructor license, the candidate must first successfully complete one test, and that was called; "Fundamentals of instruction." It was a test on the psychological aspects of learning. It was not taken seriously by the pilot community, and treated as though it was a nuisance test, simply to get out of the way. Not for me, as I considered it the most important aspect in becoming an instructor. It was during my studies for this test when I learned that understanding is the highest level of learning. I was happy to pass this test with a perfect score.

This aspect would be addressed to me later during my flight test for the instructor's license. The examiner asked me what procedure I would use before sending a student for the first solo flight. Before I could answer, she told me that I should have a discussion with the student about the responsibility and challenge, and to prepare him, or her, psychologically for the task. It seemed that the male machismo had worked itself into an issue for the certification process. After reflecting on my own first solo experience, it seemed proper that discussions with pilot candidates was important prior to solo flight, and certificate issuance. In any case it was my opinion that this woman examiner had detected this aspect in the industry. Women's intuition and experience could have told her to advise male instructors about the destructive element of machismo in the male dominated culture of aviation. I felt that she was giving me advice, as someone gave directions to a driver trying to get to a destination. The only way to know that the driver reached the destination would be to verify. The best way for her to verify was when she would fly with the candidates I recommended for the pilot's license, as she was the designated examiner for the area. She would be certain to verify whether her directions were accurate, and if I had reached my destination. She reminded me time and again, as she passed every one of my candidates, sometimes offering a compliment. I had learned how to teach from all the books, and from the good advice of important people; like her.

I made it a habit to emulate professionalism with each and every student regardless of gender, or any other aspect of his or her being. I was always on the lookout for any and all psychological characteristic that could affect someone's learning ability. It was my belief that machismo did not belong in an airplane, and I had only a few incidents with that matter. The act of flying an airplane brought its own emotional and instinctive effects, which helped diminish other unwanted psychological nuances. It was a self-regulated system where macho dudes were subdued, simply from the fright of flight.

Machismo is a male characteristic, which probably originated from male dominance in the animal world. Perhaps it represents the naturally occurring instinctive effects, originating from testosterone. It is possible that this feeling overflows into other aspects of male behavior, in subtle ways. I also experienced the effects of testosterone myself, and with the understanding of its cause and cure, I was able to deal with it constructively. It is also most likely why I did not observe it with female students. It was a delight to teach them, as they listened and followed instructions well, and they did not display any type of arrogance. I was fortunate to have acquired a strong female side from my upbringing, and it helped me with understanding in my professional life as well. It was important that females be accepted, like any male, into the male dominated society they were looking to join. I was glad to help.

RUDDER WORK

One of the more difficult techniques to teach was the use the rudder in the airplane. It was a normal human difficulty. The rudder is only effective as the airplane travels through air, and it works by pushing foot pedals left or right. The same foot pedals also steer the nose wheel on the ground. The control wheel, which looks similar to the lower half of the steering wheel in a car, is used in flight to control banking. The confusion with students was that they often tried to "drive" the airplane while on the ground by turning the wheel as though they were in a car. It was a natural tendency, and most often I had to ask the students to keep their arms folded while on the ground, which would necessitate the use of pedals for steering. Unfortunately, this syndrome occurred in the air as well, especially, for example, when it was necessary to make small corrections on final approach, where the use of rudder would be more effective. The students would try to use the control wheel, which moved the ailerons. All that accomplished was a rocking of the wings from side to side. After being subjected to this hypnosis and nausea, I would sometimes sarcastically tell them that I was not really interested in being rocked to sleep. Eventually, for stubborn candidates, I would tell them not to use the control wheel, as I would do it for them so they could focus on the rudder for runway alignment. It worked really well, as the rudder was all they were allowed to move, with their arms folded.

The use of rudder was contrary to human behavior, and did not sit well with logic and normalcy. It made many students uncomfortable, and their behavior on final approach varied from calmness, to twitching, to shoulder movements, and even whistling. They were nervous and anxious. It was slightly amusing for me. I compared this behavior to anxiety during a game of bowling. They wanted to set into motion the conditions for a perfect score, and final approach would be similar to watching the bowling ball travel down the lane, as they looked forward to that perfect score. It always seemed that the moment of truth for every flight, the moment of glory, the moment of perfection, the moment of accomplishment, was the landing. It took a bit of coaching to help them use the rudder to get that perfect score, that perfect landing, and when it worked they were rewarded. Our animal nature dictates receipt of a reward for effort, and it is how animals could be trained for tasks. It is also how humans can be trained, and it was how I trained humans for flight. The reward system really works.

THE SOLOIST

A young lady, who was one of my dedicated students, wanted to set an objective to either pass the written test required for the license, or fly the first solo in the airplane. She had already logged some hours in the airplane and she consulted with me for my advice. She would be moving out of the area in a few weeks to pursue her professional career. I considered her goal practical, and I guided her with some exploratory questions regarding flight training in the area she was moving. After considering her schedule, the challenge of locating a new flight school, and the establishment of a relationship with a new flight instructor, the answer came to her quickly. I was only the guide to her decision. She would be better off aiming for the solo flight, and not be concerned about the written test for which she could study at her leisure. The plan was made, and we agreed on it. She decided on becoming a soloist.

It was part of my strategy to prepare every student psychologically for the first solo flight, in addition to all the flight training required. It was important that they did not have acute levels of anxiety, or stress. It was like preparing them for "stage fright." During my first solo flight I could not hear the tower controller on the radio when I requested a takeoff clearance. The instructor had lowered the volume on the radio in order for me to hear his instructions for my flight. I became a bit nervous, but I figured out the problem with the radio. His version of the first solo was to tell the student the day had come, and that he would be getting out of the airplane, and then do exactly that. Perhaps he knew enough, but that was taking chances that the student was not prepared psychologically. I did not believe in taking such risks.

It was summer time, and I met the young lady after work a few times for intense landing training. We did landing after landing, time after time, until the perfect day arrived. The day had come when I would get out of the airplane, and she would fly by herself to do one landing - one landing by herself, with her alone in the airplane. It would be a day she could never forget. Every pilot has the one first landing which marks the event that could never happen again; the first solo flight. We had the firm agreement that on the day she had clocked three landings, which I did not contribute to, it would be the day for me to get out. I wanted her to fully accept our agreement and recognize it psychologically.

We had started out on this one nice afternoon with good weather. After a couple of landings I told her that I was going to slide my seat all the way rearwards, remove my feet from the rudder area, and fold my arms. I showed her what I did, and explained that she was totally in control. I also said that the only time I would intervene would be in the event of an imminent collision, or if it looked like she was going to break the airplane on landing. She was fine with everything, and she did more than three landings, to be sure. She wanted to be sure, and sure again, and again. Finally, after several landings, I said to her that I was ready to get out. She did not want me to get out. I understood her feelings. We had discussed them as preparation for her flight. I could see that she was quite calm, and I surmised that she simply needed a little nudge. She asked for another landing with me, and I firmly reminded her about our agreement, while assuring her that she was ready. I also expressed a very slight frustration of doing landing after landing. I asked her again firmly if she was up to the objective she set for herself, as I reminded her that I was confident in her. She replied; "Yes sir." It was the first time she called me, "Sir." I did not like being called, "Sir."

I had realized that she was the one who needed the push, instead of doing the pushing. She did not want to push me out of the airplane; I was her safety net. But, she needed to fly the coop, and it was time. I signed her logbook with the approval for solo flight and got out of the airplane. I instructed her to make one landing, and return to the same point, to pick me up. Her circumstances were perfect. The weather was beautiful, and there was no other air traffic at the airport.

I watched her as I had done with other students so many times before. I felt like I knew something about her that she did not know herself. I wanted to understand all that was happening to her, from her motivation to fly, to the adrenaline running through her veins, as she flew for the first time by herself. I also envisioned that after her landing, the adrenaline would be accompanied with the happy hormones and endorphins, which would make her feel like she was on the moon. The most important thing I knew, and needed to know about her, was that she could make a safe landing.

She lined up the airplane on the runway and applied full power. I watched the airplane accelerate and lift off. The climb angle remained constant. She was doing precisely what she was supposed to do. It would seem natural to her, almost instinctive. It was what training did; it was what repetition did; it made her do things naturally. I could only imagine what she was thinking, as I remembered what I was thinking when I flew an airplane off the ground by myself for the first time. I was not worried about her, as she was fully trained, and ready. I knew that she would do well. I was in her head, as I had wired her brain as though it could be manipulated by my remote control. I had all the confidence that the thought to accomplish was all she needed.

She flew the rectangular pattern around the runway as she should have done, and lined up the airplane for the final approach. I watched carefully. I saw that her angle was correct, the propeller was at a slow speed, and that the flaps were fully extended. This was routine, and she was perfectly configured; she knew what she was doing. I was hoping that she would make a smooth landing, not to please me, but for her lifelong memory. As she approached the runway threshold I waited confidently for her next action. She leveled the airplane over the runway about the height of a person, and then waited for the paradoxical procedure of keeping the airplane flying for as long as possible in order to achieve the smoothest landing. She kept it flying until the lift from the wings evaporated, and as the airplane made its final descent towards the runway she lifted the nose slightly. Her perfect landing was made with the main gears first, and then she waited for the nose wheel to settle by itself. It would be the first time she would make a landing by herself, and that memory should never fade. In our human psychology, the memory of our first significant event, or experience becomes wired into our brain, since each would be a new experience, forming the reason our minds would not forget.

The girl taxied back to pick me up after landing, and of course I could see the joy and excitement in her face and behavior. I congratulated and complimented her for her great achievement. I even joked with her by saying that we should head back to the parking spot and see if she knew how to park the airplane. She did just that, and we were done for the day, and perhaps forever. I encouraged her to go celebrate, and share the news of her accomplishment with her family and friends. She was one very happy young lady. I would not fly with her ever again, as we had completed her mission. She moved to Atlanta soon after, with her memories, and I stayed with my memories of her.

FRIEND ME

Quite often students wanted to repeatedly thank me, then hug me, because of their exhilaration, when they reached a milestone in training, such as the first solo flight. One guy even kissed me on the cheek after his first flight. I wiped it off discretely on my shirt. I always tried to discourage excessive expression of emotional outpouring from the students. I preferred to focus on their accomplishment, and that I was only the facilitator. More importantly, I felt that by accepting their sentiments I would be encouraging them to continue reliance on me emotionally. I wanted them to be strong for their future. I wanted them to have the confidence in themselves, and to focus their emotions on their accomplishments, and the challenges that would lie ahead for them. I was shaping a human mind. I wanted that mind to work for them, and for me. Sentiments, praises and hugs encourage complacency and camaraderie, which could also erode authority - a necessary ingredient in the student/teacher relationship. I expected for the next time a level of performance equal to, or above the last accomplishment. I had set the bar by which they would be judged, and it was good motivation to remind them about my expectation of them in the future. I was a nice and friendly fellow, always with a smile, but I was also the teacher, and I stuck to my guns.

THE MAN WHO WATCHED HIS WATCH

My flight training was done on weekends, and the schedule was tight. But, I also made some flexibility for each student based on the training requirements in their program. Students who simply needed to learn how to make turns, climbs, descents and such, could start and finish the lesson within the scheduled time. However, for students nearing the "solo" point, it was important to monitor their performance, the weather and the air traffic, so as to let them accomplish their first landing by themselves smoothly. In these cases, quite often such lessons would go into overtime. The students would most likely need to do extra landing practice. Such situations had a domino effect, wherein every student thereafter would be delayed. I always told students as part of my oral agreement, that when they came for a lesson there was always the possibility of a delay or cancellation. This is normal in every human endeavor. There could be inclement weather, an issue with the airplane, or the airport, and also scheduling issues.

I made it a habit to seize every opportunity to help the progress of students. One young man was attempting to accomplish the first solo when he needed extra landing practice. His flying took us beyond the allotted lesson time. The next student on the schedule came a bit early, and was waiting. From the air, I could have seen his car parked, as we circled the airport for landing after landing. Finally, I was able to accomplish the goal, and the student had his first solo flight. Upon return to the parking area the student who was waiting was nowhere to be found; he had left. He was a person who believed firmly in punctuality. He was from a European country where you could set your watch by the punctuality of the trains. I had many students from that country, and I recognized their need for punctuality. However, I always reminded them about our oral agreement, and that if their car had broken down on the way to the airport, and they missed their appointment I would understand. I must admit that I did appreciate their reliability; they always showed up. On the other hand, I expected their understanding in certain circumstances. I also reminded them that I would not forsake the opportunity for them if they were ready for their first solo flight. It was the camaraderie I fostered amongst everyone.

I wondered about this behavior in human beings who were groomed into a certain culture to strongly adhere to it without complete consideration of all of the circumstances. As an example, I wondered about the "big picture" thinking which would be lacking with such a philosophy. Why did the student not wait, and accept a shorter lesson? Secondly, why did he not understand the possibility that there could always be a delay from the previous student's situation? Most importantly why would someone cheat himself from a flight lesson after driving all the way to the airport? Why did punctuality have to triumph?

There were some things about such philosophy that I could not understand, or accept. It made me wonder about us as humans; how we can be conditioned by our circumstances. I wondered how we could be so malleable as to be shaped, while at the same time possessing the highest intellect of all species. I wondered about our arrogance, the rejection of which could bring humility, and quite possibly understanding.

I consider myself lucky that my circumstances had allowed me to think beyond the limits of what was ingrained in my brain about time, and about clocks. I detested both anyway, as I was awoken at a bitter time in the morning, every morning, when I was a youth. In addition, the clock made me late for school many times. I realized that time was a human concept, which I must, nevertheless, learn to respect. It exists because we could remember the past, and try to predict and plan the future. If I were an alligator time would be simple. There would be only two moments of time, a time to eat and a time to sleep. There would be no past, and no future. Our human penalty comes from knowing both. It is sometimes the foundation of misery on this planet.

As for the student who left because I was not available at his scheduled time, I could have only wished that he were a bit more patient, for his own benefit. If he terminated his commitment with me out of sheer disappointment, he would have to find a new place to fly. It would cost him more money to learn from this new institution, and he may also have cancellations and delays. Did he just jump out of the frying pan and into the fire? Rest assured he did. I knew the industry; I was also a student, and many times I took the time to go to the airport only to come right back home, for similar reasons that the young man experienced that day; delays and poor weather. He must have later learned the reality of taking flight lessons, or perhaps he gave up. That thought led to a new question: how badly did he want to become a pilot? His belief about the value of punctuality had probably barred him from ever becoming a pilot, as the circumstances seemed not in his favor. Our circumstances define our situation.

FLY TO MEET

I flew in airplanes quite often. I was a flight instructor on weekends and evenings, and almost every week or two my corporate job placed me in an airliner as I traveled on business trips. I donned the business suit and shoes, and jumped on a jet for meetings in Boston, or Washington, D.C. Usually, the travel and the meeting were completed on the same day. Each hour from LaGuardia Airport shuttle flights would line up like buses. All that was needed was a ticket and I would board the next flight.

I had a meeting in Washington, D.C. with some US Government people regarding the procurement of equipment that fell into my jurisdiction as marketing manager. A junior executive working for me, along with one of my company's representative for government affairs, and I, had planned to fly to meet the government representative at her office. We all agreed to meet on the eight o'clock shuttle flight. The two colleagues to accompany me were women. They did not fly very much, as it was not professionally necessary.

The ladies were prompt at the airport, and got on the eight o'clock flight as soon as boarding began. When I boarded the shuttle flight they were nowhere to be seen. It was a half empty airplane. After the plane was airborne I spoke to the flight attendant. She was free for the rest of the short flight after the beverage service, and took up a seat across the aisle from me. I verified that I was on the eight o'clock shuttle and she confirmed it. But, she added that there were two eight o'clock shuttles. She explained that when one aircraft was full it would take-off and another would start boarding. My colleagues were on the shuttle in front of me.

I asked the flight attendant to do me a favor and ask the captain to send a message to the plane in front. She was reluctant, and questioned if it could be done. I explained that I was also a pilot and there were ways. It could be done through the airline dispatch center, or on a separate radio frequency assigned for such transmissions, or through communications with Air Traffic Control (ATC). Sometimes ATC would relay a message if the workload was light. It broke their monotony of constantly giving directives, and they appreciated the gratitude that followed. Sometimes they would allow for a direct communication with another aircraft on the same frequency, as long as it was brief and did not interfere with their work.

The flight attendant did contact the captain and confirmed that the message was successfully relayed to my colleague in the airplane ahead. It made my day, as I felt the privilege to have been a member of a special group of people - pilots and controllers, who revered each other as brethren. They came through for me even though there was no crisis, and it made me smile. They eased my anxiety of wondering if I would be having a meeting or not. As I walked out of the airliner I thanked the pilots, and expressed my sincere appreciation. They were happy to accomplish something that was out of the ordinary, and perhaps enjoyed this very unusual request of a passenger. I did feel comfortable pushing their human limits.

Upon exiting I was greeted with a sign with my name written on it as though a driver was picking me up. It was the humorous tactic of my two colleagues who were waiting for me as I deplaned. They wanted to make fun of me. We laughed and went off to the meeting.

After the meeting, the younger colleague who worked for me mentioned in private that the older colleague was so impressed and excited to receive an in-flight message from the flight deck, especially on an airplane loaded with business folks. She felt so important. The two were sitting next to each other. She explained the details of the event, which started with an announcement from a flight attendant for the colleague, who was called by her name, to ring her call button, for an in-flight message from the flight deck. After pressing the button, the flight attendant gave her a note, and said that it was from the captain. The younger colleague told me; "It made her day." What they did not know was that it made my day, considering the stress I was feeling, thinking that I may not meet up with them, or that they may not have come at all, and the trip would have been a total waste of money and time. I was just being resourceful, and I concocted the best possible method to get in contact with her, by asking for a favor, and it worked. I was relieved, as I was primarily interested in getting to that meeting with everyone.

It was early afternoon when our meeting ended, so we ventured into Georgetown and had lunch at one of the iconic restaurants, at the company's expense of course. The government employee could not join us because it was against protocol, and totally illegal had we paid for her. I felt sorry for her, while I enjoyed some of the perks of private enterprise. I was quite happy that the mission was accomplished, especially noting that the meeting had to be coordinated with the schedule of several people. We flew back home on a shuttle flight, perhaps the last one for that day. The trip was all in a day's work.

LAGUARDIA LIMO

I was asked by a friend to fly his airplane from its base in New Jersey to LaGuardia Airport to pick him up after his arrival on a commercial flight. A cold front had just moved through the area and the wind behind it was very strong, and accompanied with frequent gusts. The National Weather Service issued a "SIGMET" (Significant Meteorology), which was a warning for all aircraft with regards to wind speed, and extreme turbulence. This kind of day would not be a good day to fly a blimp, for example; it would be going backwards.

LaGuardia's main runways intersect perpendicularly. On this day the winds were blowing from the northwest in excess of 25 knots at the surface, and this strength was the determining factor for the single runway operation. The selected runway with the most direct headwind was Runway 31, and all takeoffs and landings were being conducted on this one runway, causing longer wait times for departures and arrivals.

I approached the airport from the west, passing the Meadowlands sports complex (without time to watch the game). While crossing the Hudson River, I contacted LaGuardia tower and expressed my landing intention, and permission to enter the airspace, in order to obtain a clearance for sequencing. Shortly after, with the strong tail wind I was approaching Central Park and would have soon been inside the airspace of the tower controller's jurisdiction. I received a reply in time, and he instructed me to continue. By the time I passed the East River he asked me which runway I would like. I read his mind. He wanted me to use runway 4. He used this tactic to get me to choose runway 4, and not interrupt traffic flow on runway 31. Practically, it would not have been prudent for him to simply clear me to land on runway 4, when protocol called for all traffic to use runway 31, because of the high crosswind on runway 4. It had to be a pilot's request, or suggestion, and final decision. His tactfulness was necessary. I was happy to oblige, and it was also good to help out when possible. It was an unwritten language between controller and pilot that when one offers a good suggestion the other receives a benefit. Had I demanded runway 31, the controller could have had me fly ten miles out of my way for sequencing. Even though the wind was in excess of 25 knots directly across runway 4, I told the controller I would be fine with that runway. He needed to be sure, and he cleared me for landing immediately, on runway 4, while reminding me about the wind speed and direction. Interestingly, because of this clearance, I held the bragging rights that I flew directly to LaGuardia Airport and received a clearance to land immediately. That's what pilots could call, a "blessing."

Around the same time that he cleared me for landing, an airliner called in as "number one" for takeoff on Runway 31. He acknowledged the airliner with a "standby." My clearance was to land Runway 4 and hold short of the intersection of Runway 31. This intersection was about five thousand feet from the threshold of my runway – enough to land a jet. But, my airplane was high and hot, and that was what got the controller's attention. Perhaps he thought I would not be able to stop before the intersection, and that would have caused a conflict if he had let the jet go. I wanted to help out by expediting my landing so as to cause the least interruption. I knew he was holding the airliner at Runway 31 and he wanted to wait to a safe point before letting the jet go. I came in hot on purpose so as to take the least time to the runway, but my altitude was also quite high, since my initial approach was for runway 31, which was further away from the threshold of runway 4. I could be sure that the controller got his binoculars to watch my airplane land with this strong direct crosswind. It would be like showtime for him, as he was not accustomed to viewing airplanes doing the maneuver I was about to execute in order to deal with the stiff crosswind. Airliners do not perform this maneuver because of the length of their wingspan.

In the airplane with me was my student, who was also a friend and the co-owner of the airplane. He was excited to land at a big airport. I instructed him to reduce power to idle, roll the airplane to the left sharply, and apply full right rudder. I then lowered the flaps fully, and verified the correct airspeed for flaps. This maneuver is called a slip, and produces a more than normal rapid decent by exposing more of the aircraft's surface area to drag. Airliners use spoilers. These are rectangular hinged parts on the top of the wing visible to passengers sitting near the wing. When the spoilers go up they destroy lift and increase the descent rate, without affecting the airspeed of the airplane. It is not recommended to simply lower the nose to increase the descent rate, as the airspeed would also increase, leaving a net zero result. In our situation we did not have spoilers.

In the slip configuration the airplane came down like a rock, while tracking straight towards the runway. It was fun for me. Occasionally, we could feel the air trying to keep it up, but gravity had the upper hand. We also heard the sheet metal skin of the airplane vibrating from the oscillation between increasing and decreasing pressure on its surface. It was all no problem; airplanes were built to handle this. We aimed the airplane to the right side of the runway and held the slip all the way down. The objective was to touch down on the right side of the runway with left wheel first and steer the plane towards the left side of the 150-foot wide runway in order to minimize the effects of the left crosswind. We leveled the airplane over the runway to bleed off the airspeed, landed without incident, and were off the runway in a few hundred feet. As soon as our wheels touched the ground the controller cleared the jet for takeoff on runway

31, and thanked us for the help with the expedited approach and landing.

His decision to hold the jet was a subject for analysis, meaning psychoanalysis. He could not be sure that I would not land long and pass through the intersection, thereby causing a major conflict. I totally understood that he had to make all his decisions to ensure safety. Even though I acknowledged the clearance to land and hold short of the intersection, he could not trust that I would do that, especially that he must have watched my airplane approaching high and hot. He could not be sure that I would not roll beyond the intersection, or execute a go-around, both of which would have caused a conflict if he had cleared the jet for takeoff. I wish I could have told him to let the jet go, but that would not have been appropriate. It had to be his call; he was the controller. Somehow, I felt disappointed in his lack of confidence in me, while at the same time I enjoyed showing him that he could have trusted me. But, if I were he, I would have done the same. His responsibility for safety was the reason to trust no one but himself. I did get a kick out of the whole thing. I do not envy Air Traffic Controllers, as I almost became one. In my flying career I knew what they were dealing with, and I respected their area of responsibility, as I accepted my responsibility as the pilot. I always wanted to help the process and often made suggestions and recommendations, which were appreciated.

Most of the times when teaching I only get the opportunity to demonstrate the maneuvers, then the student practiced under my supervision. I was a very free and relaxed instructor who allowed students to do most of the manipulation of the controls. It was their lesson and I believed that they should get the most out of it. It was also best for them to be able to complete tasks and maneuvers, as it offered them a sense of accomplishment. Some maneuvers, such as crosswind landings were practiced under low wind conditions. This landing at LaGuardia had to be done by me, since the student was not expected to be able to accomplish it in such high winds. I coached him all the way down while holding the controls on my side to make the final corrections. We both understood that it would be that way. I did appreciate the opportunity to manipulate the controls, and feel the excitement and rush of adrenaline. Such opportunity came to me only when I was demonstrating, or when in precarious flying conditions, beyond the skill of the students. Today was one of those days. I was lucky because the winds were too high for the student to execute the landing and I got the chance to fly, even if for a little while.

I wondered about the people on the ground who may have been looking up, and what they were thinking when they saw the one wing low configuration of our airplane. Or, maybe no one was looking. In New York everyone minded his or her own business. Interestingly, while flying over New York the noise of the airplane drowned out the noise of the city. People and buildings seemed irrelevant during approach and landing, as pilots concentrated on the runway in front. New York just seemed to slide under the airplane as one big blur.

After we landed, I asked the controller about the location of the airliner on which my friend was arriving and he was happy to oblige, especially to show his gratitude for the expedited approach and landing, not to mention the free air show by a pilot who dreamed of flying a fighter jet. I found out the airliner had just landed. Perfect, the wait would not be long.

My friend showed up as excited as a young lad with a new bicycle. He would take the controls of his airplane and fly out of LaGuardia to the home base. His other friend would drive him home after a nice day in the air. They were both nice fellows, deserving of such privilege. I was happy for them, and to be a part of it.

HELICOPTER

On windy days, especially after passage of a cold front, the sun would be shining brightly, but the wind would be blustery. A wind speed of twenty knots would ground most weekend pilots. That would leave the entire sky for me. The wind would usually start to increase after sunrise, and have maximum speed in the early afternoon. Starting early in the morning offered me the opportunity to gauge the wind speed as the day progressed. It was not uncommon that the wind would produce uncomfortable turbulence, especially at low altitudes. At higher altitudes the wind speed would be normally much higher, but sometimes with little or no turbulence. The only way to know about the turbulence would be to fly in the windy conditions. The hangar pilots, who grounded themselves, did not know that, so they chatted and drank coffee all day, and called me, "crazy." Only I knew the secret of the sky above two thousand feet; that it was as smooth as a baby's bottom. Those days I would do air work with the student, and skip landing training. The students I was training would most likely not be operating in such windy conditions anyway, after they received their pilot certification, so it would not have been very useful to do landing practice.

Maneuvers were done into the wind so as to prevent the airplane from drifting far away from the home base. It would not be fair to the student to spend half the lesson time just flying back to base if the airplane drifted with the wind. One particular maneuver I enjoyed when the wind was strong was called, "slow-flight," where the airplane would be configured to travel at the slowest possible airspeed. In this configuration, the airplane would be a bit unstable, but controllable with effective use of the rudder. With full flaps it was possible to slow a training airplane to just over forty miles per hour. This meant that with a headwind speed of thirty-five miles per hour, the forward speed of the airplane would have been a mere five to ten miles per hour over the ground. It would be like a helicopter. I would tell the student to look at the ground, as the airplane was barely moving over it. It was strange, as we looked at traffic on the roadways moving much faster than us. It was more bizarre to be flying in an airplane and going so slow over the ground. It brought the sensation that something was wrong.

During this type of training I would also address the subject of wind speed and its effect on trip time. I explained the concept that once an airplane was airborne it traveled with the air, which was moving over the ground. If the direction of flight were in the same direction as the wind flow, it would be called a tail wind, which would reduce trip time. Tail winds offered free extra groundspeed. Naturally headwinds reduced groundspeed. I explained the reason a flight to Europe took less time going there than coming back to North America was that the prevailing winds moved eastward, both north and south of the equator, except for within tropical latitudes. In tropical latitudes, the vacuum left from rising hot air, as a result of direct sunlight, forms the Northeast Trade Winds. This same vacuum also pulls hurricanes westward, from Africa. In addition, as a bonus, I would explain that most of the atmosphere was in the troposphere where all these wind patterns exist. In the stratosphere it was different, as the winds there were not as strong, and one particular airplane was not subjected to the strong head winds. This airplane took about the same time going and coming between Europe and North America. It was the Concord. It flew at an altitude of 60,000 feet and above. It was a beautiful bird called, "Speed bird."

BIG APPLE TALK

The airspace around New York City has the highest traffic density in the world. There are three major airports close to each other. When I would fly out of the New York area under an Instrument flight plan I would be given vectors from the radar controller once airborne. These vectors were assignments of altitude and direction of travel required for traffic separation. I would be directed to fly in a direction sometimes opposite my destination, until the controller was able to offer a path towards my course. Eventually, I would get a clearance every airline, corporate, or private pilot yearns for: "Cleared as filed." From that point I would follow the course and altitude according to the flight plan I filed prior to takeoff.

The New York controllers have quite a heavy workload, except during periods much later in the night. Late night communications on the radio could become personal and friendly, sometimes to the point of discussing restaurants at some destinations. This type of personal communication was not encouraged on the radio, but in the middle of the night it was welcomed from a not very busy controller who wanted to feel some camaraderie.

During the day, communications consisted primarily of vectors from the controller to several aircraft with one key of the microphone. The word, "break" would be used to separate instructions from one aircraft to another. There could be three vectors issued one after the other. Airliners occupied most of the radio spectrum and usually simply "followed orders" from the controller. They had the benefit of being sequenced in a most efficient way. A small aircraft did not get such a privilege and was considered more of a nuisance, like a fly in the ointment. I would sometimes have to break-in between the transmissions trying to get a better course. The performance limitation of small aircraft was the reason the controller would have to issue course excursions, until it was safe enough for an en-route clearance. My calm response, with a mild complaint regarding consumption of fuel onboard, along with some suggestions regarding how to get me on course, often worked for a better route. The old saying, "The squeaky wheel gets the grease," worked for me.

LANGUAGE BARRIERS

ATC is conducted in the English language worldwide, and thus it is quite common for pilots on the radio to have accents when English is not their mother tongue. I had many students of foreign nationality. In addition to the given anxiety of using the microphone, they also exhibited some difficulty because of the language. Their first condition would be timidity of using the "mike" in the first place. Secondly, they were not comfortable with the phraseology and their accent. I would start them with simple replies such as, "roger." Eventually, when their confidence grew, a higher comfort level would emerge. It was their human mind I was dealing with, and patience was the key. Occasionally, some controllers would not recognize the student's communications. They would simply reply, "unreadable." There were some cases where I would agree that the language barrier caused a problem, but there were clearly some cases where the controller did not apply patience. In these cases I would take the microphone, request the clearance myself, and ask for the controller's patience with the student during the flight. There would always be a prompt response, and detectable attitude change from the controller.

When I thought about the behavior of these humans and how discouraging it could be for a foreigner, it made me think about this whole big country with all of its variations of culture, politics and religion. Somehow all of it seemed to affect individual behavior, in the air, and on the ground.

It is understandable that Air Traffic Control should be concerned with foreign pilots communicating in US airspace, as I witnessed for myself on a flight to JFK on a foreign airline decades ago. I sat in the jump seat on the flight deck of this jumbo jet, as I knew the crew in a professional way. The copilots in most airliners normally handle the communications. On this flight, the radar controller had some difficulty understanding the copilot who had a heavy accent, and the copilot also had some difficulty understanding the clearances. The controller had to repeat his messages, while expecting an accurate read back from the copilot. Accuracy was paramount, as the tolerances were not wide in the New York airspace. I was familiar with the area, and I helped with the communications by repeating what the controller was saying so that the copilot could issue the correct read back. Eventually, the rule was passed that all pilots holding licenses issued by non-English speaking countries must be certified in English prior to entering US airspace.

It is not unusual to hear many pilots speaking English in an accent on an air traffic control frequency near international airports. It is also not unusual to hear accents from American controllers, especially in the South, and in Texas. It is all about human communications.

THE RUSSIAN CONNECTION

Many years ago, I flew as a passenger on a Russian airliner on flight from the South American country of my birth to JFK airport in New York. The government of that country arranged for the flag airline to operate with a Russian fleet of airplanes and Russian pilots. The airplane was a Tupelov - 154. The government was not exactly popular with many residents as it played games with the two superpowers at the time- Russia and the USA. The use of Russian airplanes was an act of defiance against the USA. People in the Caribbean culture that prevailed in my place of origin often made fun of everything, including the Russian aircraft. As such, the Tupelov aircraft was often referred to as Topple-over aircraft.

During the flight, the door to the flight deck was wide open as it was prior to the laws requiring it to be closed during flight. There were the usual captain and first officer in the flight deck along with a flight engineer and about two other crewmembers who all seemed to be contributing to the flight. There was smoke emanating from the flight deck from cigarettes being smoked by almost all of the crewmembers. It seemed hilarious to me as I sat and watched what appeared to be a comedy about flying an airplane – loud talking and confusion. The humor intensified because they seemed to be questioning each other about procedures to be followed while speaking in Russian. I thought to myself that a prayer might be appropriate. I dared not to approach them to offer assistance in navigation or communication, as I had done previously on other airlines while occupying a seat in the flight deck. I could be sure the response would have been, "No English." However, I was comforted that this same airplane and this same crew flew the route I was traveling several times before.

The aircraft landed safely at JFK airport but was not allowed to park at a gate. Instead, it stayed on the tarmac while passengers exited via steps to a bus waiting to take them to the terminal. The US government did not have faith that this Russian aircraft would not be a threat to US security so it had to be parked far from the terminal. I could not blame the US government people as my faith during the whole flight was also diminished by what I experienced. Somehow though, I attributed my successful arrival to risk-taking and luck, and I was happy it was over

FLY OVER ONE AND TWO

One lovely summer evening, after dinner in Southern New Jersey I had to fly my friends back to Long Island, New York. In order to stay out of New York's Terminal control airspace I would have to fly north up the Hudson River then turn eastward after passing New York City. That would have been a long way, and out of my way. The short cut would be to fly directly over JFK airport. After nine in the night most of the foreign carriers would have already departed, and the traffic would not be too heavy. I contacted the radar controller and made a request for the fly over. There was a slight hesitation at first, but I was sure that he understood my situation, and the long out-of-the way alternative. He was willing to help, but his requirement was that I climbed up high. I asked "how high," as I advanced the throttle to start the climb. His request was surprising, but I accepted his 9500-foot requirement.

We both knew that above ten thousand feet I would have been responsible for a supplemental oxygen requirement, and the only oxygen in the airplane was coming in from the air outside, through the vents. The controller was a nice and considerate guy, and he knew his stuff. The camaraderie from controllers was so sweet, especially when they knew that pilot and controller would have a friendly dialog. I must have mentioned something funny to him after he issued the clearance, like; "thanks for not letting me pass out during the flight." In order to grant my request he had to use some ingenuity, as my flight was not sequenced like the airliners. I was sure he enjoyed being helpful, as it gave him a challenge to clear a path for me.

I told the three passengers to expect a recognizable temperature drop to approximately half of what was on the surface. I also explained our route, but the whole thing was a blur to them, as they looked at a sea of lights, without any situational awareness. We flew directly over JFK, and I pointed out the rows of lights under the airplane, being the runways. It did not peek any great interest, as they most likely could not identify the airport by looking at lights, and considered the flight simply routine. We descended for a landing at the airport where my friends lived, after thanking the controller for the shortcut. After I dropped them off I, took-off to return to New Jersey over Long Island Sound and the George Washington Bridge, with the New York skyline to my left the entire flight.

A few weeks later I was in a similar situation. After dinner in Southern Connecticut, the return flight would have taken me directly over Newark Airport. Again, the foreign carriers were mostly gone. The controller was more than happy to oblige, and offered me a lovely low altitude of 2,000 feet directly overhead. I would call that a sweet deal of a clearance. He mentioned that there was no air traffic, and only one cargo plane on taxi for the runway. It must have been later than nine in the night, probably closer to eleven, or even midnight. It did not matter; time was irrelevant; I was having fun. I had just enjoyed a lovely dinner and was just going to land the airplane, park it, and head to bed.

By the time the engines of the cargo jet could be spooled up for takeoff, I was overhead. I watched it roll for takeoff as it slipped beneath me in the opposite direction and went out of my field of view. Shortly after that, I descended for landing, and thanked the controller after most likely telling him where I went for dinner, and wishing him a good night. A lovely evening indeed, wouldn't you say?

BAHAMA MAMA

My good friend, who owned an airplane, and was being trained by me for his instrument license, was always trying to find ways to get training while making a trip somewhere. He masterminded a flight to the Bahamas from his New Jersey base airport during one summer, and I agreed. We took-off into clouds and went through the usual course deviation issued by the radar controllers until we heard: "Cleared as filed." That was the time to relax and not have to pay such close attention to the radio since we were done following vectors. The most likely transmission from the controller would be a final instruction to change frequency and contact the next controller in our path.

As we traveled through Southern New Jersey we encountered rain, which increased in intensity. In addition, there was turbulence, which also increased in intensity. Most small aircraft were not equipped with onboard weather radar. We had to use other sources to determine if there were thunderstorms in the area, as we would not be able to hear thunder while inside the airplane. Aviation's worst single weather hazard had to be avoided. We turned up the volume on a navigation device called an Automatic Direction Finder, (ADF). This device was the original navigation tool used for decades, since the dawn of Aviation navigation. It used a low frequency radio wave, and consisted simply of a glass-covered instrument with one needle, which pointed to a ground station. If it were tuned to an ordinary radio station the needle would point there too, and with the volume control turned up we would hear the music. Quite often that was our in-flight entertainment. During lightning strikes the needle would point to the source of the lightning. The ADF became our lightning detector. The noise on the speaker would also become scratchy when lightning struck, and that confirmed the presence of lightning.

On our flight towards the south there was no lightning. But, the turbulence was excessive, and the airplane rose and fell through quite a bit of altitude occasionally. We mentioned to the controller about our altitude excursions, considering that we did not have an altitude encoding transponder, wherein our altitude would have been displayed on his radarscope. It was not mandatory at the time. He was understanding, and reassured us that there was no conflicting traffic. The rain became so heavy that we could not hear normal conversation. My concern at that moment was for the engine to continue operating, considering the amount of water that had to pass through the air filter. I was concerned, even though the designers must have already thought of that situation. The air intake allowed for a large quantity of water to be efficiently diverted away, and not enter the engine. My mind was doing calculations as to volume of water to be diverted, and whether the design was for less than we were flying through.

We heard the controller talk to a military aircraft that had requested a deviation away from the poor weather. The controller assured the pilot of that aircraft that he had the best route through the precipitation. We could not hear the pilot of the military aircraft since the military radios used Ultra High Frequency (UHF) while civilian aircraft communicated on Very High Frequency (VHF). The radio system used by Air Traffic Control transmitted on both UHF and VHF frequencies, since both types of aircraft used the service. As such, we could hear the controller, but not the military pilot. We also requested the best route through the precipitation, and the controller replied that we had the best route. He could see precipitation on his radarscope, while we had to rely on visual cues and the one instrument, (ADF), which was not designed for weather detection.

The rain pounded the airplane as we flew through torrents. It felt like we were in a submarine. The wind tossed us around for another thirty minutes, which seemed like an eternity. We rode the weather out, and finally broke out from rain to just clouds. The ground was also visible. Pilots who are licensed to fly in inclement weather do not necessarily enjoy a wrestling match with an airplane, which is what we had to do, especially without an autopilot. Inclement weather could be also especially discomforting to passengers.

During this encounter I wondered about myself and asked the question; "What am I doing here?" I felt responsible for the comfort of my friend and his passengers. I accepted the responsibility with the expectation of having a break from work and enjoying some sun and fun. I thought it was a good idea. But, a good idea would have been if I did not have anyone else to be responsible for. Somehow, it seemed that more guilt was induced when I became responsible for others, who were also known to me, especially that I was the only one certified to fly in clouds and precipitation under Instrument Flight Rules (IFR). Eventually, the thought changed, and we pressed on with the fun portion of the trip. It was always a relief, accompanied by a sense of achievement, to fly out of inclement weather. The mood changed quickly and the bad weather became just a memory.

I was a flight instructor. It was what I enjoyed doing, and it seemed like I was doing exactly that during this flight. My friend was learning all the while, as a pilot in training. I knew that he and his passengers felt comforted that I was present. They were depending on me, and trusted me. The events that led me to this point had already occurred. I was now in my circumstance. It was my situation. I could not simply eject or escape. I was in my human condition. I simply had to press on, and so I did.

We landed to refuel in North Carolina after leaving all the inclement weather behind. We felt a big difference, the first being the friendliness of the controllers. We were used to belching orders from controllers in the New York airspace. In the Carolinas the first radio contact from them was, "Good evening" or, "Good morning." Wow! That was such a pleasure. The Southern genteel was so very sweet, as though those boys were singing the clearances to us. The greatest pleasure was upon takeoff when we contacted the radar controller and he immediately used the phrase pilots love to hear: "Cleared as filed." No belching orders, no flying in the wrong direction, just simply fly as was planned. That was nice, real nice.

We did fly our course with little communication with controllers, as traffic density was low in that area, similar to population densities. We reached Jacksonville and proceeded along the Florida coastline. Upon reaching Cape Canaveral we flew directly over the Space Shuttle landing facility. It was one of the longest runways in the world - a solid three miles long and comforting to look at. We could not land on it except for an emergency, but we could fly over it. The airspace over the United States of America belongs to the people of the United States of America. The government could not restrict or prohibit access to any of the airspace except for certain portions for security reasons. As an example, the airspace over the White House and the Pentagon are prohibited areas. Certain other areas are restricted during certain times and at certain altitudes. The area over the Shuttle landing facility was only restricted when a Space Shuttle was scheduled to land, or if some activity was being conducted. We were cleared to fly right over it, as the airspace was clear and free.

I thought to myself as we passed over miles of American ingenuity; "what a great country to live in." I was exalted, I was touched, and I was in awe, as I imagined I was flying like a Space Shuttle astronaut. I had drifted into a daydreaming state. I had become the astronaut of my childhood dreams, and the daydreaming at that moment was blissful. No one in the airplane knew my thoughts and feelings, and that I had regressed to my childhood state for that moment. After I came back to reality I thought further that I was living in the greatest country in the history of this earth. I was an immigrant, like the ancestors of all those living in it, except the Native Americans and those who came as slaves. I appreciated living in a country with true democratic values carved into its Constitution.

We landed at West Palm Beach International airport to rent flotation gear that was required for the over water flight. It was an added safety feature, which we seriously considered, regardless of the regulatory requirement. Within a short time, we were on the way for the forty-five minute flight to the island. The accent of the Bahamian controller was an immediate welcome to leisure. We set our clocks to island time - sloooow. Do I need to tell the rest of the story about the Bahamas? I didn't think so.

The return flight was naturally boring. One highlight for me was the Grand Banks of the Bahamas. Flying over the shallow ocean I saw hills and valleys under the veil of turquoise water. It seemed like a painting. I thought to myself, could it be God who painted it for me to see, or was it simply a natural formation of the earth? I had to accept the latter, as I reminded myself about the journey of knowledge that I started decades prior. I stayed on my quest.

PARENTAL PERSUASION

The father of a young man, who was referred to me by a mutual friend, called me to arrange a flight lesson for his son. The father wanted his son to become certified, and eventually advance to becoming an airline pilot. I accepted the opportunity. The young man had recently graduated from a high school that specialized in Aviation. He had already received his Aviation Mechanic certificate.

I flew with this young man, and he progressed through solo flight, and was preparing for long distance (cross-country) flights. These flights tested the pilot's knowledge in planning, navigation, communications and other aspects, in order to fly from the base airport to another airport that was over fifty miles away. After one such flight with this fellow I noticed a lack of interest in his flight preparation. His father was paying, and perhaps he did not care. Or, perhaps it was something else. I asked him point blank, but gently, if he really wanted to be a pilot, and his reply was in the negative; he was simply satisfying his father's wishes. He really and desperately wanted to be an airplane mechanic, for which he was already certified.

It was important that I maintained dialog with students, for their benefit in training, and for mine too. I was interested in understanding them, and finding ways into their heads, as I investigated how their minds worked. This young man was afraid to tell his father that he was not interested in becoming an airline pilot. That could be considered very unusual for a young man who had the ticket for a free ride straight into the flight deck of an airliner. At least it was what I thought, as I knew many who would have jumped at such an opportunity. However, it was his feeling, and I tried to guide him as appropriate. I came up with an idea that would help him to focus on his career decision. I asked the owner of the local Aviation maintenance facility if he could use a young certified mechanic in an apprentice position at a minimum wage level. The owner agreed, and off the young man went to part time work. He did all what he knew, and all that they asked. He even swept the floor at the end of the day. Hey, somebody had to do it.

I have heard from students who told me that they loved flying more than anything else in the world, sometimes more than their significant others. I always encouraged them to love what they loved, and love what made them happy. I was afraid to tell them that I did not love to fly, but I loved to teach. This young man loved to work on airplanes more than anything else, and when the opportunity came, he took it. The trick I told him was to tell his father that he had found a part time job while still taking flying lessons. His father did not have to know what he really felt; it would be our secret. Game on!

Within one year the young man was the manager of the Aviation shop where he started as an apprentice. A few years later he had his own hangar, clients and employees in his own Aviation maintenance business. He had found exactly what he wanted to do. He was no different than me. He did obtain his private pilot's license, but more importantly his father was convinced that his son had found the place where he belonged. The father had to cancel the airline career expectation for his son. The young man was happy, the father was happy, and I was a happy man as, "all's well that ends well."

SOUP KITCHEN

It was common to take advantage of poor weather to do instrument training, instead of loading up on caffeine, while waiting for clouds to lift. A student who was eager to take advantage of the overcast weather asked me to instruct him on an instrument flight. He made a flight plan to a destination about fifty miles away. We took-off and entered the soup of clouds soon after. This would be real instrument condition, in clouds all the way. The cloud layer was four thousand feet thick according to the forecast. We brought our sunglasses so as not to be blinded by the light of the sun above the white winter wonderland below. Reflection of sunlight from a deck of clouds below could make any pilot want to go back into the clouds. It takes only one time for a pilot who punches a hole through the clouds in order to get above the deck to ensure that sunglasses would not be forgotten the next time.

The surface temperature was above freezing, but at three thousand feet it was below freezing, and the wet clouds were loaded with ice. Within a short time we began to see ice accumulating on the windshield and the thermometer probe. We could not be sure that after reaching sunshine above, and vaporizing the ice, that it would not accumulate faster on the descent at the destination. We decided to return to base. Upon landing and parking the airplane, we observed one-quarter inch of clear ice on the wings. We had made a good decision. The clouds never lifted and so we went back to drinking. Coffee it was, of course. What did you think?

THE CONSTELLATION

I used a small airport in Northern New Jersey to practice landings, as there was hardly any air traffic in that area. It was located near quarries, which looked like small canyons from the air. The airport had one distinguishing feature, which was one very large airplane parked permanently near the parking lot. The airplane was flown-in several years prior, with the owners knowing fully well that the runway was too short for the same airplane to take-off. When airplanes land they could stop quickly using braking devices such as reverse thrust and brakes, but taking off required a much greater distance. The owners knew the airplane would never leave, and that was their intent. The airplane was fairly large for its time, and it was called a Constellation, or "Connie." This model was one of the first pressurized airliners, which saw widespread use at the dawn of the Commercial Aviation Age. This particular airplane was retired from the airlines and was placed at this airport for the conversion into a restaurant. It did become a restaurant, which finally served its last hamburger a few years after opening. The restaurant closed, but the airplane remained; still parked of course.

There was one runway where a quarry was dug out quite close to the threshold. On short final approach it felt eerie as we approached for landing, as though the airplane was dropping into this big canyon. To compensate, student pilots would automatically fly higher than normal, which was contrary to proper landing technique, since it was a visual aberration, not an actual hazard. The best advice I offered my students who felt some uneasiness was to ignore the canyon. I further explained that the canyon was not their business in the first place, as they were not miners; their business was the runway. Sometimes straightforwardness worked, and I really enjoyed trying every way to reach the mind of the student.

I must admit that I did get a strange and eerie feeling in my seat as well when I was over the canyon. Human tendency is to feel instinctively. Interpretation of instinct allowed for logical methodology to overcome unnecessary and non-contributory feelings and fears during the learning process. I felt what the students felt. I am human also. I had to find a way to detect the anomaly and help to teach how to compensate for it.

BUMPS IN THE NIGHT

My friend who was trained by me, loved whenever I was free, day or night, to continue his advanced training. But, sometimes his version of training was a simple joy ride in his airplane. It was all in the experience-building repertoire, and I went along for the rides. One evening while flying towards the Hudson River to view a beautifully lit up New York City skyline we encountered brief, but tremendous turbulence, which felt like we were going through pot holes with an automobile. On the ground, in New York, that was not uncommon, and almost guaranteed. Immediately after the turbulence faded, my friend turned to me with a look that carried the statement; "What the heck was that?" It was a bit unnerving. We tightened our seat belts and I calmed him down while explaining that the turbulence was caused by the rapid cooling of the earth's surface. Another, "What the heck is that?" ensued. I explained that we were flying through a low level inversion, which usually occurred soon after sunset in a stable atmosphere, after the daytime heating of the ground. The formation of a radiation inversion would start on a calm day, meaning almost no wind, as the warm air on the surface would rise quickly, after the sun had set. The air would stop at the height where it could go no further, as determined by adiabatic conditions. In this situation, the air above would be warmer than the air below, and that became the inversion, as air aloft would normally be cooler. When air of different temperatures or pressures meet, turbulence could be generated and should be expected.

We flew over the Hudson River where there was no turbulence, as low-level inversions normally form over land. We enjoyed an evening of smooth flight after the bumps. As nature would offer it, every flight brought a different experience, and every pilot in each situation learned something new. That was why I always offered a short speech, after congratulating every one of my newly minted pilots. The speech included a reminder that the pilot's license was a license to learn. Whatever my friend learned that night could help him alleviate fear and anxiety the next time he flew in those conditions.

AUTO LAND

The need to get passengers to their destinations on a daily schedule was primarily dependent on weather conditions. While airplanes could fly in almost any weather, including ice, as they are so designed, the pilot's ability to see out of the window became the significant limiting problem. Many flights were rerouted to alternate destinations, creating havoc for passengers and airlines, simply because pilots could not see the runway, or identify the airport environment. This inconvenience was alleviated by the implementation of the auto-land feature to the automation equipment (autopilot) in the airplane. This system allows the airplane to land itself as the pilots supervise. It requires the synchronization of two autopilots to execute the approach and landing to the "shrouded in clouds" airport. The pilots would supervise the decent and confirm that the airplane was on track. Once over the runway, the autopilots would reduce power, land the airplane, (better than any pilot), and slow it down to a stop on the runway.

Airports at low altitudes or near bodies of water tend to have clouds on the surface, which would be visible moisture; called fog. Fog is quite often a factor in determining the approaches in use at airports, as it affects visibility. San Francisco in the USA and Amsterdam in Holland have notorious visibility issues. One pilot friend of mine who was a captain of a foreign carrier on a very new wide-body jet told me of his repetitive experience in Amsterdam. It was the operations base for his airline. He explained that on numerous occasions he was required to implement the auto-land feature because of fog. He further said that the auto-land feature was an embarrassment to pilots, as the airplane would make a much better landing by itself, than any pilot could. It would even adjust for the wind by "crabbing," which meant pointing the nose slightly into the wind on approach, then straightening out before touchdown. It would make the softest landing that would be worthy of applause from passengers who had no idea what was happening on the flight deck. Finally, after stopping on the runway, he was not able to see the exit from the runway. He simply had to sit and wait for an airport escort vehicle. The vehicle would approach the airplane from the front, then turn around and slowly travel in the direction towards the taxiway. A large sign behind the vehicle said; "FOLLOW ME." That was how he made it to the terminal.

Amateur videos of landing airplanes, which circulated on electronic media, with some remarkable commentary about pilots' skills, must be fact checked. We must always remember that if pilots cannot see a runway or the airport environment, they are not authorized to land. But, auto-land could be engaged without regard to the pilots' ability to see outside. It would be the autopilots landing the airplane. Autopilots do not have eyes and do not need to see. It is the real "flying blind" condition, as they need only the electronic signal from the runway area. One video in particular showed a wide body airliner on a perfect track to a runway while disappearing and reappearing in the thick fog as it approached the runway. The airplane made a perfect landing in the dense fog, and the commentary on the video was about the great skill of the pilot on the landing. The airliner's autopilots were engaged for auto-land. The amateur video photographer did not know the facts, and that the auto-land feature was engaged. But, shall we leave him with his blissful thinking about the great skill of pilots? Why not?

POINTS TO PONDER

(1)   The primary reason that children under the age of two could fly for free is because FAA regulations do not require a seat belt for anyone under that age. Please do not put the child inside the seat belt with you; in the event of a rapid

143

deceleration your body would squeeze the child. Thank you very much.

(2)   Large numbers in squares at the side of runways indicate thousands of feet remaining on the runway.

(3)   Any length of runway behind the airplane is useless for takeoff, and landing too. Think about it. Pilots should consider using the full length for takeoff.

(4)   Runway numbers are based on magnetic direction and are rounded to the nearest two-digit whole number. Runway 21 would be a magnetic direction between 205 and 214 degrees.

(5)   A "set compass" sign near the runway is the magnetic direction of the runway, which would be a three-digit number between 001 and 360 degrees. Pilots should set their gyroscopic compass to that number after lining up with the runway.

(6)   "Air Force One" is the call sign for the Air Force aircraft when the President is on board. Other branches of military use their own call sign, such as "Marine One," for the helicopter.

(7)   The military is responsible for protecting the airspace within a 30-mile radius of the president's location. There, some F-16 and other fighter jet loudness could be heard occasionally, especially when pursuing intruders.

(8)   The Pope's airplane's call sign is "Shepherd One," and "Hound Dog One" was reserved for Elvis's airplane.

(9)   All US registered aircraft are assigned a number from the FAA starting with the letter "N". This is also the call sign for contact with ATC, with the exception of airlines, (which use flight numbers), and special flights such as Air Force One.

(10)   Aircraft in Italy have an "I" as the prefix while England has "G" and France has "F". "D" is

for Germany and all other countries have prefixes that do not necessarily match the name of the country, like LN for Norway. Go figure!

(11)   International airports are not necessarily large. Saba, in the Caribbean has one of the smallest. I went to Saba for scuba diving. But, I went by boat.

(12)   "Knots" mean nautical miles per hour, originally a marine measurement, now widely used in air and sea navigation. Knots are equal to 1.15 statute miles per hour.

(13)   One degree of latitude is 60 nautical miles. This was established long before GPS.

(14)   Lines of latitude are equidistant from each other, while lines of longitude converge and meet at the poles.

(15)   GPS means Global Positioning System.

(16)   GPS was deployed by the US Department of Defense for military purposes. It became fully operational in 1995 and was offered for civilian use, primarily for aviation navigation, but without the same military precision. Dropping bombs needed accurate location positioning while Aviation navigation does not have to be as accurate. Planes do not run off airways; they are 8 nautical miles wide.

(17)   SOS does not mean "Save Our Souls." It originated from Morse code as the three letters that were easily recognizable by anyone who knew Morse code, especially when repeated continuously. It consists of three dots, three dashes then three dots again (***---***). Dots are quick beeps and dashes are long beeps. It also has the advantage of being readable in both directions. Just like the letters.

(18)   Position lights on airplane wings, and on boats are red on the right with green on the left when approaching the observer. If you see that, make a turn, and quickly.

(19)   "Prohibited" airspace is simply that. For example, over the White House and the Pentagon. They are clearly marked on charts.

(20)   "Restricted" airspace has time periods and altitudes where aircraft are not allowed. Some are temporary, like rocket launches, and are not on the charts.

(21)   Most US States offer their own free aeronautical chart to the public, which should not be used for navigation. Just put it on the wall.

(22)   Sir Frank Whittle should be thanked for inventing the jet engine, which simply ignites compressed air and fuel causing extreme expansion called thrust. It is simple, reliable and full of trust, as well as thrust.

(23)   The temperature of the nose cone of the Concord in flight became hot because of friction with the air, and was hot enough to boil water. The metal of the plane also expanded from the heat during flight.

(24)   Aircraft speed limitation under ten thousand feet in controlled airspace is 250 knots, and pilots are supposed to know that.

(25)   The Cockpit Voice Recorder (CVR) is used for accident investigation and can be erased after each flight is completed, when there is no accident, of course.

(26)   The smoke that emanates from a jetliner's tires upon landing is caused from rubber burning as the wheels spin up, within a fraction of a second, from zero to the speed of the plane at touchdown. The wheels do not spin in the air prior to touchdown.

(27)   Constant and regular strobe lights in clouds could induce a hypnotic effect on pilots. The cure is to turn them off when in clouds. Intermittent strobes, which have an irregular pattern, help to alleviate the problem.

(28)   Glory to a pilot is seeing a rainbow on a cloud deck below while flying above. Double glory is seeing two rainbows. I got lucky, at least once.

(29)   The most positive way to identify an airport at night would be the light from the rotating beacon. A civilian airport shows one green light followed by one white light and repeating continuously; green, white, green, white, green white. Ok, let's stop! I'm getting dizzy.

(30)   Some airliners had landed at military airports by mistake, instead of the civilian airport located nearby. The pilots failed to identify the correct destination airport. Adding to the problem was the similar runway alignment for both airports. Seeing the military airport beacon with two quick flashes of white followed by one green, repeating continuously, would have saved the embarrassment of having to say; "Ladies and gentlemen we landed at the wrong airport, and after clearing up a few procedural matters, along with a military escort back to the runway, we will be on our way to the correct destination."

(31)   Blue lights on an airport are taxiway lights, while white lights mark the edges of the runway. The white lights turn red towards the end of the runway.

(32)   The white streaks of smoke that exit a high-flying jet are called contrails, or vapor trails. They form from the condensation of moisture exiting the engines; similarly to the vapor seen when a kettle of water is boiling. Contrails form generally in a stable atmosphere and travel with the prevailing wind movement after the jet is gone. Best viewing would be at dusk when the sun still shines on the airplane high up, as the surface of the spherical Earth becomes dark. Dawn is good too, but I'm not up that early.

(33)   The primary purpose for flight attendants is not for snacks and beverage, but for safety. That boring demonstration before the flight is a necessary requirement for each and every flight. You could at least pretend to listen if you already know the stuff.

(34)   Sometime after landing, flight attendants are notified to disarm slides before the doors are opened, otherwise the slide would deploy at the gate. That would most likely push the gate agents; who are waiting in the jet-way, right back into the terminal, along with all the wheelchairs.

GOOFBALL

A very good friend of mine had a small variety store near the school where I was teaching, and I was fortunate to visit him to burn off an hour before starting classes. I would chat a bit with him, and then venture to the back of the store to play video games - the ones where standing was required. He showed me a few tricks, as he had become a master of the games while practicing during idle time, between customers.

One evening a young lady entered his store to ask for directions. He discovered that she was looking for the school where I was teaching. He summoned me to the front to talk to her. I asked him to wait so I could finish the video game. I hated being interrupted when concentrating on my game. It meant an unacceptable score. Finally, I met the young lady who must have detected my frustration with the video game, as I was talking to it. Soon, I found out from the post card she showed me that she was scheduled to register for a class starting on that day. She had never been to the school before, and I instructed her how to get there. She had walked in the wrong direction from the train station. Before she departed I asked her if she was registering for the Private Pilot ground class, and she answered in the affirmative. I told her that I would be there within the hour to teach the class. She nodded reluctantly, and her face showed extreme doubt in my statement. I could only imagine that she was muttering to herself the disbelief that some foolish video-playing joker was going to teach her class. My friend and I had a good chuckle when she acknowledged my comment with a sarcastic; "Ah ha!" She left with a huff and a puff, after thanking us for the directions. I was only being honest, that was all. But, she did not believe me.

In about a half of an hour later, I walked into the classroom, wrote my name on the board and introduced myself as the teacher. The young lady looked at me with jaws wide open as I reminded her gently that we had met earlier. I casually mentioned to her that she did not believe me, but I was not offended. She made no comment. The other students had no idea what we were discussing as this would be the first time I would meet all of them. In my truthfulness, I realized that I had given this student a false impression of what she expected an instructor to look like. A video playing goofball that was talking to a machine saying, "come on, come on," certainly did not fit the mold for an instructor. I probably would have had the same conclusion if I were in her shoes. A person's perception could certainly influence the opinion of another. "Do not judge a book by its cover" certainly became appropriate. The young lady spent the following six weeks learning what she needed to know to become a pilot, and she also learned to accept her instructor as such. That made me happy.

MARATHON WOMAN

The New York City marathon race starts in Staten Island and ends in Central Park after participants run through all the five boroughs of New York City. In my youth, I ran a mile in six minutes, and I was exhausted. If I were to run 26 miles I would be dead. Now, I only run from trouble.

It was a lovely fall morning and I had completed a couple of flight lessons when the next student arrived. She asked me, after we took-off, if we could fly to watch the start of the marathon at the Verrazano-Narrows Bridge. I agreed, while reminding her that she had already advanced from climbs and turns and was ready for more advanced training. I explained that the start of the race was not always on time and we would simply be circling until it started. Flying in circles was a regression in her training, but she did not care. She brought a sophisticated camera, and perhaps had already decided that her flight lesson would be conducted as a photo opportunity. I really did not like when students did not show progression on every lesson, but in this case I had to oblige. What else could I have done? I was commanded by her insistence to comply with her wishes.

We flew to the western tower of the bridge where there were several helicopters with cameras for the live news broadcasts. They were not talking to Air traffic Control because they were at lower altitude where it was not necessary. I requested a clearance from the radar controller for circles at two thousand feet and I was approved. We probably exchanged a joke about whether he wanted left or right circles. He didn't care; it did not matter.

Below, on the upper deck of the bridge we saw a sea of people gathering for the event. It took a long time to corral everyone in order to start the race, and we just kept circling. I reminded the student that she was not learning anything new, but she did not care; she just wanted to see the start of the race, and that was her mission. I suspected that if I had told her one more time that she was not learning anything new, she would have slapped me. I became submissive to her mission, as she took photo after photo. The race finally started and we saw a wave of people running over the two-mile upper span into Brooklyn. It looked like a huge caterpillar with thousands of legs. They were all gone within fifteen minutes, and I headed back to the airport with one happy student.

I guess I should have considered happiness as an element in the progression of training. Flying offered a good opportunity to view the event, and was a good reason for one young lady to learn to fly. I was also happy to see the start of the New York City marathon from such a vantage point, as such a thought had never entered my mind; I always watched it on television.

GROUND RADAR

One sunny Sunday morning I was merrily driving to the airport for the first flight lesson of the day, which would be with none other than one of New York's finest; a police officer. There were very few cars on the Staten Island Expressway that morning. As I turned a corner I noticed a police car parked on the right shoulder. I immediately slowed down, but it was too late. The police car followed me, with the lights on. Not good. I pulled over to the side of the road. I had my papers ready before the officer came to my car. When he asked me where I was going I told him that I was a flight instructor going to the airport to give a lesson to one of his NYPD colleagues. He told me to wait, and so I did. I saw him return quickly with two yellow pieces of paper blowing in the wind. He handed me two summonses. I was startled. He told me that I had exceeded the speed limit above his ten miles per hour threshold, and I also had some equipment defects in the front of my car; that being two missing lights for a four head light design. He told me that he would not have even looked at my car unless I had exceeded the threshold speed, which he had set on his radar detector. He added that if I did not want to be stopped for speeding he knew exactly how I could do that. My interest perked as I anticipated such important information, especially from an extremely reliable source. When I eagerly asked, he replied: "Don't speed." I could never forget such profound advice.

The good part came when he told me that he did not issue a summons for speeding, but for the two equipment defects, which I should get fixed, and obtain a receipt to prove that the work was done. I was so happy that I did not hear the last part of what he said; that I could just mail in the receipts and the matter would be closed. In any case, I was a happy man and went off for my lesson. I told my New York police student of course, and he explained that his colleague could have really caused me a problem, but the camaraderie saved me. I appreciated that, and was happy to be regarded by one of New York's finest. I flew with many of them. These were men with guns by their sides as they faced adversity on the streets. But, in the airplane, as they flew with me, they faced a different challenge, the one from within. Once airborne they were the same human beings, with all the fears and emotions as any other. I did not judge. Flying an airplane was not about guns, or guts; it was about overcoming fear and anxiety, and whatever else could get in the way. Learning was my objective for them.

A few weeks later, since I did not mail in the receipts, I reported to court on the appointed day as stated on the summonses. I took a seat and waited for my turn. I listened, as the officer accused one motorist after another, in front of the judge, how they violated the speed limit. One after the other they lost their cases. "Guilty!" were the verdicts. After listening for about an hour, the judge decided to take a short break, at which time the officer started to walk out of the courtroom. He glanced my way as he was passing, and he called me out. He had remembered me as though it was yesterday. He asked what I was doing in the courtroom, and that he had instructed me to mail in the receipts. I told him that I didn't hear that instruction when he handed me the summonses.

When the court reconvened he took me up to the front and quietly told the judge the whole story, and that I should have mailed in the receipts. The judge simply dismissed the cases and passed the papers on to the clerk who went on to stamp each of them loud enough for the whole courtroom to hear. Each of the several stamps sounded like an act of relinquishment, an act of approval, and completion for me. But, for the guilty drivers awaiting their fate, each stamp was like a dagger in their hearts, a sort of punishment before the trial. I felt their human emotion. But, I was mostly interested in my own exoneration.

I walked out of the courtroom with my head slightly down, and with a suppressed smile on my face. I also vehemently avoided eye contact with people waiting for trial. I could only imagine what was going through their minds. They were probably saying to themselves; "Who the heck is this guy?" It was Staten Island and that was how they spoke there. As soon as I got into my car I started singing loudly; "O Solo Meo." I must have looked like I was crazy. But, then again, that was normal in New York.

I drove off with joy and happiness. I was touched that the police officer remembered me after so many weeks. He was a keen fellow with good memory, and I liked that.

HERO NEXT TO ME

Men of war have always moved me. I was not one of them, as I had been saved from the draft because it was canceled before I could be called to serve. Had I been called I could have been dead. Vietnam would have most likely been my deployment destination. Some friends I knew who made it out of Vietnam told me about some of the horrible experiences of that war. They came back shook up and messed up. I considered myself fortunate that I was not drafted, and I did not have go to Vietnam. In any case my wishful duty in Vietnam would have been to fly an F4 Phantom fighter plane. My wish vanished when I spoke to an Air Force recruiter who told me that the chances of me having that opportunity would be like a snowball in a furnace. At that moment I was not interested in going to Vietnam, and hoped that my draft number would not be chosen. I was lucky that I was not invited to that war and I did not have to attend. Had I been invited it would have been an offer I could not refuse.

I had the great fortune of teaching an injured Vietnam Veteran who walked with a cane. He took two trains and a taxi to reach the airport, and every Sunday morning he was there at his appointed time, regardless of the outside air temperature. He flew as best as he could with his handicap. I befriended him in order to make him comfortable to progress as best as possible. He did not want to talk about Vietnam, or anything about war, and I respected that. When he came close to solo flight I encouraged him, and explained to him that he should consider it seriously.

The day had come when I told him that it was a perfect day for him to go solo. He agreed. He made a couple of landings with my assistance and then I told him that I would not assist any longer. We agreed that when he had made three landings I would get out, and he could fly by himself.

His first flight was perfect from takeoff to final approach. Everything was simply beautiful as we approached the runway, until the moment he should have lifted the nose to level off and land with the main gears. He froze with incapacitance. I was tempted to pull up for him, but I waited, and waited, until it was too late. He pounded the nose wheel onto the runway. I began to smell something burning immediately; it was not the rubber from the tire, it was the vaporization of dollar bills out of my wallet for possible damage to the nose gear. It was the first time I trusted and allowed a student to go that far on a landing without taking control. I wanted to say something to inquire why he did not bring the nose up, but I held my tongue, as he expressed sorrow for the mistake. It was also my fault for not seeing that coming; I had misjudged him. I did not become angry, as I could not be angry or critical to such a humble, decent, delicate and sweet soul of a human being, who trusted me; trusted and depended on me to liberate him from the misery of horrific war experiences, even if for a short time.

I realized that there was more to the picture with this Vet, but I had to be delicate and respectful to a human who was injured from shrapnel, and traumatized by the violence of war. We spoke after the final landing and he explained to me that he may not be the best pilot, and that he was not sure that he wanted to be a pilot in the first place; all he wanted was therapy. It made him happy to fly, and it offered him a state of peace for his being. He was also interested in the camaraderie with other students in his ground class. They all became friends and met for social occasions.

This Vet never flew the airplane solo and most likely never cared to. His flying was like getting therapy for his condition; he was re-wiring and uploading his brain with better memories than those of war. The more activities he could indulge in that made him happy, the better the chances that the bad memories would fade. It seemed like he had found the antidote for his condition; it was flying, and he called it therapy; so he told me. He was a happy man, and a happy Vet, and that made me happy to have reached that human mind exactly where it wanted to be reached. There was much comfort in our experience together, for him and for me.

THE DIGITAL AGE AND OLD AGE

My Aviation teaching experience became an asset at my nine-to-five, suit and tie job. I was a professional in the Information Age, at the forefront of technology. I was leading a department of my company into the Digital Age. The work force was almost at retirement age, and many were veterans from the Second World War. These were guys who thought a "bit" was a coin and a "byte" was something to eat. I arranged several lessons in the conference room to teach them about binary code, and the functionality of computers that would run the future communication devices. It was tough, but the old heads got it. Group after group I taught them how logic circuits worked, as I had learned and built them in engineering school. I taught them how computers used four on/off switches to count from zero to fifteen, which would be sixteen possible values. I explained to them that every digital computer used this binary code to define each number and each letter.

As I explained to them, and as a quick review, let us imagine that there are four light bulbs in a row, representing four switches in a computer's logic circuitry. All the counting would start from the left. To obtain a value of zero, all light bulbs would be off. For the value of one, the first light bulb from the left is lit. For two, we turn off one and switch on the second from the left. For three, both the first and the second would be lit. For four, only the third light bulb from the left would be lit. Combining further would complete the rest, as just explained, reaching a value of fifteen. This forms sixteen possible values if we include zero, when all light bulbs were off. This sixteen-value system is called hexadecimal code.

I explained that a MODEM was a MOdulator, DEModulator. We had some examples of how to send a message using binary code. When a message had to be transferred through the medium of a telephone line, a radio signal, a cable or a fiber optic line, it must first be converted to the appropriate protocol of the transmission medium operational characteristics, also called the carrier, like a messenger. This is called modulation. Upon arrival at the destination the signal must be converted back to the digital version for the computer to process, because the computer is totally digital. This is called de-modulation. Imagine smoke signals through air. The air would be the medium, the smoke would be the transmission carrier and the start and stop of the smoke would be the coded signal or information.

All digital computers use binary code. The very first computers were analog. But, their accuracy could not be compared to their modern digital cousins. Binary and hexadecimal codes are so transparent that many of the information technology personnel of today may have difficulty explaining why every processing and storage value in a computer is divisible by sixteen, and certainly eight; it is binary and hexadecimal codes. They formed the basis of the Digital Age. It is also the basis of understanding the capability and limitation of the Digital Age, and the Information Age. It is the basis of understanding of the human brain, humans, artificial intelligence and eventually consciousness. The most powerful and advanced analog computer is not man-made; it is natural; it is the human brain. Good luck with anyone who wants to duplicate it. Artificial intelligence may just turn out to be sophisticated automation. It is human endeavor that will bring understanding of human limitation and understanding. It is good to understand, as understanding is the highest level of learning.

The old heads took my classes as required learning for the digital devices they would be working with. These guys did the best they could, as they were on their way out the door. They were headed to retirement, and out of the world of work. Soon they would be sipping cocktails on the beach. I know they took keen interest in what I was teaching, as it was something new, and they were also curious. It was more of a fun class than a vocational class. I believe they pretended to care about the company's goals, but really what they were thinking about was the clock, the clock on the wall that showed the quitting time. They were punctual with that clock, just in case the elevator was full on their way down. They could not wait to get to their homes to have dinner with their wives; the wives who simply wished they had to work overtime, as they said themselves. The next morning I would hear all the stories about the wives, and the previous evening; laughter at its best.

I had the most fun with these men of war, with their stories, and with their behavior. They also had a fantastic sense of humor, which seemed to be a compensation for the memory of war. Throughout the day there were numerous jokes all around. I loved being with them. They respected me for my digital knowledge, and at the same time, they accepted me as one of them, as we were all comrades in the same cause, for the company. I believe that these fighting men were shell-shocked by the Digital Age and felt that they were just doing time. They were waiting for the time to get the heck out of there. They were waiting for retirement time; a time when they would be home every day to irritate that poor woman; their wife, who had gotten used to them being away the whole day, as she happily got her knitting done. Soon she would become a waitress without tips, and most likely looking for a waitress job; with tips; so she could get some peace of mind from a demanding and cranky old man telling the same stories over and over again. It is what old age does to men. Trust me, I know.

THE MOVER AND SHAKER

I finished teaching the entire group, scores of men and a few women, and I moved on to a bigger and better opportunity. I was assigned with the responsibility of a million dollar division of the company, the digital communications division. The company had already negotiated with manufacturers to supply equipment, which would be used for private networks. That was the newly emerging opportunity, as companies raced to reduce costs by designing their own networks. It would be the first time that companies of any size were able to build their voice and data networks to suit their demand, as anti-trust laws barred large companies from sustaining monopolistic ventures.

My responsibility was marketing manager, which included the purchase, sale and installation process of all digital equipment. My first challenge was to train the sales force to draw them into the Digital Age. They would not be able to promote my product unless they understood what digitization was. I needed them to sell my products. It was up to me to convince them, as they were the first line to the customers. They loved to be wined and dined, as that was their lifestyle, especially with clients. I quickly became the grand host sponsoring cocktails, shrimp, and dinner, after their day sessions of the bits and bytes of the Digital Age. I had arranged training sessions with evening enticements.

I signed several contracts with manufacturers for equipment, and with the trained sales force, increased the revenue stream by one hundred and fifty percent, within a year. I hopped around and got into every aspect of this newly emerging technology for the company. I made alliances and motivated groups of people to engage the industry in an interest to shape it's future. One contractor called me the "mover and shaker," as I was everywhere, and I was the guy who got things done. I simply did not know any other way to be. It was an incredible and exciting experience to be in the right place at the right time, and at the forefront of the technology of the future.

This digital technology emerged, and private networks became the norms of the business culture. The sun had risen on the Internet, cellular and wireless communications, and a new social culture was emerging, completely facilitated by this technology. I had learned much about human desire and comfort, and what technology offered for these benefits. I am happy to have been a part of it, and I am happy to have learned more about us, and to understand humans with our immense desire to communicate. One aspect of this technology for certain was that all the professionals in the industry, including myself, did not foresee the social revolution, and worldwide connectivity it would bring into the twenty-first century.

TIME TO SHUT UP

I realized that the time would come somehow when I would stop teaching. I never predicted how it would happen, but it did, when there was nothing more for me to learn. I had begun to see repetitive behavior, and no variation or difference in students' behavior. I was done at that point; I had had enough. I realized that my mission was not career, but concept. The inspiration I received from Carl Sagan, many years ago, had motivated me subliminally to venture in that direction. My course was complete in the field of teaching people how to fly airplanes and learning about their psychology. I considered it a great opportunity, but I no longer possess the interest to teach people about Aviation. I also most certainly would not be interested in teaching pigs how to fly either.

I often reflect and reminisce about the days that slipped by and became years, then decades. My memory serves me well, and it is filled with happy ones. I still love to meet friends and colleagues from the past, and a few I still share, as buddies, in all the aspects of profession and friendship. I had trained a multitude of people, both in the classroom and in the airplane. After they were done with their training, they all went about their lives as usual, as I also did.

I remember the first student I taught in the classroom. He was the son of a captain of a major foreign airline, and he was privileged to have private lessons with me. His sister, a few years older than him was already a co-pilot for the same airline. She had come to New York for advanced training. She was absolutely gorgeous. She was tall and slim, with beautiful long hair, full lips, and a smile that could light up Times Square. I wish I had proposed, as she had made a hint to me. But, I didn't. Perhaps certain wishes and dreams are best experienced through reminiscence. I still smile at the thought of her, and the memory of that time of my life. I had made it to the moon.

George eventually progressed to professional level after moving to Europe. He had employment opportunities because of his father, and was hired by a major European airline. He kept in touch with me over the decades and until he became a captain of this airline on the 747 fleet. I could say that he lived my dream, as it was what I wanted. But, to dream is wonderful only when dreams come true. Reality is not always a dream, but when they are the same, they become the same.

I met this "first student" in Miami after one of his flights across the Atlantic, as captain of his jumbo jet. He told me of his life of being on five continents in the same month. I questioned myself; "was that the dream I wanted?" I could not be sure. In any case, we had a good chat, and a good time. George had a calm state of being as any seasoned captain should. I was proud of him, and he made me happy when he told me what he had learned from me; stuff that still matters to him. That made my day.

GENERATIONS

The flight instructor who conducted my final training for instructor certification decades ago had moved to Central Florida shortly after I was certified. We had kept in touch occasionally, then faded into our own sunsets. He began working for the FAA and had moved up in ranks to a senior level. Instructors were always teaching, as though it was in our blood. He would make speeches on safety at several pilot gatherings sponsored by the government and certain private institutions. As it came to pass, a favorite student of mine had also moved to Central Florida and was active in attending many of these gatherings. I had learned that the two would be at the same venue on a particular day. I encouraged my student to introduce himself to the speaker, which he did, prior to the speech. The flight instructor later told me about meeting a stranger who reminded him about his life, many, many years in his past. The details of the airplane, which we all had flown, were touching - to the point that the hair on his arms began to stand on end. He was excited and delighted to have discovered such a small circle. The two men and I met again and again, and we became friends all over again, all three together this time. I once told them in a humorous way that I was the father of the pilot that I trained and my instructor was the grandfather, even though our ages did not reflect such. It was laughable.

The instructor/friend also had flying duties at his government job, one of which was to protect airspace during non-military activity. One such activity occurred during the space shuttle launches. A restricted area would be designated for all flights within a specified perimeter. Some private pilots would ignore the perimeter and venture to view the shuttle launch close up, inside the restricted airspace. Radar controllers would detect targets and report them to the FAA airplane, piloted by my instructor/friend, who would then intercept and direct the intruders to leave the area, while recording the aircraft identification numbers for enforcement action against the pilot.

After all the intruders were ejected, my friend would finally have the privilege that any pilot would envy; to watch the space shuttle launch from the best seat in the world, in an airplane while on shuttle patrol. This is the kind of friend a person would want to take to any gathering to brag about. Some guys have all the luck.

TOLERANCE

A wonderful memory from my teenage years returned by coincidence after I had relocated to Florida. When I was about fifteen years of age I had joined a youth group, which held meetings every week in the town. The group leader was a respectable, knowledgeable, educated, and trusted man familiar to the community, my family and to myself. This group met for socialization and civics learning. There was one particular assignment, which I remember extremely well. We were asked to pick one topic out of several on which to write an essay. After much discussion on what subjects could expound on building and inculcating human character, the group decided on "tolerance." We all tried our best to write for a good praise from the leader, since there were no grades issued; this was not formal school. The strength of the youth group was to have discussions after the assignments. Every one was included and there was no formality. Self-esteem was the benefit for each, and was more meaningful since it was originating from the group. After the meetings, a few of us who came from the same direction continued the conversation as we rode home on our bicycles. One young man and I became friends, and we continued talking about many other subjects. He was very engaging, and I enjoyed his dialog and camaraderie.

The contents of my essay were long forgotten, but the theme of "tolerance" became a permanent member of my memory. I remembered that we discussed the meaning of the word literally, as well as its interpretation from all the points of view of the group. The take away, from the discussions, was how to accept people in their own condition, circumstances and situations, and how not to judge, but to understand. It was about how to tolerate the crying child, the angry friend, the stern father, the difficult teacher, the arrogant boss, and the misfortunes in life. It was really about how to be humble. We discussed that tolerance represented a larger spectrum of humanity, and inculcated aspects such as patience, compassion, restraint, reasoning, and most of all, understanding. It was an excellent topic, and I was happy being in the group, as I was enlightened. It was the first time I would write about human nature.

Decades later some of the people in the group had relocated to other countries. The youth who was my acquaintance had moved to Canada. As circumstance would have it, this now grown man, with wife and children, was related to someone who I was also related to, from different family ties. The world of the village was small, and the neighboring villages made it only slightly larger. This man had planned to visit my family member. I was asked to visit the house to meet him, and a few others, as a social event. I suggested a trick that no one should tell him who I was. Decades had elapsed, and we assumed that he would not recognize me. The plan was set; my family member would introduce me hastily, and make the suggestion that we may know each other.

The moment arrived. When I was introduced, he did not remember me. I spoke as though I didn't remember him either, as I questioned the place of his origin. I continued to pretend and confuse him. Finally, his brother, who was instructed to give him the clue as to my identity, told him that he should know a fellow with tolerance. Immediately, his face changed into a somber state, as he expressed complete disbelief and shock. I could only have imagined that all the wheels of the video player in his head were spinning, and his brain was making rapid electrical connections, such that within a few seconds, the complete picture would be painted. The word, "tolerance," had made its impact on the youth group, such that we would all remember it. That word had made its impact on him. A big hug followed, and we continued our discussions as though we were still in the youth group.

The entire assembly was briefed and prepared for this showdown, and was eager to see how it unfolded. They were in disbelief as to how one word could connect two people after several decades of absence. As a bonus, I was also fortunate to have met the leader of our group through a family member, some time before this event. He lived in Florida as well. We contacted him in a conference call and shared the preceding events, and our memory of the word, "tolerance." He had also remembered it well. It was a profound subject for all of us. "Tolerance" had become the mantra and call sign for the group of friends that were present at the showdown. I was happy to share it.

FINALLY

The reflection of my professional life fills me with memories of stories, events and situations, which I treasure as the benefit of my learning and my being. It was who I was, and what I was then, at that time. I have told only a sampling of stories here, but there were so many more, which would fill volumes. I often feel like the mariner in the story of "The Rhyme of The Ancient Mariner," except that I did not kill the albatross, nor do I carry guilt, and I do not have a penance to satisfy. I am like the mariner simply because I feel commanded to tell the stories of my life. I am commanded by my memory and desire to share knowledge, while he was commanded by his guilt to serve his penance. It is the human condition, which formed from the circumstances that determines the resultant of each possible future. Could it be that humans could have two opposite reasons to tell stories, one to absolve guilt, and the other to share knowledge? Both are information sharing, but with opposite motives. We are certainly an interesting bunch.

Chapter Five

TO ERR IS HUMAN

Humans probably make more mistakes than any other species for the simple reason that we take more risks. I have watched birds attempting to land during high wind conditions while they seemed to have some difficulty. Birds instinctively land into the wind as this condition offers the benefit of the slowest landing speed. They usually end up losing balance upon contact with the ground and have to adjust themselves with wings extended until they can come to a stop. Awkward landings are not an issue for the birds; they take-off, fly and land constantly in their daily lives. The risk of being hurt on landing would seem to be low for them. Humans, on the other hand, have many more activities in our daily lives that could expose us to increased risk. We could trip and fall, we could have a car accident, or we could fall off a bicycle. It's all because of gravity, one of the four known forces of the universe, which we must all comply with.

In the case of accidental events, it is not unusual for us to justify them by calling them just that; "accidents." However, if we are in a known high-risk situation where we are more likely to get hurt, could we still call that accidental? Our human logic could make some reasonable calculations, but we could never be sure. If we drive our car during a snowstorm and have a crash, could we justify it as accidental? Because of our logic, derived from our conscious ability, we have placed ourselves in an entirely different category than a bird trying to land in high winds. Whereas the bird would run for cover during a snowstorm, humans would venture out, without always calculating each activity as to the risk involved. We want to be the masters of our situation. We could justify some of those risks with rational arguments. It could be justified with logic that it would be fine to drive someone to the hospital in a snowstorm if they were sick.

One safe trip through some inclement weather could encourage us to venture out again in a casual way, even though it may not be prudent. I ignored warnings once, and attempted to drive my car to work during a snowstorm. While traveling slightly downhill, the car in front of mine began spinning around. I immediately pressed the brakes, and in what seemed to have been a fraction of one second, my car accelerated to the right, and without hesitation. It made a direct course into the concrete wall of the overpass that I was approaching. The wall was unforgiving, and the car did not accept the impact very well. It was wrecked, and had to go to the salvage yard. Perhaps I should appreciate not having to pay for the wall repair, as the damage was almost invisible. But, I did hit my nose on the steering wheel, and my knee on the window crank handle, and I had to pay for that with severe pain. There were no seat belts in those days. The same car that was spinning around had to transport me to the hospital. I swore I would never drive again, and the pain and suffering I endured simply sealed that notion.

One week out of work and a lost vehicle could have taught me a lesson. The question was whether or not I learned anything. I learned that I could choose not to drive in a snowstorm ever again, or to drive slowly in such conditions. I learned what many others would not know, unless they were also driving in a snowstorm. I learned that a vehicle skids much faster in snow; certainly not rocket science. Perhaps I also learned how to avoid skidding in the first place by not pressing hard on the brakes. What my learning would contribute to my future decision making skills would come from my analytical mind. The logical part of my brain would be influenced with the

166

subconscious part. My ego and my desire to be somewhere would play important roles in my decision-making ability. I could very well once again find myself in the same situation. It is my human nature.

We are humans always, and we will venture, and we will take risks. This spirit comes with its share of casualties, but brings a great deal of beneficial learning. Our ancestors took many risks to navigate their lives through millennia. It is the reason we are here. When we take risks we could fail. When we fail we learn. When we learn we know. When we know we can share. When we share, the information gets analyzed, and safety procedures can be established. One hundred years from now the bird would still be running to hide from the snowstorm. Humans would not; we would continue to venture.

In our society there are several organizations, both private and in government, that focus on safety procedures and accident prevention. Safety is what pilots, bus drivers, paratroopers, scuba divers, and other professionals must learn first and foremost. But, even with all the safety nets, accidents do happen. It is human nature to make mistakes. When accidents are analyzed, recommendations can be made to improve safety. A seat belt in the car that I drove into the wall during a snowstorm could have saved the injury to my nose and knee. It was an old car given to me as a gift, (as is), and without seat belts. It came easy and it went in a flash. It should be known that most accidents are caused by human error. To err is human.

MISTAKES

Humans have a strong reactive tendency. We are no different than a hyena attempting to grab a share of meat while the lion is eating, only to be chased away by a mighty roar. The hyena knows the risk, but ventures anyway, only to react to the lion's behavior. Perhaps the hyena is unable to assess the mood of the lion, and tests its limits. The proactive option; to come back later when the lion is gone, has the disappointing penalty that nothing would be left, as scavengers claim their shares and leave bare bones; hardly a hyena's diet. The reactive and proactive balance forms a challenging condition to safety, regardless of whether it occurs in the savanna or with humans. It almost seems to confirm our fallibility as we try to manage this delicate balance.

Mistakes happen in all professions and walks of life, and they measure our balance of reactive and proactive valuation. To react to a situation gone awry is to take a risk without calculating or knowing all the possible outcomes. To be proactive could mean not taking any chance whatsoever, which in turn mitigates the risk, but also dissolves the venture. Which shall it be? If the risk is not fully calculable let someone else do it. That was the reason chimps went into space before man; they were the guinea pigs. Poor chimps. I wonder what they were thinking during their space odyssey. Perhaps they did not think about anything. Perhaps G forces did not produce the fear in them, as it would be for humans. Perhaps not knowing what the heck was going on immunized them from any emotional issues, and the stress of the ordeal. Lack of knowledge certainly has its merits, indeed.

Mistakes are the conclusions of a logical analysis of a situation that shows a result contrary to what was intended. The conclusions are usually done in hindsight, hence the phrase; "Hindsight is 20/20." In hindsight I should not have driven my car and crashed in a snowstorm. But, had I not done that, I would not have learned the effects of surface snow on a moving vehicle, and braking action during such operation. I learned to be more cautious, and eventually I was able to drive in other snowstorms. Some mistakes could offer better understanding and cautious planning in the future. Others can simply be stupid and reckless. In any case, human endeavor forms the conditions for mistakes, and mistakes offer learning and correction. Mistakes are primarily the result of the incalculability of future events.

COMMON, BUT AVOIDABLE

I remember the case where a man went to the hospital for surgery to remove a diseased leg. When he woke up from the anesthesia he discovered that they had removed his good leg. Procedures failed to include verification of the surgical requirement before anesthesia was administered, and while the patient was conscious.

A man I knew was changing the oil of his car engine. After draining the oil from the bottom of the engine he proceeded to pour five quarts of fresh oil into the engine, without first closing the drain hole in the bottom. Not only a loss of oil, but a high level of contamination was the obvious result. Had he not detected the oil spill, and started driving the car, the result would have been catastrophic. The engine would have come to a complete halt, as the pistons would have fused onto the walls of the cylinders from extreme heat. It would then be called; in mechanical terms; a "seized" engine.

A high-speed train in Europe derailed because the operator took a turn with excessive speed, a human error in the risk calculation department. A truck attempting to enter a tunnel was too high and would have caused a collision with the ceiling of the tunnel. Had the driver attempted to enter he would have exited with a topless truck. A barge being pushed by a tugboat collided with a bridge simply because the tide was higher than normal. The Valdez ran aground simply because of a navigation error.

Humans are naturally prone to making mistakes, and we are not always able to help ourselves, as it is our nature. It is who we are, and how we learn each day, by taking risks.

HOSPITAL TRIP

When I was a boy of about ten years old I heard probably the loudest sound I had ever heard, except for thunder. It was a car that crashed into a bus, in the village. The incident occurred as the car was traveling at an excessively high speed. In the driver's mind, the risk of excessive speed was acceptable because of the urgent condition of transporting a very ill person to the hospital. Unfortunately, the bus driver had to make a turn that crossed the path of the oncoming car, as that was the route. The bus driver may have miscalculated the speed of the car, and not believing that it could be traveling at such a high speed, decided to make the turn. The car could not stop in time. The impact was heard throughout the three villages neighboring the crash. All occupants of the car were killed, and some on the bus were injured. The accident could easily be blamed on both drivers. The risk taker however, was the driver of the car. He did not project the danger ahead. He did not form a protective envelope around the car, especially as he approached an intersection.

I heard that the sick person being transported to the hospital in the town had come from about twenty miles away. There were no ambulances at that time, and when people needed to go to the hospital they had to be driven by a private vehicle. Unfortunately, with such an urgent situation involving several variables, including someone's health condition, the calculations became complicated.

To err on the side of caution is a good philosophy, but calculations become difficult in life and death situations. In countries that have medical emergency transport capability, it is prudent when someone is sick beyond a reasonable condition to call an ambulance, which is almost certain to have a specialist and medicine on board, as well as flashing emergency lights.

SAFETY IS NO ACCIDENT

It is not unusual for humans to become anxious when discussing human errors. However, the discussion of how human errors result in catastrophes could ease this anxiety. Knowledge is power for us. The highest level of learning is to understand, and understanding offers the optimum method of quelling our fears and anxieties. It is especially important for bicyclists, pedestrians, drivers, pilots, air traffic controllers and everyone else for that matter to take responsibility for the safety of passage. Some notable events and accidents would reveal our human behavior, and offer better understanding of our human nature. The intent here is to share information and observe methods of prevention of dangerous situations in human activities.

The National Transportation Safety Board (NTSB) is responsible for investigating accidents of all types, on the ground and in the air. Upon the completion of each accident investigation, a report is issued detailing the circumstances, probable cause, and possible remedy for the situation. Quite often recommendations are offered for changes to be made with maintenance fixes, addition and design of equipment, and training or procedure changes. Accidents happen because of unfortunate circumstances, but most often they are caused by human error. Procedures, rules, preparation, qualification and equipment are all contributory to safety. There is always risk with movement of machines, and a level of safety could always be acquired when care is taken. "Safety is no Accident." The United States has achieved the highest level of safety in all forms of transportation, especially air transportation. It is statistically safer to fly in an airliner than to travel in a car.

Investigators of several government agencies often contribute to the understanding of incidents and accidents. While most aviation accidents are caused by human error, the role of the investigators is to report their findings and offer recommendations, such as equipment failure, pilot certification, cockpit behavior and discipline. As an example, one airline flight into icing conditions caused a crash several years ago. The investigators recommended having co-pilots with more experience than the one present on this flight. The airline industry objected, but the FAA was still able to raise the licensing requirement for all copilots, which required several more hours of experience. The aspiring airline pilots had to delay their applications to the airlines until they had acquired the additional hours of flight time, and pass the exam. The

171

airlines, in the meantime, had to raise the salary of these new copilots, and most likely all the others who were already hired. It could be said that such was the price of doing business, but more importantly it was the price of safety.

I prefer to pay most of my attention to the human psychological aspects, which most times would be revealed through the details of the flight and the voice recorder dialog. Important information on the decision making process in dealing with any situation normally could be ascertained from the psychological analysis. As an example, if someone were driving a car and one tire made a loud sound because it blew out, the driver would be forced to take immediate action. Contrastingly, if the tire had a slow leak, the situation could be handled without much urgency. When machines make loud noises the conclusion tends to indicate a major occurrence or failure. In airplanes, these occurrences could include an engine blowout, or an immediate decompression.

I once witnessed a loud bang on takeoff when I was a passenger on an airliner. The pilot aborted the takeoff and all was well. He also knew exactly what caused the loud noise. The takeoff was being conducted on a runway with a very strong crosswind. The pilot determined that airflow to the engine on the leeward side of the airplane was drastically reduced, causing it to backfire, as he described it. The airplane taxied back to the runway for takeoff and off we went. This was not an emergency; it was an expected event from the conditions, and without a consequence, except for a minor delay.

Partial loss of power of an engine, or a slow decompression would not be considered with great urgency. However, the bigger issue with non-urgent situations is that they could spell bigger problems as the occurrence becomes exaggerated after the initial event. Maximum interest should be placed in determining the cause of the occurrence, and until such is ascertained, treatment of the condition should be precautionary.

Smoke in the cockpit in most cases would intensify, and inasmuch as it may be considered non-urgent, such occurrences had incapacitated pilots on several occasions. Immediate emergency action should be considered for smoke, and any loud noises that create immediate reactions, or is of unknown origin. It is the psychology of humans, and animals as well, to behave differently in urgent and non-urgent situations. When the alligator in my yard was approached rapidly, it jumped into the canal quickly. If it were approached slowly it would simply crawl into the canal, slowly. Humans, however, have the conscious logic to analyze a problem and act accordingly, especially when a minor occurrence becomes intensified. Trusting the unknown is the risk-taking aspect of human psychology. The alligator in the meantime takes no risks. It will run for cover every time, and at the pace of which it's approached.

WITH YOU, FOR SAFETY

The amount of knowledge required for pilots regarding safety is intense. Piloting an aircraft is an activity that does not offer much tolerance for errors. When I was teaching pilots in the classroom there were few subjects that were fairly the same in scope for all the levels, from private pilot to airline pilot. All aircraft operate in the same atmosphere, and knowledge of the weather was paramount for all pilots. Some pilots could qualify to fly in the clouds under instrument flight rules (IFR). This qualification was not an invitation to fly into hazardous weather, such as thunderstorms and hurricanes. Common sense and prudence must be exercised to achieve the highest level of safety. Federal Aviation Regulations was another subject matter affecting everyone in achieving safety in the skies. These regulations affect all pilots regardless of certification level.

There were a few important ideas I had to communicate from the get-go. I explained that there was a government body called the Department of Transportation that has the mission to develop transportation infrastructure that was fast, safe, efficient, accessible and convenient. That meant on the ground and in the air. The group responsible for the Aviation sector was the Federal Aviation Administration (FAA). A major part of the FAA was Air Traffic Control (ATC). When discussing ATC, I insisted that each student understood exactly what it meant, and not simply the translation of the acronym. Air traffic control meant the separation of aircraft while in the air and on the ground, simply said. ATC is not meant to relieve a pilot of the responsibility for navigation, or terrain clearance, again in simple terms. When ATC assumes the navigation, traffic separation, and terrain clearance for a flight, it would be to organize a smooth flow and sequencing of aircraft. Under this condition the controller would provide directives known as "vectors," to the pilot. Clear communication during this condition must be established between pilot and controller.

Both groups use a phonetic alphabet when using letters, such as, alpha for the letter "A" and whisky for "W". In busy airspace, it is often necessary for a radar controller to issue vectors in order to separate and sequence arriving and departing aircraft. These vectors are not always in the direction of the intended destination of the flight, and sometimes may result in a holding pattern. Pilots become familiar with these procedures quickly as they operate in high-density airspace. The objective of ATC is safe passage of all aircraft from origin to destination.

The rules set forth for the conduct of safe flight is well established in the Federal Air Regulations (FAR). Each pilot and controller has specific authority and responsibility. There may be times when the responsibility portion overlaps. In such cases neither party should assume that the other has full responsibility. The safety of any flight is a cooperative effort by controller and pilot. However, it is imperative that all pilots know that they have final and full responsibility for the safety of their aircraft. As such, the pilot has the final authority whether to comply with ATC directives or decide alternative options, especially in an emergency. The two groups customarily work harmoniously together to achieve the safest result. When pilots make specific requests, and controllers offer options and recommendations, the result is improved safety. As such, the relationship between pilot and controller is expected to provide safe passage of the aircraft. The relationship also places the controller in a subservient position, as the pilot always retains the responsibility for the flight, and has final authority. This also means that the pilot could refuse the controller's clearance. I would dare to tell any pilot that there had better be a good reason for refusing a controller's clearance. The last thing any pilot needs is to be at odds with a controller. Inasmuch as the pilot would simply need to say that he is refusing the clearance while asserting his authority, the refusal should make sense to the controller, or at least have some diplomacy when offering a reason for the refusal. It's not nice to hurt a fellow's feelings.

The pilot and controller relationship is best when both participate as team members. There were several times when I made corrections to ATC directives, as they were not accurate. Errors could be minor or significant to safety, and controllers always appreciate input for safety. When both members participate for a common goal, the result is often satisfactory. A good example would be the FAR requirement that all aircraft reduce speed to 250 knots when below ten thousand feet in airspace controlled by ATC. This way the controller would be separating targets traveling at the same speed, and aircraft would not be able to overtake each other in the event of controller's negligence. Pilots are required to know this rule and comply, but could quite easily forget if workload is intense. Radar controllers may include the phrase; "reduce speed to 250" anytime a vector is issued for a descent below ten thousand feet. This overlap of responsibility along with courtesy ensures compliance for safety.

When I operated small airplanes from LaGuardia Airport it was common, while taxiing behind an airliner, for the ground controller to issue a statement to the airliner to use thrust sparingly so as not to blast me. As soon as the airliner turned for the number one position it would be the first time the pilot could see my airplane. It also would not be uncommon for the engines to be spooled up about fifty percent before the takeoff clearance. The runways are not very long, and takeoff power is necessary as soon as possible. When I became number one for takeoff it was necessary to wait for turbulence from the preceding airliner to abate. Finally, when I heard, "Cleared for takeoff," from the tower controller, it would be accompanied by the phrase; "caution, wake turbulence." It was the rule, and his job, to notify me of any hazards. The small plane I flew required a shorter takeoff distance than the airliner. To be cautious, I would turn into the wind as soon as practical, and then climb parallel to the runway. Wake turbulence drifts with the wind and is extremely dangerous, especially at low altitudes; it could place an airplane in an uncontrollable position.

LIGHTS OUT

One night over Long Island Sound, along the Southern coast of Connecticut I was flying back from dinner with two friends. One was already a pilot, and the other a student pilot. The airplane's electrical system failed after approximately thirty minutes into the flight. There was no panic, and no need for panic. Let me say for non-pilots that an electrical or battery failure in an airplane does not disable the engine, as would happen in an automobile. It would cause the exterior and interior lights, the radio, and some instruments not to function. In addition, the transponder, which was used for radar detection by Air Traffic Control, would be non-functioning. Oh! I forgot one other device that would not be functioning, and that would be the electric clock that we never used.

We discovered the failure from the garbled radar controller's voice on the radio, as the low battery power could not modulate his voice. He reported that he was no longer receiving our transponder signal. It was time to investigate like a detective. I surmised that the first thing that happened was the alternator failed shortly after we took-off. With a fully charged battery there was enough energy to operate the electrical devices in the airplane, but naturally for a fixed amount of time only. I knew that the lights used the most energy from the battery, and we had the landing light on the entire time, since it was a requirement of my pilot friend. I used a landing light for landing, but my friend preferred that the airplane be as lit up as possible on the outside. The landing light was the cause of the rapid loss of electrical energy, as it had the highest continuous wattage consumption of any component or instrument in the airplane.

I knew that the burden of responsibility was mine, as I was the senior pilot, and instructor. The first objective was to tell the controller what was happening. We informed him that we would continue to our destination in this stealth condition, meaning no lights would be illuminated on the exterior of the airplane, and the radar return would be primary only, not transponder assisted. We turned off all the electrical devices, including the master switch, and flew on.

Simulating an electrical failure was part of pilot training. It was simply turning off all the electrical devices one by one so the student could understand the effect, detect it, and make corrections. At night, since navigation lights were needed, the exercise would be abbreviated, with only some components turned off. Several landings would also be practiced with the landing light in the "off" position. The most important details to learn would be the loss of navigation instruments, radios and interior lighting on the instrument panel. In addition, electrical flaps would not function. A flashlight was a good substitute for interior lighting and it was a recommendation for night flights.

It was good for each student to see that during an electrical failure, the airplane's engine would not stop, and the airplane would not fall out of the sky. Instead, it would fly the same as it did before. The airspeed indicator and altimeter would function normally as they are pressure instruments and do not require any type of power. On a visual flight, the consequence of a complete electrical failure could be minimal, especially during daylight. There is even a procedure to follow at an airport with an operating control tower in case the pilot is unable to make radio contact. It would simply be to join the flow of airplanes and rock the wings. Controllers would know what that meant, and would use a light gun to show signals to the pilot. Of course a steady green light would mean, "cleared to land."

I was always cognitive of each student's human nature and decisions. I would never discourage the use of a landing light during the day or night. Each pilot must make that decision. My friend's decision was based on his consideration that it would improve safety by illuminating the airplane to other air traffic. The unfortunate circumstance was that the same safety feature he considered important became the cause of the airplane having no lights whatsoever. A delicate balance of features tarnished by an unpredictable event. My decisions for the use of a landing light was for what it was intended, landing at night. However, traffic density in the area at any given time, and visibility, were factors to be considered.

We humans make safety decisions based on many variables including fear, confidence level, and analysis of the circumstance and risk. We incorporate a set of standard operating practice in a particular situation. Whenever I flew with licensed pilots I was either providing instruction for a more advanced license, or occupying the seat as an extra level of safety. We would agree before the flight regarding who would be the pilot in command. In this light I would be contributing to the flight by instructing or advising as the case may be. I would never usurp the pilot in command's authority unless an urgent or emergency situation occurred, and then by agreement. I wanted them to do the planning, the navigation, and the communications, in addition to making all the decisions concerning the flight. Those were my principles, even though I was their instructor at some time in the past. I followed my idea that even though I could be a motivator or influencer, it would be better if they simply learned from their own routine and experience, while continuing to become independent. It was my understanding of human nature that the more I contributed, the more they would expect from me. It would be no different than feeding an alligator. Dependence is every creature's natural tendency.

Our situation on this flight became interesting only because it was at night. We were not perfectly legal to fly because the navigation lights were not illuminated outside of the airplane. The only way for it to have been legal would be to declare an emergency. There would be paperwork to follow. I was not interested, and no one suggested it. We made one last communication to the controller that we would terminate radio contact and navigate to our destination. We did not need the controller anyway. My friend always liked to be in contact with ATC just as he liked to keep the landing light on at night, as an added level of safety.

Aircraft are well lit up at night and easy to see. It is the same for airports. I preferred to depend on my eyesight in order to be accustomed to not being dependent on a radar controller. I did not want a controller to tell me there was an airplane a few miles to the left or right of me when I could clearly see it. In addition, I would scan every sector including above and below for air traffic. At night, traffic density was lower to begin with, and targets were easy to see.

This evening was clear, with no traffic in sight, and the radar controller offering traffic advisories, until we lost him. We proceeded on-course, crossing the Hudson River slightly north of The George Washington Bridge, while keeping a close lookout for traffic at the nearby airports. We continued to Patterson and positioned the airplane on a long final approach to a very nicely lit runway. Now it was time to reflect on my engineering skills. With the master switch turned off, the battery had a zero current drain. During the minutes in this condition some residual power would be restored. The radio used a very small amount of power, and so we turned on the master switch and the radio, and then contacted the tower at the destination airport. Immediately, the words: "Cleared to land any runway" came back over the speaker. The radar controller had already contacted the tower controller by telephone, and explained our situation. It is not usual for controllers to get a chance to deal with urgent or emergency situations, and they use every opportunity to practice what they were trained for. Our situation

179

placed the tower controller on alert, and offered him an opportunity to exercise his talents as well. He was extremely cooperative and even showed us a light gun signal while we were on final approach, a "cleared to land," solid green light.

We turned off the electrical system again to preserve whatever power could be saved. We continued straight in and landed without incident. Then came the most embarrassing part of the journey. We slowed the airplane down to taxi speed, but could not see the taxiway to exit. Only few of the taxiways had lights at that time at this small airport. We had to open the door and shine a flashlight on the ground. I wished the tower controller, knowing that we would not be able to see, had sent a car to greet us, with lights on. However, that would be beyond the jurisdiction of his responsibility. Every situation brought its merits for learning about humans. We thanked him before we shut everything down. Eventually, the friend in the back seat of the airplane walked to his car and turned on the headlights close to the airplane. We parked and left. Drinks all around.

SHOW AND TELL

I once made the mistake of not demonstrating a maneuver to a student prior to asking him to execute it. He was a very educated young man who demonstrated an accelerated learning potential. I had assumed that his intellect would compensate for the absence of demonstration. The maneuver was to place the airplane in a stall configuration, and then recover from it. When the wings stall there is not enough airflow to produce the desired amount of lift to maintain flight. The airplane would begin to lose altitude and exhibit a pronounced shaking. A loud stall warning horn would also be activated. The recovery would be to lower the nose, apply full power, and level off in cruise flight.

I neglected to explain to the student that the nose of the airplane should be lowered slightly below the horizon; I thought his intellect would suffice. He executed the stall with effective positive control and after the shaking began he pointed the nose down very sharply towards the ground. The earth filled the windshield, and was rushing up to meet us. We transitioned from zero gravity to negative gravity in a split second. The airplane was descending faster than the objects inside. Our seat belts kept us from a head strike against the ceiling. All of the unsecured objects in the airplane were now firmly planted on the ceiling. I immediately yelled, "Not that low," and took control. I arrested the dive, and all the objects fell from the ceiling and settled wherever they landed. He was a bit rattled and so was I. It was not what I expected.

I was happy that we had good communications, something I established from the beginning of training. I needed him to listen to my instruction and relinquish control of the airplane anytime I requested. He did so immediately, as he felt there was something wrong. We had a good laugh after discussing what happened. Thereafter, he was able to execute stalls and recovery with confidence. From that day forward, I never, ever, neglected to demonstrate every single maneuver to every student, even if they had a PhD, or if it was Einstein sitting next to me. I had learned my lesson on teaching. My misunderstanding of the psychology of the human led me to assume that intellect could supersede other learning aspects in humans; perhaps a few, but not stalls in an airplane.

FOOLISH BOY AND THE BIG AIRPORT

One student, a young man, who I considered quite airplane smart, was already approved for solo flight, by me. I asked him to ferry an airplane back to the base airport from the airport where it was serviced by the maintenance facility. It was late afternoon when I drove him to the airplane. I offered specific instructions regarding his flight, including instruction to park the aircraft after landing, since he would be arriving before me. I watched him take-off and I began driving. Upon arrival at the base airport there was no airplane, and no student to be found anywhere. I became nervous, but I had confidence in this student. It was wintertime, and it became dark quickly. After a few minutes of waiting, it became night. I saw an airplane overhead and I was relieved. However, the airplane was not following the traffic pattern, but circling instead. This airport did not have a control tower, but the radio operator at the airport's office mentioned that the pilot of the airplane had previously called in for advisories. That was a standard practice, which was prudent on the student's part. I tried to contact the student on this airport radio, but he did not answer. I went back outside to look, and I noticed that the airplane did not land. I saw it fly towards the huge airport to the north. That would be Newark Airport; one of the busiest in the New York area, with tons of airline traffic, literally. It was six miles to the north. I was alarmed, but all I could do was wait for a phone call to get information. The phone call came about thirty minutes later. The student had landed at Newark Airport.

In the series of events, some were favorable, and others unfavorable. The first unfavorable event was that the student did not promptly fly to the base; he decided to practice a few maneuvers first. Darkness set in on him and he was not trained or approved for night flight. He could not identify the base airport even though he was right above it. He made a favorable decision to fly to Newark Airport, which was lit up like a Christmas tree. He called Newark tower on the radio and declared an emergency, but the tower did not hear his call. Another unfortunate situation was that the radio in the aircraft had a weak transmitter because of a blown power transistor. Fortunately, the speaker in the airplane could receive radio messages loud and clear, and the student could hear them well, as the receiving transistor was fine.

There was an airliner waiting on a taxiway for take-off on runway 4-Left; the same runway that the student was lined up to land. The fortunate event that took place was that the airline pilot had heard the student's radio calls, but the tower was much farther away, and the controller did not hear him. The tower controller cleared the airliner for takeoff, as he did not hear the student's declaration of an emergency. The airline pilot must have been confused that he got a conflicted clearance. He did not know that the tower did not hear the student. The airline pilot replied to the tower with a bit of humor; "You mean we're cleared for takeoff after the airplane on final approach with an emergency?" The tower controller must have immediately and carefully looked to verify, and he saw the small airplane on final approach, at which time he asked for the aircraft identification numbers and intentions via the radio. The student would have heard and replied, but again the controller did not hear the response because of the weak radio transmitter in the airplane.

This was an urgent situation; it was about safety. The fast thinking controller quickly surmised that the aircraft radio was most likely inoperative, and he asked the student to flash the landing light if he could hear the radio. The final factor to this flight was that the airplane was returning from routine service. The landing light bulb on the airplane was burnt and inoperative, and it was on the maintenance list to be replaced. When the student flashed the landing light it was operational. Luckily, it had been replaced at the service shop the very same day. The controller cleared the student to land, and the landing was uneventful. As the student reported to me after; every fire truck at the airport was racing towards him. They surrounded the airplane and escorted him to the General Aviation ramp.

I drove my car to Newark Airport to fly the airplane out, and the student drove my car back to the base airport. The controllers had already known the aircraft identification number and the radio issue. They also knew that my acknowledgements during takeoff would come from the use of the landing light on and off positions. An airport official vehicle escorted me to the takeoff position of the runway. The controller asked me to flash the landing light if I could hear him. I flashed the light and was cleared for takeoff. Within ten minutes I was on the ground at the base airport.

It could seem that I should have been angry with the student for not following my instructions. I was not angry for what he did, I was unhappy that I had to cancel my dinner plans.

I was actually relieved that the circumstances were favorable for both of us, overall; I called it luck.

One of the considerations for any flight instructor was the immense responsibility that went along with the title. It could seem like a privilege to be in the "under one percentile category" of the population who were pilots and instructors. But, such were the responsibilities I accepted, whether I was in the airplane with the student or not; the privilege had its price.

A week later I received a phone call from an inspector of the local Federal Aviation Administration office. After each emergency, the pilot and the controller must file a written report. Since the pilot was a student, the inspector wanted my input. I explained that the student was quite intelligent, and his youthful indiscretion should be forgiven, but should be accompanied with a warning, instead of action or suspension. I was lucky that I didn't have to file pages and pages of paper, as the inspector accepted my verbal summary. I told the student that I had covered his butt, and that the inspector would close his case. He appreciated it enormously as he was very interested in finishing his licensing course. I especially appreciated his appreciation when I handed him an envelope that came to the owner of the airplane. It was a bill with an alarmingly high landing fee from Newark Airport, which he was expected to pay. Luckily, there was no extra cost added for the fire trucks' dry run. I explained to him that he would be one of the few people, if not the only one in the entire world, who would have had the experience he acquired from this flight. I suggested that he put the bill in a photo frame (after it was paid of course). The young man did get his license and went off into his sunset, not necessarily with an airplane this time.

JAW DROP + ADRENALINE

Safety was paramount for flight training, and I had to teach with close observation to rules. I had to be the example. Rarely did I get to "have fun." When the opportunity came to demonstrate some difficult maneuvers, such as stalls and steep turns I felt good. I felt better when the student was able to complete the maneuver within the prescribed tolerances. I used caution as my guiding light while teaching. I rarely took chances beyond the scope of the requirements for a maneuver, as there could never be too much caution. It was also not appropriate to indulge in unnecessary and unsafe practices while teaching someone to fly. It could certainly be considered counterproductive, not to mention dangerous, especially if the student tried to copy it.

In a sixty-degree bank, while keeping the airplane level, two G's of force would be produced. It was like being twice as heavy, and the pressure in the seat could be clearly felt. During this maneuver I would tell the student to try to put one hand towards the ceiling of the airplane. It would be more difficult as the weight of the hand had doubled. Another exercise was to open the mouth, then attempt to close it. Sometimes the mouth would have to stay open until the maneuver was terminated, or shut by hand. The jaw muscles with a wide-open mouth had difficulty under two G's of force.

Another rule that must be strictly followed was height above the ground. The only exception from altitude rules was during takeoff and landing. Some of the fun I invented would be taking off and then holding airplane at a low level (ten feet over the runway) with full power, and for some distance down the runway, then pulling up for a steep climb. It was fun to be traveling at over one hundred miles per hour right over the ground, and then climb steeply for a short-lived rush, as the G force pressed me into the seat. Of course, student approval was necessary, as I did not want them to be fearful or anxious. In addition, it was good for them to feel some excitement and learn the characteristics of the airplane.

Another maneuver, to prepare for emergencies, would be to simulate engine failure by requesting a landing on an adjacent runway shortly after takeoff. Once approved by the tower, the engine power would be reduced to idle, and a steep turn and descent would follow towards that runway. This would be good fun for the instructor and good learning for the student.

Proper judgment of distance, altitude, and wind conditions were essential. The added safety measure for this maneuver was that the landing was not obligatory, as the clearance to land also included the clearance not to land, and to "go-around," instead. We always made the landing. Why waste a good opportunity?

CRACKED JUGHEAD

A student who was progressing quite nicely towards achieving his license, and who was also very self-motivated, had reached the point of completing the final long cross-country requirement, which would include one leg of 100 nautical miles maximum. It was general policy not to allow any aircraft to fly beyond the 100-mile limit as a precaution, in case of poor weather conditions or mechanical issues. I authorized this student's request to do his long cross-country trip way beyond this limit - to North Carolina, to visit his family. He was quite competent, and had a constructive and serious attitude toward his responsibility as a pilot. I had the utmost respect for him and my compassion prevailed over any other element of my psychological state.

As a flight instructor, safety was extremely paramount, and I regarded it seriously, without wavering or concession. His flight would take him through the Philadelphia, Baltimore and Washington, D.C. airspace. That would be like entering the lion's den and coming out safely at the other end. I prepared him for it, as he was quite capable from practice in the New York area. He needed me to sign him off for the trip, as required by regulations, and I did, especially after confirming that the weather window for his weekend trip was quite good.

He took-off and contacted the radar controller with his intentions once at cruise altitude. The New York controller issued vectors for the most direct route then handed him to the Philadelphia controller, as he was traveling into a new jurisdiction. Each new controller would have already received the destination and route of flight from the previous controller. Eventually, he would speak to a Washington, D.C. controller and finally one in the Raleigh area, until he reached his destination. He arrived safely, closed his flight plan and called me to check-in. He then spent a lovely time with his family for a few days.

On the return trip, he took-off, climbed and leveled off at his cruising altitude, and was in contact with the radar controller in the area. Within the first hour of the flight he encountered an unusually rough engine, and decided to make a precautionary landing at the closest airport. It was a major airport. He had followed the correct procedure as I had taught him. The student contacted the control tower and reported that he was a student pilot and was requesting a priority landing because of a rough engine. Had he declared an emergency the paperwork to follow could have choked both of us. After a descent from a 5,500 feet cruising altitude he landed safely. Fire trucks were lined up at his point of touch down and followed him like shadows to the General Aviation section of the airport. The firefighters didn't get to do that very often and it was good practice for them.

He called me after landing to report the situation. I wondered how he felt, and I asked him. I wanted to know and understand his feelings, especially feelings of fear or anxiety. He explained that he was confident with his ability to make a safe landing and fear was not paramount, inasmuch as he also realized that I was not sitting next to him to handle the situation. He was a good student and relied on his training, which worked well for him. He told me the thought came to him about how I would have felt if the airplane was unable to make the flight back. It was his reaction to the 100-mile rule, and the possible repercussions of such deviation from protocol. I appreciated his concern as to the possible inconvenience of such a situation, with special recognition to him for his Southern genteel and respectfulness. However, it was my decision and I would have to own the consequences.

He was able to arrange for a mechanic to check the engine thoroughly, and nothing was found to be inconsistent with normal operation. We spoke about continuing the trip and he felt comfortable; and that was my main concern. In addition, psychologically it was better for him to get back in the saddle. By taking the bull by the horns and not letting the experience diminish his confidence, he could learn to overcome the negative effects of the experience. It reminded me of the first time I crashed my car; I told myself that I was never going to drive again. I did drive again, and again, albeit much more safely ever after.

He proceeded cautiously to continue the return trip, and climbed to cruise altitude within close proximity to the airport before turning to his course. His return to the base airport was successful, and we were both relieved. It was possible that a slight amount of water had condensed in the tanks overnight and found its way to the carburetor. Water and fuel do not mix well, and the engine would be sure to inform the operator immediately if that had occurred.

Upon the next scheduled inspection of the airplane the mechanic discovered a cracked cylinder. When asked as to the cause, he responded that it could have been from rapid cooling. It was possible that the partial loss of power, plus the introduction of water could have caused it during descent. Performance was not inhibited, but the crack could have expanded and caused the cylinder to fail to a point beyond repair. The smell of burning dollar bills would soon ensue for a complete replacement. After the mechanic detected the crack, he grounded the airplane, as was his duty and responsibility. He reported that the bad jug (a mechanic's term for a cylinder), had to be removed and refinished at a machine shop.

The mechanic removed the cylinder by undoing several bolts at its base and sliding it out. That was; after spark plug wires and other attachments were first removed. Airplane piston engines are designed with the same principle as automobile engines, but with different cylinder arrangements, whereby each airplane cylinder is individually installed onto the engine. This makes it easier to work on an airplane engine. The airplane cylinder could be compared crudely to an opened tin can.

The mechanic asked me to drive the cracked cylinder to the machine shop so as to expedite the completion of the engine. I agreed, as this would save time. In addition, he had already made arrangements with the machine shop for an exchange. Finished cylinders could be matched with the cracked one to verify proper fit and simply exchanged. The mechanic had also informed the machinist that I was the flight instructor for the airplane.

I believed that this machinist had some resentment or disdain for flight instructors. Upon arrival, I had to listen to his lecture regarding the torture I put the engine through during training, from acceleration with full power, followed by sudden power-off at high altitudes. It seemed that he treated engines like they were his babies. He was a man perhaps two decades my senior, and whom I surmised had nuts and bolts in his diet for quite a long time, as it showed on his face. He was stern looking, with an expression that could scare a gorilla. He seemed like a guy not to mess with, or start small talk with. Instead, it was best to just simply swallow the insults and get the heck out of his shop. I gladly agreed with all that he said and left with the refinished cylinder, while muttering to myself the appropriate response to his lecture, for which I had stood there tight-lipped.

As I drove off extremely happy to have a finished cylinder that matched, I continued the response to myself about the lecture I had just listened to. If that jughead thought for one second that I was going to baby an engine during training he would be seriously wrong. That was what training was: maximum applications of power, and at best slow reduction when needed. He sounded like my father, when he reminded me not to torture his tools.

We were two humans on opposite sides of the spectrum, each with our own perspectives. I already knew I was not going to follow all of the advice he offered during his lecture. I was a flight instructor, and what I had to do with an airplane and the engine was part of training, and that was all. To me, a cylinder was just a hunk of steel and aluminum required to perform as I wished. I didn't really have feelings for a piece of metal, but I was, nevertheless, cautious that my negligence could produce a financial penalty. That part got my attention.

UPSIDE-DOWN: IN A SEAT BELT?

Turbulence is difficult to predict, except in high wind conditions, storms, clouds and the vicinity of the jet stream. Clear air turbulence (CAT) is something usually reported by pilots already in flight. For that matter the most accurate weather report comes from a pilot in flight. It is simply called, a pilot report (PIREP). These reports are taken seriously as they are considered to be extremely reliable. Air traffic controllers are obligated to inform other pilots flying in the same airspace what a PIREP states. The PIREP eventually becomes part of the official weather report. When the pilot of an airliner turns on the seat belt sign and informs passengers and cabin crew that the controller provided information about turbulence ahead, it is most likely because of a PIREP.

Turbulence is classified into three main categories - light, moderate, and severe. Pilots are encouraged to understand these classifications when making a report. Light turbulence would be bumpy and choppy, with minor deviations requiring minor corrections. The first recommendation in turbulence is to ensure that all occupants tighten their seat belts. Moderate turbulence occurs when noticeable excursions of airspeed, altitude and direction occur. Pilot input should be constant and deliberate to ensure that the aircraft remains in a controllable state. Pilots are recommended to adjust speed to "maneuvering speed" during turbulence. This allows for the least stress on the aircraft. Severe turbulence is just that; it is severe, and could result in damage to the aircraft and loss of control. It should be avoided completely.

Inexperienced pilots often describe turbulence based on how they feel, and not as defined. This confusion gets transferred to the controller through a PIREP, and then to all the other pilots. Each and every pilot was inexperienced at one time, and some pilots cannot help but make fun of others on the radio for an inaccurate PIREP. They stretch the radio privilege a bit with sarcastic comments. Controllers do not indulge in such communications, even though they may be tempted to. It could put their job in jeopardy.

One afternoon while on final approach, I was informed of a PIREP from the pilot of a preceding airplane. It stated that there was extreme turbulence on short final. There was a hill on the final approach path of this runway at my base airport, and the wind had increased as the day progressed. This condition always caused turbulence, and sometimes it would jostle the airplane around. The best option was to ride it out and not over-control the airplane. That day the PIREP was incorrect, and all pilots at the airport knew it. It was not the controller's job to question a pilot as to his report. The controller's responsibility was to pass the information on to other pilots. All pilots heard the controller broadcast the PIREP as he called it out to "all aircraft on frequency." The pilot behind me replied with a question asking if the guy who reported severe turbulence was hanging upside-down in his seat belt. It called for a good chuckle, and a reminder that because a jolt of wind scared someone, it did not qualify as severe turbulence. But, perhaps it was also not nice to make fun of a fellow.

PINK SLIP + MURDER

The Traffic Collision and Avoidance System (TCAS) was implemented as a technological improvement to safety for aircraft in avoiding mid-air collisions. The system works in a short-range environment when there could be a possibility of a mid-air collision. Pilots could only wish never to have one. But, the sad news is that many TCAS alerts had happened in an environment where they were totally avoidable. TCAS works when one aircraft is within close proximity to another. An alert would be issued to both aircraft directing each to change course and/or altitude in order to avoid a collision. Several incidents have occurred since implementation of the system, with some catastrophic results. Most notably are those, when in hindsight were avoidable.

A foreign airliner flying over Hawaii received a TCAS alert within a radar environment, and with an active radar controller on duty, whose job was to separate targets as his first responsibility. The pilot immediately complied with the directive of the TCAS and alerted his course as directed by the alert. The pilot then contacted the controller on the radio stating that he was altering course as per the TCAS alert. That was good for the airline pilot who avoided a collision, but a clear accusation as to the controller's negligence. I could not be certain about the controller's job after the incident. Pink slip?

A second notable event occurred when a radar controller was handling two airliners over Europe, in the dead of night. They were his only targets, yet they both received a TCAS alert. The rules pertaining to TCAS alerts were different for each airliner, and were based on the country of origin. One was required to follow the alert, while the other was required to follow the directive of the controller. (Some nations do not agree on many issues). This situation placed both aircraft at the same altitude and going in an almost opposite direction. The controller failed to confirm that condition, and perhaps he was also not aware of the different rules.

The pilots thought that the controller had everything under control. But, he was distracted while trying to contact the destination airport by telephone for the benefit of one of the arriving airliners, because it was late in the evening. Some airports in Europe close at a certain time in the evening, and adherence to this regulation is strictly enforced. The consideration for the rule relates to sleep disturbance from jet noise for residents living near the airport area, as published in the findings of the World Health Organization. Decades ago, I was a passenger on an airliner headed for a European airport that was closed. We had to wait for personnel to return to the airport. They even had to turn the lights back on in order to process documents and handle baggage. It would seem that every culture forms rules for human rights, including the human right to sleep in peace. It is all about being human.

As the two airliners neared each other, the controller pointed out traffic to both by radio, and asked for a visual confirmation. Both replied in the negative. The airliners were approaching each other in an almost opposite direction, which meant that the closing speed would have been approximately 1,000 miles per hour; an equivalent of one mile in four seconds. That meant that the pilots would have had to make a visual identification and turn away from each other within the ten seconds it would take to see a target, to the time it would fill the windshield. In addition, if they made a mistake and they both turned in the same direction, the collision would not be avoided, only delayed.

The two aircraft collided, where the odds of two objects colliding in such vast airspace were totally astronomical, and could have been avoided by a simple turn by only one aircraft. The controller was eventually blamed. Unfortunately, the angry father of one of the passengers assassinated him some time later. It was very sad for all concerned, indeed. But again, it is human behavior, and it is not always logical.

CUMULONIMBUS

Aviation's worst single weather hazard is undoubtedly thunderstorms. They have a huge record of extracting tin cans out of the air and crushing them. Thunderstorms start when moist air continually rises because of heat energy from the ground and in the atmosphere. It is the reason thunderstorms are most prevalent during summer months. The rising air would cool, and then fall, only to rise again with the already rising air. Eventually, the top of the storms would condense, and rain would fall. If the storms rise high to the freezing level ice would form. As the rising air falls and rises repeatedly inside the small columns of these storms, the ice particles would get larger and fall to the ground as hail. The size of the hailstones could be a reasonable measure of the storm's intensity. Storms could reach heights of up to ten miles while the bases are only a few miles wide.

The beginning of thunderstorm formation is called the updraft stage, which is a cumulus cloud. Airplanes could accrue some nice and free altitude gains with the updrafts. The cumulus would continue to grow higher, while assembling enormous amounts of moisture. When the storms mature, the tops fall back to the earth forming tremendous downdrafts, in which airplanes have no chance of escape. When the air reaches the ground it has nowhere to go except out in all directions. It would be like pouring water on the floor, which would spread in every direction. The outward rushing air provides the first sign of danger for pilots. The increased headwind during landing would seem like a blessing, but the landing would have to be expedited, especially if the storm was moving towards the airport. Soon after the rush of outward air, pilots would find themselves in the downdraft column of air, called microburst. That would be "Houdini" time. The best way to avoid the dangers of thunderstorms would be to avoid thunderstorms completely. It is as simple as that, and no magic required.

It was unfortunate that the science of thunderstorms was not studied until after several accidents had happened. Notable, was one crash in New York, and one in Dallas, due to thunderstorms. I followed both of these cases closely, as they prompted investigators to focus on avoidance of dangerous weather, especially microburst. After these accidents, sensors were installed at major airports to improve safety, and "microburst" was added to the Aviation weather vocabulary.

In addition, one problem originally arose as simply procedural, where pilots were responsible for all decisions regarding weather, while Air Traffic Control was responsible for providing traffic information only. Airports would stay open as long as the visibility and height of clouds were suitable for approaches. This led pilots to fly into thunderstorms because it appeared only as heavy rain. Unfortunately, being able to see did not necessarily mean it was safe. Since those accidents occurred, procedures have changed. A joint effort to provide a wider safety margin was instituted where ATC would prompt aircraft to hold outside the area of thunderstorms, or proceed to an alternate airport. Inasmuch as this cancelled the pilots' authority to make all decisions, a safety margin was established that benefited everyone.

DAY AT THE BEACH

Landmasses near bodies of water tend to cause the formation of local weather conditions because of the two factors that form weather, which are, moisture, and the uneven heating of the earth's surface. The Atlantic coastline of the United States runs north and south generally, and areas where heating from the sun becomes intense, such as Florida, there are strong weather patterns. Land heats up faster than water, and also cools down faster. As the heat over land rises, a vacuum is formed, simply from the evacuation of air. The vacuum gets filled with air drawn in from the ocean. This air flowing from the ocean towards inland is called a sea breeze, and is welcoming for beach goers, surfers and kite fliers. In strong sea breezes sunbathers could also get sandblasted, and swimmers pounded by waves. Important for pilots is that they are aware of the sea breeze, which would be the most important factor in the runway selection. Because of the sea breeze conditions along the Florida coastline, many of the runways are aligned in an east/west direction.

At nightfall, the land cools quickly, and the sea breeze would diminish, quite often into a light breeze, or become a land breeze, where the wind blows back towards the ocean. This could spell trouble. The thunderstorms that would have formed over the center of the state from the high heat and humidity would now drift eastward, and out to sea. The best option when flying while thunderstorms are caged during the day is to be sure not to get caught offshore when they become un-caged, and begin their eastward march, even with a seaplane. A submarine plane may be acceptable, if it could become submerged for safety, when and if that becomes available, perhaps for a certain British secret agent with a double zero status.

SITTING DUCK

One piece of advice I offered during taxi to the runway for takeoff was to keep a lookout for traffic on final approach to the runway. Since the route on the taxiway would be towards the takeoff and landing edge of the runway, all the airplanes in the air that were either on final approach, or preparing to enter final approach, would be clearly visible during the day or night. The ability to observe incoming air traffic offered the advantage that in the event the controller made a mistake and issued a takeoff clearance to us while an airplane was close in, we would have the advantage of correcting the situation. I had made many such corrections before, and have avoided unpleasant situations. I also decided to adopt certain techniques that would enhance safety.

One of the clearances, which I always encouraged my students to refuse, especially at night, was the "position and hold" clearance, which was to go into takeoff position on the runway and wait for the takeoff clearance. This type of clearance placed me in a precarious position, like a sitting duck. I always wanted to be in charge of my situation and would prefer to be certain that any clearance issued did not come with a possible conflict. I simply did not trust another human being with my life. Instead of the "position and hold" clearance, I would prefer to request an immediate takeoff clearance instead, after I could ascertain that there were no conflicts. I did not like the idea of occupying a perfectly usable runway, especially when it was in use. At night, this situation warrants extreme caution.

The unfortunate condition of pilots who simply comply without question came to pass one evening when this exact precaution was not taken. At a major Southern California airport, an airliner was cleared for "position and hold," and the pilot complied. He taxied into takeoff position on the runway and sat there, awaiting a takeoff clearance. A takeoff clearance never came. Minutes after waiting, another jetliner landed on this sitting duck, as the controller cleared that airliner to land on the same runway. The pilot could not see any incoming traffic behind him, and perhaps did not listen on the radio that another airliner had received a clearance to land on the same runway he was sitting on. The controller had forgotten that there was a sitting duck, and cleared the other airliner to a collision. The back-side of airplanes are not very lit up, and thus the pilot of the incoming airliner did not recognize that there was a sitting duck, as all the lights may have seemed like airport lights. I can compare the "position and hold" clearance to someone standing on a train track, and who must always be vigilant that a train could be coming at any moment.

WRONG SURFACE

Night flying offered the great advantage of having the skies to myself, pretty much most of the time. Also, turbulence often diminished at night, and the scene was beautiful. The disadvantage was that the options for emergency landings disappeared, as the light of day faded into darkness and blacked out the ground. That was the risk of night flying, which must be accepted for such activity. Night flying to me was literally like night and day. The entire scenery became different as only lighted objects could be seen. Navigation lights could identify aircraft, and their direction of travel ascertained visually by the movement of those lights.

A rotating beacon, similar to a marine lighthouse beacon, is used to positively identify an airport at night. For a civil land airport, the beacon would have one green light followed by one white light, and repeating continuously. The light is angled upward for pilots to see. Too often pilots use other means of identification, especially within close proximity, or within suspected close proximity to the airport. The latter usually spelled trouble. The identification of runways are the white lights lining both edges, which eventually turn to red at the far end. Taxiway lights are blue on both sides.

On a clear night, while conducting navigation to another airport with a student pilot, I learned how anxiety could affect judgment. It was the student's first night flight, and he was excited. He was well briefed on the airport identification process before we left the ground. However, shortly after takeoff and level off, he suspected that he had reached the nearby airport. It was only a few miles away. He proceeded to set up his approach to two rows of white lights, which he told me was the runway. I allowed him some latitude, as well as some altitude, until he lined up and descended a bit. In a short time, I had to alert him as to his situation, and then break off his descent to the unidentified airport he concocted. He discovered that he was approaching a straight portion of a road that was well lit up.

I would not say that I enjoyed watching him make a fool of himself, as he regressed, with embarrassment. What I really enjoyed was that he had learned in an effective way, never to ever forget to identify an airport positively before descending. The only comment I needed to make was a reminder of what we had discussed on the ground a few minutes earlier, about airport identification. He was an educated man, and he understood his error. He was really anxious and excited to land at night, and I believe that his anxiety could have contributed to his error. These opportunities rarely presented themselves. But, when they do, they become valuable lessons, which help me with the psychological aspects of teaching. I doubt that my student, who did become a licensed pilot, would ever forget to use the rotating beacon to identify an airport in his future night flights.

At a Northern California airport, during nighttime, an airliner made an approach to a taxiway, instead of the runway. The pilot most likely did not see, or could not identify the taxiway, with its blue lights, and certainly neglected to identify the runway, which had white lights. The tower controller most likely could not see the airliner approaching the taxiway and could not issue a corrective clearance. The airliner did not land. The pilot aborted the approach and climbed out for a "go-around," finally returning for a landing on the runway.

The pilot most likely did not see the other airliners lined up for takeoff on the same taxiway he was approaching, as they most probably had their landing lights off. Pilots train for their licenses by complying with all the regulatory requirements, but in addition, some training in courtesy always proved helpful. I made it a point to teach every student, while waiting on a taxiway for takeoff at night, and facing the landing traffic, to keep the landing light off, so as not to interfere with the flight visibility of the landing pilot. Most pilots learned this as well. It would be like dimming the headlights for oncoming traffic while driving. Please do it.

ALTITUDE UNKNOWN

There are more general aviation airplanes in the sky at any given time than airliners. General aviation includes training, charter, sightseeing, banner towing, parachute jumping, crop dusting, fire retarding, experimental, dinner trips, hundred-dollar hamburger lunch trips, business trips, and any other activity humans could find to do with airplanes. It is not unusual for mixtures of these types of traffic, along with airliners, to form conflicts, which are caused, not only because of the differences in speed, but also rules and communications requirements with ATC. Often, it is the results of accident investigation that prompt improvements in aircraft separation technology.

A collision of an airliner with a small plane over Cerritos, California would prompt an almost immediate change for improvement. On this particular day, the radar controller could see both targets, but he could not ascertain the altitude of the small plane, as that pilot was not required to communicate with him, according to the rules. In this case only the airliner would be receiving alerts. It was at a time when there was much heads down work for the airline pilots as they prepared for a landing. Most likely the pilots did not look diligently for the traffic as alerted by the controller. The collision was imminent since both aircraft were at the same altitude, and traveling towards each other. If the controller could have ascertained the altitude of the small plane he could have instructed the airliner to change altitude and avoid the collision.

The FAA thereafter mandated that all aircraft within certain dense airspace, and within certain altitudes, must have a transponder that sends an altitude-encoding signal for the display on the controller's radar screen. With this technology controllers could see the altitudes of all air traffic, whether in radio contact or not. Traffic alerts would still be issued to pilots via the radio, and pilot confirmation of visual sighting makes a controller's day. There is nothing better for safety than eye contact, even at a four way stop sign on the ground while driving. It is always good to verify that the other driver is not in a hurry, and who simply ignores the presence of other vehicles. Safety is everyone's responsibility, and it is never a good thing to be "dead right," and still be dead.

THE MOUNTAIN BETWEEN

In Southern California, late one night, a charter jet needed to fly East to its base location. There were no passengers on this flight, so the pilots had the flexibility to decide what type of flight plan was most expeditious. They filed under Instrument Flight Rules (IFR), but could not get a clearance by radio on the ground because the tower was closed. They decided to take-off and contact the radar controller for a clearance once in the air, which was perfectly legal. As they climbed out they made radio contact, and the controller acknowledged radar contact. However, he did not have a clearance as yet, which would have been generated by the computer system. Herein lied the problem. During the time that the aircraft was flying while waiting for an IFR clearance, all navigation decisions as to altitude and direction had to be made by the pilots, as they were operating under Visual Flight Rules (VFR). The controller would only issue alerts for other air traffic in the area, until he had the clearance for them to follow. The one variable that changed the dynamics of this flight and sealed its fate was that the flight was at night, when only lighted objects could be seen. The pilots flew into a mountain. They had neglected to accept their responsibility for navigation under VFR, and assumed the controller had their backs, thinking he would also issue advisories or vectors for terrain. But, that was not his job. He was an Air Traffic Controller, not a terrain obstruction controller. The IFR clearance they were all waiting for would have placed the jet at a safe altitude and course, and the controller's responsibility at such time, and only at such time, would have been to offer vectors, to place the airplane at that safe altitude and course. In the meantime they were on their own, and these professional pilots did not realize that they had that responsibility.

When pilots fly under IFR regularly they are usually in constant contact with ATC, and receive directives/vectors as such. This tends to form a dependence on ATC, which sometimes causes confusion about areas of responsibility, while at the same time breeding complacency with pilots. All clearances issued by ATC are generated without conflict with terrain or air traffic. However, until a clearance is issued, pilots beware, and certainly be aware that there is responsibility for you, as you are on your own.

RUNNING ON EMPTY

In the mid-nineteen-nineties, an airliner from South America was on approach to JFK airport in New York in low visibility conditions. The pilots did not see the airport on the first attempt and executed a missed approach. The aircraft was directed to fly several miles out of the area, and to be sequenced back for landing. Imagine a multitude of airliners being sequenced as far out as 25 to 50 miles, and this airliner would have to join in somewhere in the line. This airliner finally made it back for the second approach and crashed only a few miles from the airport. There was no fuel on board.

The pilot had two options that could have saved the day. After the first attempt to land he could have declared an emergency, or a fuel emergency. Pilots tend to resist these options, as they would have required paperwork and reports, causing questions regarding the airline's procedures. In this case, hope and prayer did not work. The pilot should have at least informed the controller of the low fuel situation. Most likely that would have solved the issue, as they are very cooperative in urgent situations, and without paperwork, only mano-a-mano.

STRAIGHT IN PLEASE

The pilot of an airliner on its way from North America to a South American destination made contact with the Air Traffic Controller and was issued a straight in approach to a particular runway; with the aid of a ground based navigation station. The frequency of the station was entered into the autopilot and the airplane made a turn immediately towards that station, as expected. Autopilots are subservient to pilots always, and without question, of course. After several minutes, the pilots questioned why the autopilot made a turn when it should have been a straight in approach. Minor turns for straight in approaches are not uncommon, but this was a huge turn. The pilots discovered their mistake; they had entered the frequency of a different navigation station - an incorrect one.

It was not unusual for pilots to simply dial in a frequency of the ground navigation station and simply fly it. The autopilot follows what the pilot enters. The problem occurs when they enter the incorrect frequency. The verification method, as I taught every pilot candidate, was to turn the volume up on the frequency of the navigation station selected and listen to the voice or Morse code identifier for the station, which was printed on the charts. Failure to do this could have the airplane flying to the wrong station, which was what happened on this flight. The pilots corrected the navigation error and the autopilot turned the airplane immediately back on course, directly to the airport, from that position.

The pilots thought all was well, and that they had corrected the problem. Minutes later, the airliner crashed into the side of a mountain. The pilots did not see the mountain as there were no lights on it, and the flight was at night. The initial error was what started the crisis. The first turn to the incorrect station placed the mountain between the airplane and the airport. When the error was corrected, the autopilot flew the direct route to the airport from that point, but it did not know it would be through the mountain. Autopilots do not have eyes or noses, and as such, they can neither see, nor smell trouble.

CORRECTION! CORRECTION! CORRECTION!!

Autopilots were designed to relieve pilots of the many tasks in aircraft control. They are often used to keep an aircraft level, or at a certain speed, or on a certain course. Some autopilots are connected to navigation equipment to facilitate control of the route to be flown. Others can even land the airplane by controlling all the functions of a human pilot. Most often the autopilot does a better landing than the pilot. In fact, autopilots do not make mistakes unless there is a malfunction beyond their ability to control the aircraft. They do a good job of relieving pilots of the control burden even during a failure of an essential component. For example, if one engine on a two engine aircraft loses power or fails completely, the autopilot would apply rudder in the direction of the good engine to counteract the adverse yaw induced by this asymmetrical trust.

Problems occur when pilots turn off the autopilot while it is making a correction. When the autopilot is disengaged the pilot would have to make all the corrections that the autopilot was making in order to fly right. Sometimes pilots are not aware of all the corrections being made by the autopilot, and the aircraft goes into an unusual condition referred to as an "upset." When upsets occur pilot skill is often the best way to correct them. Here is where training comes in. Several upset scenarios can be introduced during training so that pilots are able to recognize them and make immediate corrections. One upset that I showed every pilot candidate was how to recover from a stalled configuration. Another scenario included inducing an unusual attitude, then instructing them to recover to normal level flight. The application of effective rudder to counteract induced rolling during some maneuvers was also very important. Steep dives and loss of power are others. The immediate action to correct the unusual flight condition is what I looked for. This immediate response is what saves upsets when an autopilot is turned off, as the pilot is able to recognize the condition and take immediate action.

One notable incident regarding an upset was analyzed and documented. It was a jumbo jet of a foreign airline over the Pacific Ocean on its way to the west coast of the USA. One engine failed, and the autopilot made the best correction for the resulting asymmetrical trust. However in that model of aircraft at the time the rudder was not connected to the autopilot control functions. As such, the autopilot was not able to correct the situation completely, as ailerons do not have sufficient effectiveness. The airplane became erratic as the pilots desperately tried to figure out the problem. All that had to be done was an application of rudder in the direction of the good engines.

All airplanes, from small training types to jumbo jets are controlled the same way, and this type of training would usually be done during the early years of any pilot training program. However, pilots tend to depend on the autopilot for flight control and navigation to the extent that they become complacent, while resisting the almost instinctive benefits of their training that could save the day.

The pilot in this jumbo jet decided to disengage the autopilot. This could have been a good decision if the correct application of rudder had been applied. However, the pilots never touched the rudder pedals. The aircraft went into a steep bank and rolled over through an inverted condition while the nose was pointed straight down at the ocean. Prevention of this condition is exactly what pilots are intensely trained for, especially if the condition occurs on takeoff. In this critical stage of the flight, immediate response to any asymmetrical trust issue must be promptly addressed, or the airplane will roll until inverted and with a nose down attitude as one wing (with the good engine) produces more lift and chases the other wing into a corkscrew towards the ground.

After wrestling with the aircraft and stressing the airframe to the point of damage, they regained control in time to avoid a big splash in the ocean. The aircraft eventually landed safely with all the scared passengers. Inspection of the aircraft revealed serious visible damage to the tail section. Further inspection of damage may have placed it in an un-airworthy condition. Good for parts only. Investigations eventually revealed the cause to be the pilots' lack of the correct response to the flight condition that was induced by the loss of power from one engine. The question now is, "did the pilots all forget that the rudder was not connected to the autopilot?" Human memory or recurrent training may have contributed to this incident.

BIG APPLE EVENING

Two pilots on a charter jet landed at Philadelphia airport on the last revenue leg for that day. The aircraft had to be repositioned to Teterboro airport, about a hundred miles north of their position, for another flight. They filed a flight plan for a flight of less than 30 minutes at 27,000 feet. That would be like trying to get to the other end of your house by walking upstairs, then across the top floor, then walking downstairs to ground level again. In addition the traffic density in the area of New York could have well forbade such an altitude. They were given a clearance for 4,000 feet from end to end. It's like staying on the ground floor of the house to get to the other side.

The flight took-off and soon reached Newark, when the radar controller told the pilots to contact the tower at Teterboro.

The weather was fine, but the winds were strong. The airplane was cleared to land, but it was not flying the course for the runway. A right turn followed by a left turn would have aligned the jet to the runway. The airplane came close to the airport then made two very sharp turns to align with the runway and crashed into a parking lot.

The voice recorder revealed some problems. The dialog in the cockpit was not conducive to safety. There were quite a bit of accusations directed towards the radar controller from the copilot as he spoke to the pilot. The copilot was conducting the flight, and he seemed to have a sense of urgency and hot-headedness. The controller had asked about their airspeed, as he must have noticed that they had exceeded the 250-knot limit below ten thousand feet. The co-pilot was venting to the pilot about the frustration of not arriving sooner, with fault directed at the controller, and was concerned that there could be a report of a possible speed violation. The co-pilot must have kept up the speed on the jet in order to get his evening started in the Big Apple.

Perhaps a bit of common sense could have helped them. If a trip took only twenty minutes, how much time could they have saved by going thirty miles per hour faster, or even fifty miles per hour faster? Even without a calculator it could be ascertained that to place oneself, and others, at risk would not be a valuable trade off for the few seconds or minutes of time gained. The pilots' lack of situational awareness, coupled by serious emotional issues, contributed to their demise. Ego, arrogance, anger, anxiety and urgency do not belong in the two front seats of any airplane in flight. A slight bit of fear could regulate non-productive emotions. I always looked for some fear in every student.

There were few special words I would leave with newly minted pilots as I offered my congratulations. After the pat on the back, I would explain that they had just acquired a license to kill. I intended to startle them into the remembrance of their responsibility to passengers. With laughter from the confused look on their faces, I would offer some consolation that they should be proud of their accomplishment. Secondly, I would encourage them to build experience and enjoy the privilege of being a pilot. Further, I would explain that ego did not belong in an airplane. Finally, I advised that complacency was contrary to safety and that safety was not an accident.

SLIP SLIDING AWAY

It was a rainy day at LaGuardia Airport when an airliner was cleared for takeoff on a very wet runway, with standing water. Airplane wheels don't spin with power like automobiles; the wheels simply roll as the jet engines move the airplane. In this case it is not difficult to take-off on a wet or icy runway, but careful and positive steering control must be maintained. On wet surfaces the problem of hydroplaning could ruin a perfect day.

The airliner began its takeoff roll and was accelerating down the runway. It would have been fine had it taken-off. But, the copilot, who was conducting the flight, was uncertain of obtaining the correct airspeed in time, and he decided to abort the takeoff. Herein came the major problem. Upon deceleration, especially with brake application, the tires began to hydroplane, effectively rendering the braking action: zero. The airplane was floating on the runway, at least until the speed was reduced below the hydroplaning threshold. Unfortunately, that did not happen soon enough, and the airplane slid off the runway and into the water. LaGuardia is known as the "aircraft carrier" of an airport because the runways are not very long, and all of them, but one, stick out into water. The airliner stopped with the front partially submerged in water, while the rear remained on the airport surface. It was cracked in two parts at that point. I was able to view this aircraft during taxi, as a passenger on an airliner, the day after the accident.

The captain was blamed for not exercising command authority, meaning that he did not supervise the copilot. The most important consideration on a wet runway is not during acceleration, but deceleration. The force on the tires would be increased from torque, and hydroplaning would be almost certain once the hydroplaning speed was reached. Both pilots should have known and calculated the hydroplaning speed in order to make additional consideration on aborting the takeoff.

Automobile drivers also could encounter hydroplaning in standing water. This is called dynamic hydroplaning, and is caused when water fills all the threading of the tire so as to render it, "effectively," smooth, while at the same time resisting the tire to the point that the tire is lifted off the surface. The tire literally "floats," and does not touch the surface firmly. The drive wheels of the automobile could begin to spin without traction. The front wheels could lose directional control, as the tires appear to skid on the water's surface. Most times slowing down would solve the problem as the water would be diverted away from the tires, while keeping them firmly on the road surface.

The speed for dynamic hydroplaning is not very high. It could be calculated by multiplying the square root of the tire pressure by the number 9. Knowing the hydroplaning speed of an automobile would be good for drivers also. Most tires for passenger cars are inflated to approximately 35 pounds per square inch. For convenience, if we use 36, the square root would be 6. Multiplying 6 by 9 results in 54 miles per hour. To be driving on the safe side, the hydroplaning speed should be considered 50 miles per hour for the average automobile. Slow down below that speed for safety on a wet roadway.

CLEAR SKIES ABOVE

Airline passengers are briefed prior to each flight, as required by aviation rules worldwide, on the use of seat belts and decompression. Airliners are pressurized with air so that passengers do not pass out from lack of oxygen. (Some flight attendants may not mind such a flight.) If a cabin depressurizes suddenly because of a valve failure or other structural issue, a mist would form, as the moisture in the cabin air condensed, because such amount of moisture could not be supported as a vapor under the lower pressure. The pressure inside the cabin after depressurization would be the pressure at the altitude of the aircraft, which may not be supportive of life, and oxygen masks would have to be deployed.

The innovation of the pressurized cabin decades ago during the advent of the jet engine enhanced the flying experience by allowing airliners to fly higher and faster in order to reduce travel time. It was called, the "Jet Age." The first aircraft designed with this concept was plagued with failures, as the cabin pressure exceeded the strength of the structure of the airplane, and it simply exploded in flight. This design flaw was corrected, and the airliners of today are perfectly safe and comfortable.

One issue with pressurization would not surface until decades after the first failure of the pressurized cabin. A discovery was made with airliners that were used for short distance flights. These aircraft would be pressurized for takeoff then depressurized upon landing. The frequency of this procedure, because of the short flights, caused the cabin to expand and contract more often than normal. One such flight caused a cabin to rupture. A small section of the top of the airplane literally flew off as the securing hardware and rivets simply gave way. Luckily, the airplane was still controllable, and it landed safely. Metal fatigue was attributed to the final conclusion as to the cause of the situation. Manufacturers learned from incidents such as this so that modifications could be made to improve safety. Human endeavor is always a learning experience.

SEE AND AVOID

FAA law requires the separation of traffic in any condition to be done by seeing and avoiding, as far as possible, considering weather conditions. Simply put, it means looking outside for traffic. Pilots with radar help from ATC often become complacent and depend too much on the radar controller for directives. While the controller is clearing a path, it allows the pilots to presume that there is no traffic. Bird strikes become the issue in this situation. Even though uncommon, they are in most cases purely avoidable.

Two birds may be difficult to see, but a flock is like a starship. Birds, especially geese, may do forty to fifty miles per hour at best in flight, but an airplane travels several times that speed. Birds do not fly into airplanes; airplanes fly into birds when pilots do not see them.

Geese are large animals and sometimes show up on primary radar, especially when there is a large flock. Perhaps in the future some geese could be tagged such that when flying they could amplify the radar return for a controller to see.

UP AND DOWN

Two notable incidents from which movies were made have been widely publicized. Both were caused by human error because of miscalculation and risk taking. The Hindenburg was an airship that was filled with hydrogen, which is one of the most explosive gases. The airship was to be filled with helium, an inert gas, but the government commerce control did not allow availability. The decision to fill with hydrogen would prove catastrophic, after a spark from a storm ignited it and sent it upwards in flames.

The Titanic, on the other hand, was designed to be unsinkable, with such precaution implemented into the design. Perhaps the ship was unsinkable as a seagoing vessel for passengers, but it was not designed as an icebreaker. When difficult situations present themselves, human ingenuity often cannot remedy the crisis that follows.

It is believed by investigators that accidents and human error could be traced along a line of continuous failures. In the case of the Hindenburg the first failure was to fill it with hydrogen. The second was to expose it to a lightning storm. The people who built and operated the airship knew very well about the dangers of hydrogen, yet they decided to go forward with the venture. It is human risk taking.

The maiden voyage of the Titanic was scheduled for a winter crossing, when icebergs were known to be present in the Atlantic. The second failure was that the high speed of the ship at night, and in fog, made it difficult for the lookout seaman to see the iceberg in time to issue a warning for corrective action.

LET US PRAY

With all the safety systems we could institute, safety is never guaranteed. Humans still make mistakes; it is our nature. To err is human. Some people pray when traveling, to relieve fear and anxiety, or perhaps they pray that God would save them in the event of an accident. I am not sure what criteria God would use to save only selected individuals. Perhaps only the ones who pray would be saved from injury in an accident. Perhaps those who pray could induce additional safety during travel. It would seem proper for those who pray, that they pray for everyone, while paying attention to safety information and measures that could save them in the event of a mishap.

ASSESSMENT/ UNDERWRITING

Risk can be determined by the amount of our activities. Insurance companies assess risk for drivers with the amount and type of driving conducted. A lower risk on the scale means less driving; it is simple. A man who stays in his house all day is unlikely to be struck by a car. But, contrarily I have heard of airplanes landing on top of houses. Life is not without risk.

It is understandable that as the intensity increases on high-risk activities, a corresponding level of mistakes and mishaps would be expected. Activities in professions such as astronauts, police, pilots, firefighters and the military lend themselves to higher accident and causality statistics. Human error with these professions and other high-risk activities would be significant. Aviation has a lower tolerance for safety, but is still very safe. Hindsight is the best tool available to analyze incidents, accidents and mistakes; it makes it as clear as 20/20.

Logical analysis brings out better understanding, while common sense most often could be the sixth sense that could save the day. Please be safe.

Chapter Six

MA AND PA

"A reflection of life lived"

Oh, mother, mother, where art thou? Oh, mother, where have you gone? Your child still needs you. You are the healer, the comforter, and the nurturer. There is no one else like you. There is only one you. No one can take your place. But, you have left this place. I do not see you anymore. You do not bring me hot cocoa when I have a fever. You do not put your hand on my back when I go to sleep. I do not feel your comfort any longer. Oh Ma. Oh Mama. Oh Mom, why have you left me? I know you love me and you care about me, but I do not feel your warm touch anymore. Or do I? Silly me. Of course you are here with me, how could I forget? My memory could never allow me to forget you Ma. You are by my side anytime I want, or need; all I have to do is think about you. Thanks Ma.

In all the years I have lived I have not met a more genuine woman than my mother. I needed to say that not only because it is true for me, but also because I owe that to her. I never told her those words, inasmuch as I felt the emotion. I also know that she knew what I felt. She had the most genuine and sweet smile that was like a hypnotic beam attracting friends, family and even strangers. Her smile commanded the attention of many people, including passers-by in some foreign places she visited. Strangers would stop and talk to her with a

213

sense of curiosity about her. I miss this woman in my life. I miss my mother.

She was the epicenter of the lives of many, not just her children's. She was the matriarch for all the neighbors' children, all the children in the family, and all the women in the village. She was their confidant, their advisor, and their friend. She never relented from what she considered her duty - to help others, especially women. I never saw my mother physically or mentally exhausted from her duties; the duties she acquired all by herself. She was always there, and always watching over her offspring, and all children and women, all around. I took her for granted during my youth, and my youthful indiscretion got the best of me. I have now become a grown man who still misses his mother.

FAST TRACK

My mother was a young woman when she married the man she barely knew, and ten years her senior. The village in the nineteen-thirties was a different time. There was only casual courtship, until the parties decide to go all in. There was no in-between. My father however, had a ten-year head start. He was a man from the town, and he was a man about town. He played musical instruments, like the violin, and he danced well. Those ten years would come to play in their lives together.

My father had his glory before he met my mother. My grandmother told us some of it. He had done the stints of staying out late with friends, and jumping through the window in the night so as not to wake anyone. He avoided reprimand by his clandestine behavior. It was his age of youthful play and he played with the big boys, and perhaps the big girls, but no one could ever know; he kept that private, and so he was entitled.

My mother had to wait a bit after their marriage, until my father accepted his role as husband, and then as father. She was patient, and he eventually changed, for good, and for goodness. But, not before she went with him to social events where he would be dancing, and she would be sitting, with child in arms. She told us so. She could not dance anyway. I presume that she enjoyed herself, and hoped for the best. I would think that she did not complain either. Perhaps she felt privileged to be married to an experienced and popular man in the town.

She was a country girl, and she knew she was no challenge for the town culture. Her family had a different heritage than most of the population. They probably had some ancestry to the people of the old silk trade. They were natural at becoming hucksters and farmers. They were very industrious with a natural affinity to business dealings, and deal making, but the suave of the townsfolk was not in their personalities.

TOUGH TIMES

My parents lived through both World Wars. The second war would have been more significant since they were older, and already had children. I have heard accounts of scarcity of food supplies and the rationing of goods. The news came twice daily from England over short-wave signals that were picked up by the local radio station. The Caribbean was patrolled by war ships and warplanes because of the precious cargo needed by the British and the Americans. Oil and bauxite from South America and the Caribbean were carefully guided through to ports in America. Cuba was on the American side of the war effort, and formed a formidable barrier of protection to the Gulf of Mexico. German and Italian effort to disrupt the supply of oil and bauxite from South America and the Caribbean were thwarted. These were some of the small intricacies of history that could have changed all of human history. But, it is history, and it must stay as such.

The bauxite was smelted to extract the precious aluminum needed for the thousands of warplanes to be built, and it came from the British colony where Ma and Pa lived; the place where I was born years after the war. The Caribbean Sea and the Panama Canal were strategic, and well protected. My parents were in one of the safest places. Supply ships found their way easily to support the population that never resisted, or complained about war, but simply cooperated and complied.

The proximity to the Caribbean, in addition to having the best grade of bauxite in this British colony meant the sightings of warplanes above. One landed in the pasture of the village not far from our house. It either ran out of fuel, or the pilot lost his bearing. That was excitement to the local people. They had never before seen an airplane on the ground. All of this happened before I was born, and I enjoyed listening to all those who told the stories, and the many versions of it as well. It is amazing to me that four humans could see and hear the same thing, and yet there would be four versions of that same thing. Welcome home to humanity.

DON'T MESS WITH MA

My mother was simply tough. No one intimidated her. No one got in her way, and she always got her way. On occasions where my father would observe my mother during a negotiation for a purchase of something for the house, he would be battling two emotions; one of subtle embarrassment, and the other; respect for my mother. Finally, he would accept the way she was, and consider her admirable. Her children were also not spared from her negotiation skills. When we needed something, or wanted to go somewhere, timing was important. We had to approach her when she was in a good mood, or busy with something else. We learned the tricks and mastered the system. We were children, and we learned fast. As soon as she would approve our request for something or somewhere to go, we hightailed out of sight, just in case she changed her mind a moment later. If she happened to say something as we departed with the travel visa she just issued, we would pretend not to hear. Our focus was intensely on our mission.

Ma was as strong as an ox, gentle as a lamb, and as firm as jelly, with her sons. We got away with anything and everything, but she was tough on the girls. We outsmarted her and tricked the poor woman into confusion, to the point that she relented her authority, such that the final decision on what we wanted would be ours. She was helpless with the mastery of young boys wanting to have their way. Poor thing. She also had to accept the blame for any of our misgivings when Pa found out, since she was the approval officer for our actions. But, she also knew how to play him. She had her own talent for survival.

We walked barefoot everywhere, in the yard and to the shops. We were children, and we did not care. At nightfall, we all assembled by the doorway for feet washing. It was barefoot in the house by the authority of the masters - Ma and Pa. Barefoot meant washed and clean feet only. My mother would inspect our feet and reject any abbreviated washes with a U-turn command. Everyone wanted to be first in the door, not that it mattered; we all ate dinner at the same time and at the same table. As I got older, shoes were purchased for outings and for school. It would be the first time I learned what a callus was.

COEXISTENCE

My mother was happy to be with my father. She got to know and accept him; his routines, his likes and dislikes, and especially the importance of his doctrine. He was very firm, proper and mannerly. He did not speak loudly, but when he spoke everyone listened. Perhaps acceptance would be the cornerstone of their union. Ma had a very peaceful co-existence with Pa, and she complied with all his requests as best as she could. There were some instances where she would just shrug him off because she considered his demands to be unreasonable and excessive. She would simply dismiss him, walk away, and start muttering something under her breath. That was how she asserted her territorial boundary, and that was how Pa knew where the no-crossing zone was. Everyone has limits. Still, with occasional disputes, she was successful in being calm and peaceful in all situations. My father exuded that state as well. I never heard them in angry discourse with each other. They were happy together, especially because each knew the responsibility undertaken with the role each had assumed. My father was the breadwinner, and my mother was the homemaker, and that was it; no further questions.

My father ate the food that was served to him and he never asked for more. He believed that he was given his share, as everyone else had a share. Ma would be sure to examine all plates heading to the kitchen after a meal. Edible food was not allowed to pass her. Nothing was thrown out except that which was not fit for human consumption. Ma would feed the un-edibles to the chickens and ducks, as they ate anything and everything. We would watch them all rush to the food as each tried to claim their share. Somehow human food tasted better than the corn and husk they had to eat daily. I couldn't blame them.

If my father had to enter the kitchen it would never be for something big to eat. He believed that cooking and serving food was the responsibility of the woman of the house, or one of her subordinates; one of my sisters. He entered the kitchen only on rare occasions when he needed to get something quickly, such as a spoonful of honey. I could characterize that my father considered the kitchen like prison; if he must go in he would get out as soon as possible. It was the norms of society back in the old days; very old fashioned would be the best description.

FEMALE SIDE

I grew up around many females. In addition to my mother, I had many sisters, aunts, neighbors, family and friends. One significant memory I have is being rocked to bed at night, when I must have been four years old. It would be either my mother, or one of my sisters, on the rocking chair upstairs. I have come to believe that women are the true masters of the human race. They bear all the offspring, and provide nurturing, training and support. When male offspring grow up they look for women to mate with, for family, and again women become in charge. Inasmuch as my father, or another man, could assert their power, it is mothers and women who possess the true intrinsic power - the power of instinct, to raise the young and protect them. It is the ultimate power.

I was fortunate to have had the experience that would guide me, in the future, to have the utmost regard and respect for women, considering that I grew up in the male dominated macho world of the village. The influence of the women in my life at an early age offered me appropriate perspectives.

GRANDMAS ALWAYS LOVE

When I was a young boy, my grandma had already turned blind. She was a lovely woman with utmost love and humility. A simple operation in today's world and she would be able to see all her grandchildren. Her hearing was keen for a ninety-year-old woman, as it had improved to compensate for her loss of sight. She was able to hear us coming up the stairs. She would call us with hand stretched out, until she was able to feel us, then she hugged us, but we always tried to escape her hold. During our elementary school years we were of the age of fun and games. We did not care about an old blind woman. We just wanted to take off our school uniform and go down to play in the yard. What I could only wish for is to return to her time zone and hug her, and let her hug me with all of her frail might. I feel that loss now in my life, and it is saddled with a terrible feeling of disappointment and guilt. But, it is what the age of childhood delivers upon all of us, the age of child's play. A young boy does not want to be with an old woman, he wants to go outside to be with his friends. He wants to play.

As a consolation, my grandmother now comes to me in my thoughts and dreams, and with her smile. In addition, she also gave me the gift of knowledge. She contributed greatly to my understanding of how one important human sense (hearing) improves when another (sight) is diminished. For that matter, I often close my eyes to hear better, especially when listening to music. It is human nature, animal nature, and nature as well.

HAND-MADE

In the village, toys had to be hand-made, not store bought. Store bought toys came only at Christmastime. As boys, my brothers and I would have to create our own form of fun. Whatever object we could find became an item to manipulate into some form of fun, toy, or game. We often would take a small cardboard box and attach wheels on the sides to make a truck. The wheels were simply caps from soft drink bottles. A string attached to the front was used to pull the truck and deliver stones from a make-believe quarry. Eventually, when the cardboard truck disintegrated from over-use it became a boat, and was placed into the small canal near our house and pulled along with the string. Soon, the cardboard vehicle would totally disintegrate from being waterlogged. The final action remaining would be to use the string to spin it around over our heads, until it flew out somewhere. Often, it would land on, or near, another child who would jump after being startled. Giggling would soon ensue.

A creative use of allowance money before spending was to spin them on a flat surface. Glass was preferable. As the coins spun, they would each make a sound, which would change pitch as they slowed down. We would have contests to see whose coins would stay spinning the longest. We were boys, and we actually enjoyed the sounds. We would be imagining that we were driving a sports car. To us the sound was exciting; to my mother it was torture. She had her own idiosyncrasies. She did not like any kind of noises, unless she was making them herself. Ignoring her notification of becoming annoyed at the torturous noise of the spinning coins, we would continue spinning them until she had reached her limit of patience, or irritation, or both. Finally, she would approach with clear and purposeful intent. My mother was not a small woman. She would approach like a mad rhino to cancel our Olympics and seize our wealth. We would have to run off with our coins, or suffer the loss. Running away after grabbing all of our coins

220

was also part of the challenge. The last one who left before she arrived was surely the bravest. It was amazing how at a young age we develop our limits of fear, and our risk assessment skills.

NO BIRDS AND NO BEES

By the time I was ten years old my mother's authority waned by the authority of the king of the house. I became my father's property. He would groom me to his standards, drum responsibility into my head and inject it into my veins. It would seem like he wanted to make me the carbon copy of himself. Or, it could be that he simply wanted me to take on some duties, and relieve him of some of the responsibilities. I had to comply, even though reluctantly at times. I was a young boy, and this young boy needed to play with his friends.

I must admit that my adolescent years were no different than it was for any other boy, with regards to the relationship with the master of the house. Rebelliousness was natural as a young male asserted his power to the more powerful master. It was a natural power play in homes as it would be in the savanna with lions. My father believed that as children grow, they must learn all the aspects of themselves on their own. That included puberty. There was no talk on that subject. Perhaps he believed that sooner or later, instinct would reveal the aspects of our anatomy, just like it would be in the savanna.

I had to learn from my friends how to shave my face. I also learned the explanation of some aspects of adulthood from the same friends, who tried to convince me that babies did not come by stork. I was naive. It was in due time that I would learn how to be a juvenile, and it was not difficult to unlearn some things that the friends were wrong about; it seemed just natural, and it came with age. It had also become easy for me to understand humans, and the misinformation that consumes our lives in so many other ways, as adults. We pass it on from generation to generation and the same nonsense continues as truth and fact.

221

MALE CHALLENGE

I had some resentment to my father about his demands. It lasted all my teenage years. He insisted that I follow his example of believing in the religion of the one invisible God. He could never venture outside of the envelope of the safety of God. He could not accept the world in any other way. He was not a man of many words, but every word meant something. He was a strong disciplinarian and when he spoke the ground shook; the ground I was standing on. He was not a man to be challenged, only to obey and comply with. "Yes Pa" was the most common phrase of compliance heard when he spoke to any of his children.

While I was learning about science and having questions about matters beyond the realm of God, my father was consistent about his firm belief in his maker. He would not entertain even the slightest inclination of an alternative philosophy, even with all the facts that could be presented. My father was set in his ways. This only caused me further confusion in my life about my own existence, as I realized it was I who needed to learn more. This balance between religion and science would become my quest. I would have to investigate and choose the philosophy that suited me. But, I would also have to be an independent adult before I could break any bounds. As long as I lived in my father's house I would have to abide by his philosophy, and his rules. He was the king of his kingdom, the master of all his children, and the mastermind in his house. He was my master, and the master of my mind also.

A GOOD MAN

My father was a wonderful, upright, decent human being. He never judged, criticized or caused harm to anyone, or anything for that matter. He was conscientious, kind, generous and helpful in every way. He was a man of quiet speech, and he believed firmly in the saying: "Quiet speech is a mark of refinement." He followed the God of his belief in the best possible way. Not just by praying and doing all the traditional actions, but by living the life. He walked the walk, and talked the talk. He was respectful, and highly respected as well. He was the epitome of a thoughtful person. He was extremely aware of the environment in which he lived. He never followed any politics, or accepted any position in any system of governance. He was encouraged on several occasions to join a political party. The only party my father cared about was one where his God was present. He educated many people in the village about the goodness of his God. He encouraged them to always be good, and he led by example. My father minded his own business, and wanted to know someone else's only if he was asked to help them. He was a good example of a good man.

He was self-taught, worldly, and very disciplined. A very remarkable achievement, considering that he never went to high school. My father was regulated and regimented. He woke up at the same time each and every day. He worked every day of the week. He ate at the same time each and every day. He took a nap at the same time, each and every day. His most important device was a clock. Somehow he got his body and mind to adapt to his clock. His digestive system, sleep requirements and work schedule all fell into this clockwork. He was very predictable.

My father was knowledgeable in most religions, especially the big three - Christianity, Judaism and Islam. He accepted and respected all those who believed in monotheism. He regarded all the great people who came to guide humanity, beginning from Adam. He believed from the family tree of Adam came Noah and eventually Abraham and also Jesus. He believed that Abraham was sent to change the world from Paganism and idol worshiping, to the belief in the one and only God. My father believed in that same one God, the God of the world; the God of all humanity. He believed that the opposite of good is not bad; it is evil. "Bad" to my father would be a rebellious teenager, or a drunken man cursing in public. "Evil"

223

to him was like Hitler, the Pharaohs, slave traders, and people who do intentional acts of barbarism. My father believed in Heaven and Hell, and that someday one of those places would be the destiny of all humankind. He was truly his God's follower, in belief and behavior.

DRESS CODE

My father was a neat and impeccable dresser. Inasmuch as he worked in the shop that was attached to the house, he always had a professional presentation - neat and clean. He encouraged his children to dress presentable, and if one of my sisters would depart from his standard he would report it to Ma. She was the one to discipline the girls, while he was in charge of the boys.

After having listened to his lecture about proper dress code on a previous day, I suggested to the boys that we all get dressed up with shirt and tie when we go to work for him in the shop the next morning. It was a Saturday morning, and we got dressed for the goof. Upon entering we all said, "Good morning Sir." My father was surprised when he saw our attire, and pretended not to look too closely. He kept it casual, as we waited for his comments. He made none, as he would have simply cracked-up while looking at us. Pa did not laugh loudly; he considered it insulting, as he firmly believed in the saying, "Empty barrels make the most sound." Pa smiled when he saw us dressed up, and it took much effort for him to suppress his laughter, which he was compelled to indulge in, given the humor in our gesture. We watched him as he only giggled silently at what he must have considered hilarious, until he finally recomposed his demeanor.

We never played that trick again, as we had already known what the reaction would be. Many people had made Pa smile, giggle, and show excitement. But, no one could get Pa to laugh loudly. He thought it was rude and un-gentlemanly. The behavior training of the English was firmly planted in him, and he exuded it always.

SPIRITUALITY

My father believed that animals were innocent, and could never commit intentional acts of violence or harm. He believed that if an animal ate someone's plants, or destroyed someone's garden, it would be the owners' fault - the owner of the animal and the owner of the garden, both. He was a fair person, and would have made a fair judge. But, judge he could never be. He never judged. He always remembered that if he were to judge another human being it would insult the God who made that human being; the same God he believed in. What audacity and arrogance it would be to judge one of God's creations? My father walked a careful, narrow path, and he stayed on it for all the eighty years of his life. I miss my father's presence, but I do not miss his insistence that I should have followed his way of life. Yet, had I not been exposed to his doctrine and life, I would not be able to write about it. It is a paradox in my life, one that I must accept.

I thank my father for teaching me about doctrine. All I have learned cannot be unlearned. It is fortunate for me that I had him as a father. This knowledge now matters to me. I needed to make sense of all of it; for me, and for what I write here. I needed to understand religion and science both. My father was the best teacher of religion. He took no sides; he was objective. All of those who believed in the one God were his brethren, no matter which religion they followed. If a man came to my father's door and indulged in conversation, my father would want to know everything about the man's philosophy, and the reasoning of the man's decisions. He would want to learn from the man by learning about the man. Many men have also learned from my father, with regards to civility and behavior. Many have spoken about him for all the years of my life regarding the example he was for others, an example that was worthy of emulation.

My father ate only what his body could hold. He always said that people should eat and leave room for water, then drink and leave room for air. He was truly spiritual in that way, never taking more from the planet than he needed to survive. He was never wasteful, and he resented wastefulness. His discipline was strong with the values of good manners, respect for elders, kindness, quiet speech, proper dress and presentation of self. His behavior in being cordial, quiet chewing, proper speech and all of the rules that govern a civil society were his steadfast principles. He was a serious man most of the time, and he exhibited imposing power and authority simply by his presence. Although he never judged, he was quick to discipline his children about our behavior, as any parent should. We dared not embarrass him. He would not let us slide. But, we knew better, and we became better, because of him.

THE ONLY SON

My father did not want me to do anything dangerous. He especially did not want me to fly airplanes. He thought it involved too much risk. The memory of the loss of his only son years before would be the paramount factor in my future. I had a brother who lived and died before I was born. He was ten when he died. He was the only son my parents had, along with several girls. My brother had younger sisters and older sisters. I was told that there could be no better child than my brother. All the family, the village people, the school staff and children loved him. He was simply an angel, I surmised.

He fell sick on a Sunday and died two days later. His only symptom would be a fever, which would normally be treated, in those days, with rest and aspirin. The germ that entered his body would be some form of bacteria, virus or fungus. At that time there were no treatment for this type of rapid decline in health. To this day some children still die from encephalitis or meningitis if not treated in a hospital promptly. The germ that caused his death had DNA. It was a parasite that had found a host and it did what any parasite would do; it multiplied at a rapid pace and caused extremely high fever and lethargy. The diagnosis for my brother's death was vague from

226

those who remembered; meningitis was what I heard. It was a rare ailment and perhaps the best guess diagnosis.

The important consideration, as I wondered about this, was that the parasite invaded the host and found a suitable place to multiply. It is what germs do. It is what DNA does. Multiplying did not guarantee survival of the parasite. In fact, the germ caused so much damage that it caused the demise of its host, and eventually of itself. What a foolish germ. But, the germ had no brains, and could not think, or regulate itself in order to survive.

Microbes are everywhere, on our skin, in the air, in the water, in the ground, and in our bodies. If a germ enters our body it could multiply and create havoc in our lives. The common cold and flu are such examples. Others are deadly. Walking on the beach could cause a person to contract warts; a virus left by an infected person. Keep your slippers on.

My father was a firm believer in his God. He was not a man of science. The science of acids and metals in his jewelry profession was the extent of his scientific knowledge. He did not understand microbes, and how they could invade a human body and cause it to cease existence. My father prayed for his son, but all the prayers he offered to his God did not save the life of his son. He expected that his prayers would be able to heal his son. He did not know that prayers do not extract germs from human bodies. If such were the case there would be no need for doctors and medicines. Prayers are a means to console oneself. Then again, if my father could understand scientifically that a germ invaded his son's body, like a doctor would, it still would not take away the immense grief that came from losing an only son - a good son. Neither science nor God could have removed the pain, grief, and immense suffering for my father, mother, and all those who felt it.

The only hope for my father to quell his disappointment or anger towards his God would be his faith and his firm conviction in the story of Abraham. He told this story as though it was his own; the story that God commanded Abraham to sacrifice his son as proof of his fear of God. My father feared his God and would suffer the loss of his son with firm faith and submission rather than to defy or criticize his God. He would grind his teeth in anguish, accept the pain, suffering, guilt, anger, depression, despair, and all the possible emotions that a human soul could experience from the misery that came with such a circumstance. Such feelings and emotions all had to be dismissed and suppressed. He could put his head down in disbelief, but he could not reject his God. He had to swallow the bitter pill of intense pain from which his God would not save him. It was not his place to question, but to accept and show no weakness. It was he who had to show strength and faith in his God, and console himself, and others too. It was he who would have to accept that his God knew best, and that he was being tested; in the same way that Abraham was tested. Such were his beliefs.

The magnitude of the loss of my brother shocked and vibrated throughout the village and beyond, as though an earthquake had occurred. Sadness consumed every human heart that learned of my brother's death. His funeral had the longest procession the village had ever experienced. On the day of his funeral the school was closed, by order of the Headmaster of the school. Every person in the village, every schoolchild, everyone who had the means and availability came to join the procession to the cemetery. It was a procession fit for Royalty, not a ten-year-old boy. The brother I never knew was somewhat of a celebrity, and definitely the Prince of the village.

All the mourning and lamentation of the people in the village, the school children, and the friends and family could only offer some consolation. I am certain that the suffering my parents endured was unrelenting; they must have been shocked into disbelief. They probably did not sleep for days. I could only imagine sadness beyond the range to consolation. The entire village mourned; teachers wept, along with family, friends, neighbors, and the people in the village. I am weeping now as tears run down my cheeks. The aftershocks still come.

THE REPLACEMENT

In time, my parents adopted a boy, but not officially. My father was the type of man who wanted a son around. It was, I suppose, a true test of his manhood. The boy they adopted would grow and become a permanent member of our family. His name was Deo. He did everything my parents asked of him. He was loved by my parents, respected by my siblings, and regarded by the villagers as the true son of my parents. But, my father knew that this boy could not be the one to take the place of the deceased son. This boy could only fill the void, inasmuch as time had eroded some of his memory of the loss of his son. He wanted his own son.

The next child to be born in my household arrived dead. That would be two children's funerals one after the other. My parents must have been devastated all over again. They must have felt that God had cursed them and wanted them not to have any more children. But, I believe that my father's goal was to have an heir to his kingdom, his small kingdom in reality, but a huge kingdom in his mind.

It is the thinking of men to have a male heir, and perhaps that has an instinctive origin. Even Henry the Eighth of England wanted a son, an heir to his kingdom, and a kingdom he had; a huge kingdom in mind, and in reality. He wanted a son so desperately that he divorced many wives who did not bear him the son he so desired. He married woman after woman trying to have that male heir. He went as far as to break from the doctrine of the Pope, because the Pope would not grant his divorce from Catherine of Aragon who did not bear him a son. He fixed that problem by forming his own Church of England. Oh! The lengths men would go to get what they wanted. Henry did get his son, who died only after a few years after ascending the throne. Eventually it would be Henry's daughter Elizabeth, who became queen, and had one of the longest reigns in English history - great proof that it is okay to have a woman do things.

My father was no different than the King of England. He was a man, and the son he must have. The child who arrived dead was a girl. I wish that she would be alive now, and I could give her a hug and tell her that it was okay to be a girl, and it was the same as being a boy.

I could only imagine that the pain of the loss of their two children would have faded in time, but I doubt that the pain of losing their only son could have faded easily. In due time, my mother gave birth again, and it was a boy. Finally, he would be the boy who came to replace the dead one; I was that boy. There would be joy and celebration at my birth, but I am sure that the memory of the other boy would surface occasionally, and sadness would invade. This sadness would prompt the deep desire to protect this newborn little boy such that he would not have the same fate as the other. I would become the heir my father always wanted, and he would protect me with all his power. He could not lose me as he lost the other. My father's feeling in this matter would shape many of the events of my future, and condition me to the person I would become. He would mold me into his own likeness, as God did when he created Adam, as it was written, and as my father believed.

OLD FASHIONED VALUES

I grew up in an old fashioned society where everyone was safe. Eight-year-olds could walk to the candy store alone. Believe me, when I went to the candy store I intended on being alone. I grew up in a society where children had to share their candy. Need I say more? I grew up in a society where each adult person was a citizen of the community, and watched over all children. Especially, they watched out for children who were not in school. It was not a good idea to skip school. The repercussions were worse than the benefits. The crime did not fit the harsh punishment. We were in the British system. It was mandatory for every child to be in school until the age of twelve. Any citizen had the right to question any child who was not in school as to the circumstances for the absence. The worst thing that could happen would be a complaint to the parents about the absence, most likely by a person in the village. The fury from parents, especially, in addition to them refusing to write a note for the teacher, would guarantee a "do not repeat" clause in the violator's constitution. The same clause would prevail for not behaving according to standards. One of the social elements handed down from the British rule was that each child must obey rules and have good manners.

The British were instrumental by indoctrinating the masses into their system of thought and governance. Their influence was commanding, yet subtle, and the masses simply followed. I felt that my father thought that British blood ran through his veins, even though his own mother, as a child, arrived in the colony on a British ship. To be disobedient, or to embarrass him was like a death sentence, for him, and then for me. He did not know, or cared about what his ancestors endured under the British, similarly to others in the village who were focused on survival, not history. They had no knowledge, or cared to have any, of the treatment of their ancestors by the British. The history had faded through the generations. The British were successful in conditioning a population to abide by their rules, and everyone accepted without question. The British were the masters of rules, etiquette and respect, and they lived like that for centuries. The villagers had joined their captors; survival was more important than resistance.

Every person in the village obeyed these principles. It was not uncommon for people to be judged by the way they spoke. There were certain special exceptions, such as when someone got drunk at the corner bar and staggered home. There would be several of these characters having entire conversations by themselves, as other villagers looked on and laughed. In fact, the main road of the village was like a television screen. There would be every kind of drama unfolding, with characters from every background. The plot was always interesting, and only unfolds as the drama happens. This was our entertainment. On the main road there would be fish sellers, hucksters, horse drawn carts, cars, buses, cattle, dogs, chickens, and people, all

231

at the same time. It would not be unusual for drivers of cars to yell out of their window for people to move out of the way, as their car horns were totally ignored, and became benign. It was the way of life then. It was a time gone by. But, I was living in that time; it was a time of innocence, a time I miss dearly, to which I could never go back.

I learned much during those early years of my life. I learned the values that would shape my thinking, my future, and my character. I consider it a privilege that I was immersed into this environment as a child, and I hold no resentment or anger towards British people for the shaping they did.

WHAT ABOUT ME

Every time my mother talked about the son she lost she would break into bitter tears. I could not understand her emotions, as I was just a child. I did not know my brother. I only knew him as a child of someone. I knew him because he was frequently talked about. Ma cried easily for the sadness of losing her first son. Otherwise, she did not cry easily, or frequently. It did not mean that she was stone hearted. She was just a tough and strong woman who had been through it all. By the time I was old enough to understand, I could only remember my mother crying at funerals. Compared to me she was one hundred times stronger. I cry for everything.

I would not be educated had it not been for my mother. My father wanted to groom me in his own likeness. He wanted me to follow him in his business, doctrine, and profession. He wanted to own me like his possession. I had become the son he had lost. Pa was a soft-spoken man. He believed in the saying, "Quiet speech is a mark of refinement." Ma believed in the saying; "I'm having it my way, thank you." Ma challenged him, and thought differently on certain matters, and he did not mess with Ma; her voice was louder. She took me to register at the local high school after I finished elementary school. Ma had the foresight that education offered the best opportunity for children's future, all children's future.

The tuition for high school was fifty-two dollars per year. That was quite a sum in those days, and I heard about it every time my report card showed a grade not acceptable to the payer of the tuition - my father. He would suggest that I quit school and revert to working for him. I was not going to accept that, especially since all the teenage girls were at my high school and within close proximity to where I was sitting in class. I picked up my grades really quickly.

FAST CASH

As a young boy I had to work in my father's shop after school and on weekends. Many people came to the shop to purchase jewelry, and others came to visit. I remember an incident when a familiar woman came to talk to my father about a difficult situation her family was experiencing. They had a money problem, but had made some plans that would clear up the problem in the near future. The woman explained in detail what had happened, and what was going on in her family. My father listened, and listened. I also listened, and kept listening intently, and that was all I could do. I could not say anything; I was a youth who was allowed to be seen, but not to be heard. I continued doing my work.

I was amazed that my father, a man not short of words, stayed silent as this woman pleaded her case for a small loan. My father was known to be dependable and helpful to neighbors, friends and family. He was generous, but he was not wealthy. He worked hard and provided for his family, and was never short on assets. He planned well, and always thought of the future. He had small sums of money set aside in several envelopes. There was one envelope marked for petty cash, one for charity, one for donations and so on. Each had its own purpose and accountability. He believed in tithing a percentage of his wealth every year.

The woman pleaded and pleaded. She explained how she would pay the money back, and she confirmed when she would. My father listened, but he would never let her plead to the point of begging; he just wanted to hear the whole story. Finally, he came to me and whispered his instruction that I should take twenty dollars - which would be like two hundred of today's dollars - from the envelope marked for charity and give it to her. I was perplexed. I was confused. Mostly, I was surprised. This was supposed to be a loan, not charity. I thought he would ask me to take the money from the business drawer, not from one of the envelopes. I followed his command and gave the woman the money, without question.

My father believed that every person whose hands would help to transfer money or goods for charity to the final recipient would receive a blessing from God. He also believed that a smile was a greeting, an invitation, and the easiest form of charity. The woman was extremely grateful, and continued thanking my father and promising the return of the money. Finally, she left quietly. I waited to hear what my father would tell me. He said nothing. I was afraid to ask. I did not want him to feel as though I was questioning his judgment. He never said a word, and I never asked.

Less than a decade later I would learn the lesson my father taught me. I would encounter such situations, as it was not unusual for people to want to borrow money. I would eventually learn, the hard way, that my father's lesson was not a lesson on how to issue a small loan; it was a lesson in psychology. My father listened to the woman for a very long time. He wanted the opportunity to qualify her need, and more importantly, understand her motives; he was analyzing her. The lesson I had to learn was how to take the time to analyze any person so that when a decision is reached there would be no regrets.

I made my mistake with a work colleague by lending him some money, much more than my father loaned the woman. I listened to the man's humble words and difficulty providing for his children, and I was moved. I was young and inexperienced. I would have to learn. My difficulty came when it was time for me to get my money back. My colleague made me feel like I had to wait, and that I was being unreasonable by asking him to repay his debt as he promised. What I lent that dude was not charity money; it was my whole paycheck. I had to plead with him for my own money. I became the person who was in need. But, I had to learn on my own so I could never forget how to understand people, as best as possible. I painfully, and finally got my money back, but there was a sense of compassion that I still felt for that man with children; I still had some guilt about him and his family. I also finally understood why my father asked me to give the woman the money from the envelope marked for charity. He never expected to get it back. By listening to all the arguments the woman made, he was able to ascertain that her story did not qualify her for a loan, simply because her repayment plan was not assured. However, she was in need, and so it became a charity case. I could not afford to write my loan off as charity; it was a lot of money for me. I hounded that colleague to the point that I became the pain he did not want, and in the place he did not want.

The final take away from my father's strategy, which I learned for myself after many years, was that the money the woman received, was still a loan; in her mind. That was why my father whispered his instruction to me. Had she known it was charity she would not be obligated to pay it back. But, the genius of my father was that his strategy was a carefully thought out plan. As I wondered why my father would care if the woman knew it was charity or not, I concluded that he wanted her to believe it was the loan she requested. The benefit of his plan was that the next time the woman needed a loan she would not be coming to my father, until she had paid the first loan off. My father would ascertain all of the facts before he made his decision. His decision also included the prediction that the woman would default on the loan. Somehow, he knew this was case for charity.

I learned my lesson, and I admired my father for his intellect and wisdom. I wish I could tell my father what I had learned, and how much I admired him. But, the opportunity never came. The feeling to tell never came. I missed my chance.

The memory of him would have to suffice for the legacy he left. But, is that not what legacy is - the memory of him in others?

NIRVANA

I know that when he was a boy my father had chores to do before he went to school, no different than I. His family owned a livery service. I heard stories about him having to take animals out to graze in the pasture then rush home to get ready for the eight o'clock school bell. He hardly spoke to us about his childhood. Perhaps that conversation was for him and his friends, quite similar to me now. I never wanted my children to feel any guilt regarding the disparity between my childhood and theirs. Actually, I am happy for myself that I had many more experiences than them.

At an early age, my father had reached the stage and state of mind that he would keep for the rest of his life. His humility, routine, and belief in God would be the pennants of his peacefulness. He did not chase happiness, but he was truly happy. His happiness was a derivative of his way of life, and his state of mind. My father had achieved a euphoric state of being by simply eliminating all the elements that were contrary to his peaceful state of mind. Feelings such as greed, arrogance, jealousy, enmity, and prejudice were all totally dismissed.

I often wonder about how this state of happiness could be achieved. Perhaps it is our personality, or our circumstance, or our beliefs, or education. Perhaps it's a perfect blend of all these things. I am always wondering about things. I yearn for the state of mind that my father possessed. But, was it boring to be like that? I do not want to be bored. I like to be peaceful at times, and engaged at times. Perhaps my father was not bored at all. I know he had a good balance of peacefulness and engagement. I would never know how he felt. He never told, and I never asked. Now, I will never know.

My father was a worldly man. He could have had a conversation with anyone, and at anytime. When he was not an expert on a subject matter he would listen, and he would ask questions. He wanted to learn all he could, about people, and about his world. He spoke about everything. He tried, and in my mind, succeeded in understanding people. He was such a master of psychology; I mean everyday people's psychology. I aspire to be a worldly man, but I live in a much bigger world than my father. I can only try, and hope to meet the challenge.

DECISION TIME

In time I realized that my father could not let me go. He had already lost a son. My leaving would mean his loss of control of my safety, and he felt that he could end up in the same place once again, by losing another son. The pain and suffering was not an option for him. The reconciliation of this dilemma would be one of my father's major decisions of his life. He already had other sons after me. He must have thought this through and through, and over and over. He must have considered that I was also a human being, like himself, with aspirations for my own future. He had consciousness and memory, and he must consult and confront both of them. There would be no choice, but confrontation. It was the paradox that he must resolve in order to make a constructive decision - the decision that could punish him for making a mistake. A paradox indeed it was.

It seemed that my father needed help. He needed a little discussion for the decision he had to make. He solicited the opinion and support from a man who was in the family, and a man he trusted. This man was pragmatic. He was a straight, no-nonsense type of man who called it as he saw it. I would find out decades later about this consultation my father had with this man, who also knew my brother who died.

On the subject of me leaving the village to pursue educational goals in a foreign country, the man asked my father if he had the power to save me, like he had (not) saved the other son. The man, in blunt and sarcastic terms, told my father that he could not save me from whatever would happen to me. This man understood that my father was fearful because of my

237

deceased brother, but that he must not allow that fear to jeopardize my future. It would be unfair to me. My father finally reconciled with the forces that played in his head, and confidently signed the authorization for me to leave the little village, after sleeping one night with his dilemma. I was under the age of consent, and I was happy that I needed his permission; it was more like an approval for me to leave his kingdom.

SNEAKY

I took flying lessons without my parent's knowledge when I came to America. Only when I became certified they would find out from the family and friends who had taken an airplane flight tour with me. They could not find out otherwise, as I was tight-lipped about it. We lived thousands of miles away from each other. I had to keep my secret for as long as I could, until, spoonful-by-spoonful, my parents, especially my father, would accept this passion in my life. I had to do what I wanted to do, with all the inspiration, passion, and goals I expected from my life. I was defiant to any person who would forbid, or resist my mission. I was on my own quest to accomplish what I wanted, and no one was going to dictate what I was going to do. Inasmuch as I felt the confidence and independence, there were subtle reminders of thought going through my mind, with regards to the authority of my father. Ma was game for anything I wanted to do; she did not feel the need to suppress me. She wanted me to fly like a bird. She was okay with anything that would make her proud of me.

By the time they would visit America I was already a flight instructor with quite a bit of experience. They had already heard from the grapevine about what I did. They even told family, friends, and village people that I was a pilot instructor, not realizing that it was a secondary profession. My main profession had drowned in the glory of piloting. I did not consider it to be glory, but for people from the village it would be glorious for the village boy they knew. It is our human nature to react to sensationalism. In addition, the village people could not conceive of my main profession as a marketing manager. They simply could not grasp the business of New York.

THE MOMENT OF TRUTH

The day I took my Pa for a flight in an airplane was the day I yearned for so dearly. It would be my day of liberation from his bondage. He agreed for me to fly Ma and him up the Hudson River to visit his sister who lived about thirty miles north of New York City. I drove them to the departure airport and readied the airplane for flight. With all the objections my father had about my flying interest, I had expected some questions as to my qualifications and capabilities as a pilot. There were none, not a single question. My father entered the airplane and took his seat, as though he had done it a thousand times, and with the comfort of a baby that was just fed. "Really Pa?" "That was all there was to it?" "After all the inflicted guilt from your objection to my becoming a pilot how could you not offer some validation for the objection?" "How could you not simply say that you had accepted it and offer some sentiments of consolation to me?" He left me with two conflicting feelings; I was disappointed that after all the fears he injected into me about flying that he would not query me, and at the same time, I felt relieved that he accepted my venture to become a pilot. He had accepted my defiance to fly without his blessings, and he had accepted the invitation to fly with me, and without hesitation. I was perplexed, and he left me with my mouth open as to what the correct sentiments should have been. I said nothing, and simply treated my parents as two passengers under my responsibility. I would have to process the emotions at a later date.

I proceeded to take-off, and I flew towards the Hudson River, where I showed Ma and Pa the New York City skyline. They both looked carefully as I pointed prominent landmarks including the Empire State Building, the Twin Towers, and the Statue of Liberty. They seemed only curious, and not deeply interested in details; perhaps that was a sign of their aged feeling and thinking. What I did see was a proud man, and a proud woman, both totally fearless, and without any questions as to the qualification of their pilot. Especially, I saw a man who knew he had done the right thing for his son. My mother sat quietly in the back looking outside the airplane in total comfort. She asked no questions the entire trip, she trusted her pilot completely. My father sat looking outside with the wide-eyed curiosity of a first time student.

I made a sharp bank in Pa's direction to line the airplane up for the runway at the destination airport. He jumped back, as though he felt like he was going to slide off the wing and fall. I quickly corrected the angle and apologized, so as to comfort him. I also explained that what I did was not unsafe. I did not want him to have a problem flying with me in the future. He did fly again with me several times. I flew Ma and Pa to Canada nonstop, and landed at Island Airport at the base of the CN Tower, where family members picked them up. I returned to bring them back a few weeks later.

Decades ago when I made the flights to Canada I did not bring my passport; the only document I showed the border personnel was my pilot's license, which did not even have a photograph. Those were the days my friends, we thought they'd never end; we lived the life we choose. That was nice and dandy, until the turn of the century, when the world changed, and photographs, passports and ID became required for everything, except sneezing.

Pa was not fearless, he was comfortable and trusted me as a pilot. Each time my father would make a trip by car, bus, train or airplane he would verbalize a short prayer for safe journey. That would be him placing his life into the hands of his God. He would proceed with confidence that his God was watching over him and all those who traveled with him. He trusted his God more than anyone, or anything else in his life.

In all the time I flew with my father I wondered how this man could have injected his fear of my flying into me; a fear that plagued me for years and years, even as an instructor, many, many times, as I would enter an airplane. I felt each of those times that my father was coming in the airplane with me to remind me not to fly. I finally realized that my father had resolved his issue with my flying and that I was the one unresolved. He had handed me his issue and it was mine now to deal with. What possible course of action could I have taken, but to accept the condition that was placed upon me, by a man who cared and loved me so much, that all he wanted was to save me from that which he had no foresight or control over; in the same way that he wanted to save the son he had lost before?

RITA

During the later years of my parents' lives a young girl from the village was asked to live-in and care for them. She did the chores like shopping, cooking, cleaning, and laundry. She became like a daughter to them, and a trusted child in their eyes. She was honest, kind, loving, sweet, and simply wonderful. My parents could not have had better. Rita would be the angel who descended into the house; sent on a mission by the God of my father. She stayed day and night to care for them. She talked to them, ate with them, gave them their medication, handled their finances, and had many sleepless nights when they did not feel well. She was their angel, and an angel she was. She stayed with them for all their lives, and took care of the house when they traveled away from home. People such as Rita, are simply special, and who ever crosses their path, the angel in them would touch, as I always feel, every time I see Rita. She is still that angel.

PACKED SUITCASES

My parents traveled to Europe to visit their children. They also came to America, and then visited Canada. They spent one year in New York and were cared for by an in-law family member. This woman who cared for my parents was the other angel sent by the God of my father. She showed them love, cooked for them, talked and laughed with them, gave them their medication and made them comfortable. She told me it was easy for her to do all that because she had great respect and admiration for them, and she loved them dearly. Most of all she had a learning opportunity with both of them, about doctrine and family values.

The time in New York proved beneficial for my parents to have some good medical treatment. A student of mine was a doctor at a hospital. He asked me to bring both of them in for a thorough check-up. After a battery of tests that could make a lithium highway glow in the dark, several prescriptions followed, like from a printing press. There was a pill for everything. It was like the doctors were trying to turn back the clock, and correct all the mistakes and diet for two people over seventy years old. It all was good; my parents took their medication as recommended, and were as happy as could be.

They also had many visitors from the local areas, and from overseas, as they were well known. Finally, when winter came they decided to return to the village. Pa had already refused to accept a recommended heart procedure, even though it had a high success rate. He told the surgeon that he did not want to be in any discomfort, and that when God was ready for him he would be ready to go.

THE FINAL MOMENTS

My father had lived a full life, and he had made many good decisions in his life. He had done well, he was happy, and he did not want anything to interfere with the flow of the rest of his life. His children were all well, and on their own. His affairs were in order. His health was his only concern. Pa had already foreseen this final chapter of his life and had taken precautionary measures. Several years prior, he had already begun to sell the house lots and land he had acquired during his early life. He had kept the properties like a bank account, in case of difficulty, as they paid decent dividends. When he made the decision to sell, the first offer went to the existing tenants for a fair and affordable price, to be paid over several years. Everyone accepted, as they knew that they were being offered a once in a lifetime deal, and were treated with respect, by a man they knew did not have an ounce of greed in his soul.

When Ma and Pa went back to live in their house in the little village, after they had traveled, Rita was there waiting, and ready for them. Pa was born there, and he wanted to be in the house that he lived in for so many years. It would seem that Pa went back with the knowledge that somehow his time was near. He was right, and after about one year, he went to meet his God. I could only suspect that my father died within a few feet of exactly where he was born. It could seem almost instinctive that he would want that, but I would have to accept that it was with intellectual desire that he planned to be there to die.

I was in an airplane conducting a flight lesson when the news came from the village in South America, from my family. The urgency would have to wait until I landed. But, when I called in for a clearance, the controller in the tower told me via radio, that I should contact the office of my school for an urgent message. He had recognized my voice, and he knew me from my previous visits to the tower when I brought students to learn about how the tower operates. Somehow, I knew immediately what the message was going to be; I felt the urgency in the controller's voice, as though he was the one telling me the message - in code. I believe he was told what the message was, as his voice reverberated with such emotion. But, he did not want to let the cat out of the bag, and certainly not on the radio. The next day I was on an airliner headed south, to the village where I was born.

It was Pa's wish to be buried in the place where he was born, and his final wish came through. When I arrived I met many people who were in tears and shock. Especially, I met neighbors who hugged me and told me how much they would miss him. More importantly, as a tribute to Pa, and being the appropriate time, they told me how he was the reason they became property owners, and what a noble deed he had done for them. They said that his deed would be something they could never forget. I was happy to know that his legacy was noble. I knew Pa as my father, and the man that he was; the man everyone else also knew - a noble man.

Ma was very sad, and found comfort in her children. She did not have much to worry about, as all matters were being handled for her. Her children simply wanted her to be happy, and at peace. She accepted those benefits gladly, and after spending some time mourning Pa she began to travel around the continents to see her children and family. She spent the last years of her life enjoying time with children and grandchildren, and helping others. She knew no better, as she did not know how to be idle. After several years away from the village Ma went back for the final time. She said that she had traveled enough, and had been in too many houses. She went back to her own house, and Rita was there again, waiting patiently for her.

Ma followed the path that Pa took, and she followed him all the way to that place where everyone has to go someday. I cried bitter tears on that day, more than I did when Pa was buried. I don't know why, even though it was I doing the crying. My conscious mind did not know the reason, as that information was tucked away in my subconscious mind. I know that those two parts of my mind don't always talk to each other, and that was why I did not know. The subconscious knows me more, as it records everything in my life, and it knew why I was crying so much. I was in my human moment, and I must accept that I don't know many things, and I will never know many more things; such is the nature of humans; we are simply robots of the universe; compelled by its formation and rules.

TIME TO ALWAYS REMEMBER

With all of the issues that could affect the relationship between a child and a parent, it is imperative that I remember what all children must also remember - the power of the father and the mother. The mother is the nurturer, the healer, the comforter, and the one who always forgives. She is the one to come to for all that hurt, and all that troubles us. She is the knower of children, the knower of her children. My Ma must be remembered for her influence on her children, the village people, and the greater community. She must be remembered for the values of family that she encouraged and shared. She must be remembered for her laughter, especially the laughter enticed by her silly boys with their tricks.

The image of a successful father is represented in our judgment of his power, strength, knowledge, understanding and protection. He is the ultimate man a child must come to terms with. He is the ultimate challenge. He is always known as the father, the master, the adviser, the provider, the knower of all things, and no one must speak unkind words about him. He is the king who must always be remembered as the lion of his pride.

I am glad about my upbringing with this man I call Pa. He is my hero, especially for his example of being upright. I try to model my life as best as I can with his principles. Especially, I do not like to waste anything, as it all comes from the earth. Respect for the earth must come together with respect for everyone, and everything; it is true spirituality. I am a simple man with a circle of friends and family who are important to me. I try to be happy always. I have a sense of humor. I am rarely ever annoyed with anyone or anything. Instead, I try to understand the person, or the thing that would be annoying. I strive to be calm, and calm I am, most of the time. Of course I will have a burst of emotion and pain on certain matters. But, they are short-lived. As I describe myself, I realize I am also describing my father. I am my father's child. The apple did not fall far from the tree. I wonder about all of this. Was he such a powerful influence on me, or is it that my character is similar to his? I could be certain that some of his principles and values did rub off on me, as it was inevitable, having spent so much time in close proximity to him. I could wonder about it, or simply accept that such is being human.

I have become regimented in my own life, and I follow a daily routine. I try to stay calm and relaxed as much as possible. I try to be kind. I am compassionate for all those who suffer. I take no unnecessary risks. I mind my own business. I hate no one. I do not want conflicts, with anyone, or with anything for that matter. I have become the man I must appreciate; a man with regulation and regimentation; a man with a mission to protect that which he loved as dearly as nature would allow - his children. I became my father. I follow his spiritual concept with regards to consuming the least from the earth, but with a different perspective - one of compassion for the earth's resources. My father's belief was that his doctrine commanded him to his spirituality, whereas for me, it is my compassion, my feeling for Mother Earth. I can offer no logical explanation, except that my compassion originated from my circumstances and conditions, and perhaps conditioning from my Pa himself. Whatever it would take for me to understand my father is what I must do, as a father, and as a son. The one thing for sure is that Pa was submissive to his God. I am submissive to the universe, which defines my existence and my future, as is the same for all that exists. Whatever resentment I had did me no good. It is in my memory now, but I must forget it, for Pa's sake, and for me too. I should recognize that it was noble for a father to protect his children from anything and everything, including that which is incalculable. I am also a father, one no different than any other, and I must do what the generations of past fathers had done - be a father.

The inability to qualify or quantify risk is also a father's responsibility. Pa did what he knew, and that was the best he could have done. I am certain that the fears and memories of the loss of his first son plagued him constantly. I am sure that Pa was happy to get my letters after he let me go, so he could be sure that I was fine, and that he did not make a mistake. I could never tell him about my difficulties with money and school, and my suffering in cold weather. That would have caused him more suffering, and I did not want that for him. It was my life that I was trying to build anyway. I must always remember that what Ma and Pa taught me helped with what I needed to know for my own understanding, inasmuch as they never knew I felt that. I must always remember that it was what Pa taught me that created my conflict, and drove me on my quest to resolve my philosophy. I must accept the figurative and paradoxical pain from the exercise he induced upon me, which made me realize that my muscles for life have grown stronger. It is best for me to tell my father and my mother now in their graves that I love them dearly, and I thank them dearly for raising me, educating me, tolerating my toddler tantrums, as well as my teenage rebelliousness. I do miss them dearly, and I wrote a short poem to honor them:

SEQUOIA

The greatest person in the world is not a king or a queen.
Not a president, or a ruler either.

The greatest person in the world is not an actor.
Or a singer.
Nor a poet, or even an artist.

The greatest person in the world is the most powerful,
and the strongest.
The biggest, and the mightiest.

The greatest person in the world is a good parent.

NOTES:

CONTINUE THE JOURNEY WITH BOOK TWO

"the philosophy of existence"

A book about human existence from the perspective of the reality and facts of our origin, existence, and future, with a multi-disciplinary approach, including doctrine, science, anthropology, history, psychology, consciousness, spirituality as well as other aspects. Follow me as we explore who we are, what we are doing here, and where we are headed in this vast universe. You get to decide. Knowledge is power to understand.

ISBN for book two: 9781702412322

I

THE AUTHOR

Ralph B. Bacchus is a retired Corporate Professional, a former Airplane Flight Instructor, an Advanced Ground instructor for Pilots, and an Electrical Engineer. He also researches in other fields and disciplines.

ACKNOWLEDGEMENTS

I wish to extend sincere thanks to my friends Michael, Andrea, Judy and Nancy for their support, encouragement and motivation. I appreciate their inspiration greatly. Special thanks to all those who contributed to all of the knowledge I have acquired throughout my life. A special tribute to my parents for showing me the love, kindness and guidance each human being deserves. I thank them for being good examples of that instinctive desire to provide and protect their offspring by exhibiting one of the most fundamental aspects of human existence.

DISCLOSURE

The ideas, opinions and information expressed in this book are those of the author. No acknowledgement is made with regards to accuracy of facts and statements, and no sentiments are directed to any individual, group or entity. No intention is made to encourage or discourage a behavior, or belief, and no judgment is intended of any individual, group or entity. The reference of any entity is solely for information only, and without bias. No intent is made to affect encouragement to change, or alter any belief, or system, and no criticism is intended of any belief or system. Reference of any entity is made from a neutral perspective and only to foster understanding.

Contact: beinghumanbeing2019@gmail.com